TWELVE NEW FACES OF
PHILOSOPHY

An Anthology Featuring Classic Texts
Seen through the Eyes of
the Next Generation of Thinkers

George David Miller

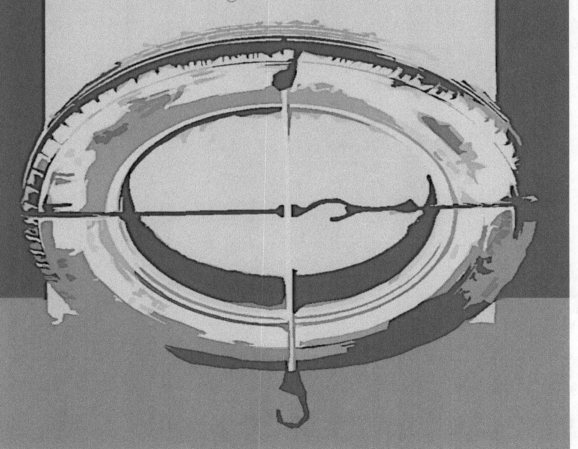

Kendall Hunt
publishing company

live/dead hypothesis
writ idee
language game
blank slate
reductionism
Free speech

ataraxia

philosophical approach

Cover image: George David Miller

Kendall Hunt
publishing company

www.kendallhunt.com
Send all inquiries to:
4050 Westmark Drive
Dubuque, IA 52004-1840

Copyright © 2020 by Kendall Hunt Publishing Company

ISBN 978-1-7924-1350-6

Published in the United States of America

Contents

Chapter 1 deconstruction   Chanol

Chapter – dead vs dead hypothesis   content
                                      parse

What is my purpose

delete comma

The title of George Miller's book is, *Twelve New Faces of Philosophy*. It is a philosophical anthology like no other. It introduces philosophy in general and major philosophical themes, figures, concepts, and arguments in particular through the perspective of non-specialists. By "non-specialists," I mean they are not necessarily philosophers who specialize in a specific area, which is typically established by earning a PhD in philosophy. This is not a criticism but must be seen as a compliment. Twelve individuals are philosophers in their own right. A PhD in philosophy does not make one a philosopher. More precisely, but it is also a compliment because a philosophical dialogue with such thinkers will allow undergraduate students and any layman to connect with the major philosophical themes, figures, concepts, and arguments and their stories in a more organic fashion. This is one of the greatest merits of this anthology constructed by Miller.

Each topic is introduced by an interview. It makes the topic—seemingly abstract and esoteric—very relatable and concrete. Miller typically gives details about his interviews, particular details that highlight their humanness in their very singularity—that is, as *this* specific individual with his or her specific history and everything in that history that makes this person as *this* person. Texts by famous philosophers in Western and Eastern traditions and non-philosophers are placed in between the explanation—by the interviewee him- or herself.

The reader—whether an undergraduate student or a layman—should be able to clearly and distinctly see that the twelve interviewees—although not philosophers by intensive training and precisely because they are not philosophers in this *narrow* sense—discuss philosophy in a non-abstract, non-theoretical, and non-esoteric way. I have been teaching philosophy since 2009. Reading these interviews and the texts woven in and through them from some of the greatest thinkers in the Western and Eastern traditions makes this anthology *more accessible* to the average everyday individual than any *Introduction to Philosophy* anthology that I have ever read in my entire academic career as a teacher.

Dialogue is key in this anthology. Twelve individuals are interviewed by Miller. I could not help but notice how the dialogical nature of the interviews was very much like the one that is found in Plato's dialogues. Miller in this text is doing philosophy that is very much *like* how Plato's Socrates practised philosophy in Plato's *Dialogues* and where Miller does not follow Plato's Socrates to the letter, he does so in spirit. Miller and Plato's Socrates are cross-examiners even though very different ones. It is well-known that Plato's Socrates claims that he does not know what he does not know (i.e., Socratic ignorance). By contrast, *for the most part*, Miller lets his interviewee know what they claim to know even though, from time to time, Miller will question the sense in which, and the extent to which, they claim to know what they know. Miller is also very much like Plato's Socrates in that he creates a dialogue between him and his interlocuters. But the greatest virtue of Miller's texts over

Contributed by Arsalan Memon. © Kendall Hunt Publishing Company.

Plato's dialogues and Plato's Socrates is that Miller does not "win" (for lack of a better word) at the end of the interview. Miller does not come out of the interview showing that his interlocuter does not know anything about the discussed subject matter. Like Plato's Socrates, Miller lets the interviewee guide and lead. Unlike Plato's Socrates, Miller follows the interviewees in their claims and lets his interlocuter speak in an *honest* way that Plato's Socrates does not let his interlocuters do. Plato's Socrates always seems to win or have the last word (sometimes literally and other times, metaphorically). This is not the case in Miller's text. You genuinely get the sense that these twelve new faces, who are people from all walks of life, have genuinely thought about specific issues that have motivated them to turn to philosophy.

Furthermore, it is not entirely clear to me if Plato's Socrates had a single method of doing philosophy that remains consistent or explicit throughout Plato's early, middle, and later works. It is also not clear to me if one can simply—or exclusively—define Plato's Socrates as having a specific method (i.e., ἔλεγχος [*elenchos* or *elenchus*], a way of cross-examining and refuting others). But one thing that remains consistent and explicit throughout Plato's dialogues is that Plato's Socrates almost always asks what can be called the *what is F-ness question* (i.e., What is X-ness?). Socrates asks the following questions in Plato's dialogues: in the *Euthyphro*, "What is Piety?"; in the *Republic*, "What is Justice?"; in the *Meno*, "What is Virtue?"; in the *Hippias Major*, "What is Beauty?"; in the *Laches*, "What is Courage?"; in the *Charmides*, "What is Temperance?"; in the *Lysis*, "What is Friendship?" and the list goes on. Although Miller's book is very dialogical, it remains different from Plato's dialogues and this must also be seen as one of its *merits* or greatest virtues. When Miller interviews these twelve individuals, he does not ask the Socratic *what is F-ness question* but some variations of the following questions: *What does philosophy do? What has philosophy done for you? How has philosophy impacted your life*? If Socrates asks the *metaphysical* question (What is X-ness?), then Miller asks the *archeological* question: "What got you into philosophy?", "Do you have time to chat about what got you into philosophy?", "What "drew you into Philosophy[?] (implicit question), "What aroused your interest in Philosophy?", "When did you catch the philosophy bug?", "What got you into Philosophy, Evan?", "What roped you into philosophy?", and "Why do you think we've reached this point? More specifically, Miller asks the question of the ἀρχή (*archē*), the origin, which connects him with the questions asked by the thinkers that we call the Pre-Socratic philosophers, or if we follow Nietzsche's description, Pre-Platonic philosophers. But even then, there is a difference. The Pre-Socratic or Pre-Platonic philosophers were mostly interested in questions of the origins of the universe. None of them interviewed people to ask about their encounter with philosophy. That is another great merit of this anthology.

To Miller's archeological question (What got you into philosophy?), the following are the responses provided by the twelve individuals. Before listing their responses, I want to provide two quotes from two French philosophers that I believe unite all twelve thinkers. The two quotes thus follow:

> Something in the world forces us to think. This something is an object not of recognition but of a fundamental *encounter*. What is encountered may be Socrates, a temple or a demon. It may be grasped in a range of affective tones: wonder, love, hatred, suffering. In whichever tone, its primary characteristic is that it can only be sensed. In this sense it is opposed to recognition.[1]

---

[1] Deleuze, G. "The Image of Thought." *Difference and Repetition*. Trans. Paul Patton. London and New York: Continuum Press, 2001. 136.

A certain man loves a certain woman today because his past history has prepared him to love that particular personality and face, but also because he *met* her, and this meeting awakens possibilities in his life which would have remained dormant without her. This love seems like fate once it has become established, but on the day of the first meeting it is absolutely contingent.[2]

In the first quote, Deleuze rightly tells us that thinking does not happen in a vacuum. The world forces us to think. If philosophy involves thinking, which I believe it does, then these twelve individuals are thinkers in the Deleuzean sense. Philosophy is an event that takes place. It happens. As an event, it is also an encounter, an encounter between an individual and the world. As an archeologist, Miller traces the origin of their encounter with philosophy. In the second quote, although Merleau-Ponty is talking about love, what he says about love can equally be applied or extended to philosophy. As a side note, it is well-known that philosophy in its Greek sense (φιλοσοφία) means love of wisdom, where the word for love is φίλος (*phīlos*). Even though Merleau-Ponty is talking about love that can be categorized as romantic love, it can be extended to any form or kind of love. What connects Merleau-Ponty's quote with Deleuze's quote is that they both emphasize encounter. What is emphasized by Merleau-Ponty and not by Deleuze is the dialectical or *bi-directional* nature of an encounter: not only is it the case that the world forces us to think (as Deleuze rightly argues), but also and most importantly, something in our individual "past history" prepares us for such an encounter and the encounter itself "awakens possibilities" in one's life. This is what I see in all twelve interviewees. The encounter with philosophy eventuates because of something in their life leads them to philosophy and in turn, philosophy provides a response that "awakens possibilities" in their respective lives. Now let me turn to their responses to Miller's archeological question (What got you into philosophy?).

It seems that each interviewee finds in philosophy a kind of *response* to life in general or life events in particular. Something in their life or their life as a whole demands some sort of response and that response is found in and through philosophy—at least for these twelve individuals. Chapter 1 deals with the issue of self-identity and the question of "who am I?". The first interviewee, Joy-Ray, said what got them into philosophy "was looking for something for a long time to explain to myself exactly who I was. In this society, people fit into neat categories and there didn't appear to be one for me." Chapter 2 deals with the issue of philosophical creativity and expressing oneself philosophically. The second interviewee, Jorge, said that it was the search for, and articulation of, truth that got him into philosophy.

Chapter 3 deals with the issue of wisdom. Brandon, the third interviewee, said, "That's one of the most important things Philosophy taught me. Knowledge is objective and public. Wisdom is subjective and private." Chapter 4 deals with the issue of the environment. Jedda, the fourth interviewee, said that "Philosophy is how I am going to save First Nation Persons—our people and our culture. It is also the way to make it clear to everybody what is going on and hopefully make the earth perpetually habitable. By the way, we're coming up to our ship now." Chapter 5 deals with the issue of miseducation. The fifth interviewee, Herbert, said that education had the greatest philosophical impact on him. In his words, "Education. Once I began reading stuff by Whitehead, Dewey, Freire, Gardiner, Mill, and Bloom, I encountered that changed me at the core. I learned the value of education to me and began to see how miseducated I had been. For me, this was a revelation. It's like you've been trying to do this thing that just didn't work and being miserable because of it." Chapter 6 deals with the issue of anxiety. The sixth interviewee, Carolyn, said that philosophy was a response to, or antidote for, anxiety. Chapter 7 is about the issue of

---

[2] Merleau-Ponty, M. "The War Has Taken Place [1945]." *The Merleau-Ponty Reader*. Ed. Leonard Lawlor and Ted Toadvine. Trans. Hubert L. Dreyfus, and Patricia Allen Dreyfus. Evanston, IL: Northwestern University Press, 2007. 45.

human relations. The seventh interviewee, Gentry, said that what got him into philosophy was a problem, notably, why human relationships didn't work and how philosophy can *respond* to or solve such a problem. Chapter 8 is about the issue of reality and the question, "can I know what's out there?" For Margaret, the eighth interviewee, it was what can and must be verified by experience that got her into philosophy. Chapter 9 deals with the issue of the meaning of life. Evan, the ninth interviewee, turned to philosophy to find values to structure his life. Chapter 10 deals with the issue of nature or nurture. The tenth interviewee, Jin-Sun, traces the origin of her encounter with philosophy to the "idea of tabula rasa." Chapter 11 deals with the issue of physicalism. The eleventh interviewee, Katrin, was attracted to philosophy by "how other people use arguments." Chapter 12 deals with diversity and free speech. The twelfth interviewee, Woke, says: "Philosophy is not about ending dialogue, but beginning it, always going back to the beginning, reexamining one's premises. Without that reexamination, you can't begin to be woke. Philosophical reexamination is the manner in which the blinds are drawn and the eyes opened." And, Woke adds: "If you're woke you're philosophizing. If you're philosophizing, you're always going back to the beginning to retrace your steps and wondering whether the path you took is the right one. This involves the positive as well as the negative, the whole range of human thoughts and emotions, which PC severely limits. Then you're woke." Last, but not least, the book ends with an Afterword written by a former student of both Miller and mine, Kyle Paup. He has taken at least seven philosophy classes with me and he is one of the most intellectually engaged students I have ever met in my entire life. Kyle's assessment of the entire book:

> Personally, as all twelve voices ahead will affirm, philosophy is a life-changing experience. It allows us to reflect on ourselves as much as it allows us to reflect on the world. The person I am as a result of philosophical learning, a person who questions the nature of the world, questions the ethics behind our every action, questions what we can do to make the world a better place, and questions the limits of my own mind, is not the same person I was before being subject to it.

Overall, what I see in these interviews is how philosophy is neither abstract nor esoteric, which I am assuming may be the common perception of philosophy by non-philosophers. In teaching philosophy since 2009, I have learned that most of the time I have to bring philosophy to the students rather than the other way. This text exactly accomplishes what I could never accomplish as a teacher to this day: to bring philosophy to students in a way that connects philosophy with actual human beings and their real-life problems. Through these twelve new faces, Miller does an excellent job of showing how philosophy is and is not what can be called *trans-mundane*. Philosophy is not trans-mundane if by "trans" we mean "beyond the mundane." By contrast, philosophy is trans-mundane if by "trans" we mean "across the mundane" where across is taken in the sense of permeating the mundane in all of its aspects. Miller does a beautiful job in showing how these twelve individuals together form what can be called a *textual community*, a community formed in and through this text, even if they do not know each other at all outside this textual encounter. They may not have anything common outside of this text, but what they do have in common is the *encounter with philosophy*—encounter in the Deleuzean and Merleau-Pontian senses. What I also find to be common in all of these twelve figures is an axiological element that connects them, notably, the *value* of philosophy. It is not merely that one does philosophy out of habit, although one can. It is not merely that one follows a specific norm to do philosophy, although one can. It is not merely that one follows a specific desire to do philosophy, although one can. Perhaps, the habit, the norm, and the desire to do philosophy is motivated by the encounter with philosophy, which has led all these twelve figures to value philosophy itself and find or create other values through philosophy. I highly recommend this anthology to be used by any professor in an *introduction to philosophy* course if the professor wants to *introduce* philosophy in the *most accessible* way possible.

Introduction

As a philosopher heading off into the sunset as they like to say, I wanted to focus my remaining energies on finding the new Socrates, Hegel, or Derrida among young people.

I started with this vague notion that I'd like to see what's coming up next in philosophy. The project stayed on the back burner on low heat for several years until I figured out what I was doing.

How would I find these people—that was the main obstacle. I don't have a winning personality—that is how people have phrased it. Yet my desire to put this anthology together made me into a friendlier person and that result was welcome relief, especially to my wife.

How did I find these budding thinkers? Only one was a former student of mine. Others I found floating out there on the internet, especially by becoming their followers on Instagram, their friends on Facebook, and their connections on LinkedIn. Some colleagues made recommendations. Some people I met while traveling and just starting up a conversation. I met one at a Starbucks after overhearing her mention Socrates during her order of a Grande cappuccino and another who saved me from drowning in the Great Barrier Reef off the coast of Australia. You just never know.

I interviewed over one hundred philosophy students from all over the world and had a hard time whittling down the number of people to a manageable twelve. There are lots of great young thinkers out there. I was so happy that my interviewees were so diverse, including trans person, immigrant, assistant district attorney, marine biologist (and First Nations Person), border guard, stay-at-home mom, executive administrator, physicist, entrepreneur, counselor, politician, and cyber security expert.

These young people understand: philosophy matters. They understand more than philosophy matters: philosophy is essential for saving the world. It takes a superhero to step outside norms and traditions to see and craft a vision of the future. We definitely need young people to step up and actually practice philosophy.

This book has twelve chapters. Each chapter addresses an important philosophical theme. These themes are addressed in unique ways by each of the young philosophers. They were my guide; I was not theirs. These kids knew their stuff, but in order that readers can follow along, I decided to include the referenced texts. This is not such a bad thing inasmuch it provides context for the readers and offers them a unique kind of anthology: driven not by traditional themes in the history of philosophy but emerging from the narratives of our young thinkers. This makes the key points so much more vivid and accessible to students who are going through similar things in their lives. Our young philosophers express how these ideas are important to them and I think the readers will pick up on that and will be swept along by their narratives. I am wary of thick anthologies that achieve their goal of plurality at the expense of showcasing crucial points with new juxtapositions of texts and ideas. In this way, an anthology is not tomb for old texts, but a pressure cooker for the expression of ideas.

I came up with eight basic questions to ask each thinker:

- What got you into philosophy?
- What problems do you have that philosophy helped you with?
- Which philosophical ideas have had the most impact on you?

- Why is philosophy important to you?
- How did philosophy change you?
- Why do you think philosophy is important to the world?
- What was your family and friend's reactions to you becoming a philosopher?
- Do you have any suggestions for today's students?

How have your family and Friends reacted to you becoming a philosopher.

I got better at interviewing as the process evolved, so I don't necessarily ask every question in every chapter. But there are some lame and awkward moments due to my inexperience, though sometimes on purpose I did not ask each person every question if my interviewee was rocking it!

Self-Identity

Who Am I?

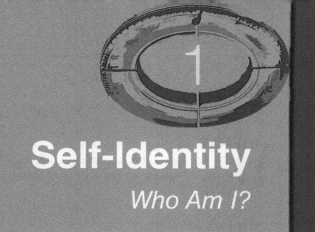

With platform shoes, Joy-Ray is at least a head taller than I am. Straight platinum hair and large hoop earrings accent an oval face and a long black lace dress is the height of fashion. I know Joy-Ray through a friend, who employs Joy-Ray as his accountant. We meet at a very famous Chicago restaurant. I can tell Joy-Ray is nervous, but so am, since this is actually my very first interview.

◇◇◇◇

JOY-RAY
You're odd looking.

MILLER
People have always said that about me.

JOY-RAY
I'm only saying that because that's probably what you're thinking about me.

MILLER
I'm not judging. I'm here to hear what you have to say.

JOY-ROY
As a philosopher.

MILLER
As a philosopher.

JOY-RAY
Alright, you sound safe.

MILLER
What got you into philosophy?

JOY-RAY
I was looking for something for a long time to explain to myself exactly who I was. In this society, people fit into neat categories and there didn't appear to be one for me.

MILLER

What prompted you to turn to philosophy?

JOY-RAY

Frankly, because the Philosophy Club at my university was the only club that didn't judge me. I felt safe there. I'd come to the weekly meetings and there's been accepting people and the topics did not disappoint.

MILLER

And was there one problem in philosophy that really helped you as a person to explore?

JOY-RAY

Self-identity. This was my major issue as a trans person. And I found a path to understanding myself and being okay with myself. If I couldn't solve this problem, life would be unbearable.

MILLER

Philosophy, then, did something important for you?

JOY-RAY

It saved my damn life by changing my viewpoint.

MILLER

And that saved you?

JOY-RAY

It stopped me from doing things I really don't want to share with a stranger.

MILLER

Would you share the philosophical ideas that have most impacted you? A short list perhaps.

JOY-RAY

Okay. First, intersectionality by a lovely person called Kimberlé Crenshaw. Second, the idea of double-consciousness by W.E.B. DuBois. Next, the unconscious projection of oppression by Iris Marion Young. Deconstruction also helped me map out my identity. Thank you very much, Jacques Derrida. My final two influences are as different as night and day: A German philosopher Immanuel Kant and an ancient Indian philosopher—Patanjali. Both taught me about my self-worth and identity.

MILLER

If you'd like to identify your favorite texts and tell how they inspired you, it would be instructive.

JOY-RAY

The idea of intersectionality was the first idea that rocked my world. In her 1989 paper, Kimberlé Crenshaw explains why it is misleading to think of discrimination coming from one direction when it could be coming from many directions. For example, I can be discriminated because I am trans, Black, an immigrant, and as a member of a lower socio-economic class. It is easier to identify one cause and one effect. However, in the complex social world of intersections, the impact could be from different directions at different times with varying forces. Those who are discriminated in one respect (e.g., race) are less burdened and more privileged relative to the multiply-burdened:

> This apparent contradiction is but another manifestation of the conceptual limitations of the single-issue analyses that intersectionality challenges. The point is that Black women can experience discrimination in any number of ways and that the contradiction arises from our assumptions that their claims of exclusion must be unidirectional. Consider an analogy to traffic in an intersection, coming and going in all four directions. Discrimination, like traffic through an intersection, may flow in one direction, and it may flow in another. If an accident happens in an intersection, it can be caused by cars traveling from any number of directions and, sometimes, from all of them. Similarly, if a Black woman is harmed because she is in the intersection, her injury could result from sex discrimination or race discrimination. . . .
>
> Sometimes the skid marks and the injuries simply indicate that they occurred simultaneously, frustrating efforts to determine which driver caused the harm. In these cases the tendency seems to be that no driver is held responsible, no treatment is administered, and the involved parties simply get back in their cars and zoom away.[1]

It's easy to personalize oppression and make it about the intentional action of evil individuals or groups. The intersection analogy would have us believe that there are specific drivers of oppression who purposely collide the oppressed. But this is too simple an explanation, which I got from "The Five Faces of Oppression" by Iris Marion Young. Oppression can be embedded within the norms, habits, and symbols of a society and followed unreflectively. The slaveholder with a whip is replaced by people and organizations who by habit and tradition unreflectively oppress others, for example, in language identifying me as "he" or "she" or a clerk who's following me around a store because these Black folks, they all thieves, or immigrants and poor people as freeloaders. Instead of having a new road system where drivers easily avoid one another, old road systems with dangerous intersections and traditional traffic patterns are retained and crashes are inevitable.

> I have suggested that oppression is the inhibition of a group through a vast network of everyday practices, assumptions, behaviors, and institutional rules: it is structural or systemic. The systemic character of oppression implies that an oppressed group need not have a corresponding oppressing group. . . . The conscious activities of many individuals daily contribute to maintaining and reproducing oppression, but those people are usually simply doing their jobs or living their lives, not understanding themselves as agents of oppression.[2]

From the ideas of intersectionality and structural oppression, I learned that social identity is formed at an intersection of societal forces. Some people can go through the intersection without a mark. Others, like myself, are hit from many directions, with some of the collisions more violent than others. While intersectionality explains to me what's going in the social world, it does not speak the inner world of

---

[1] Crenshaw, Kimberlé. "Demarginalizing the Intersection of Race and Sex: A Black Feminist Critique of Antidiscrimination Doctrine, Feminist Theory and Antiracist Politics." *University of Chicago Legal Forum* 1989.1 (1989), Article 8. <http://chicagounbound.uchicago.edu/uclf/ vol1989/iss1/8>.

[2] Young, Marion Iris. "Five Faces of Oppression." *Political Philosophy: The Essential Texts*. Ed. Steven M. Cahn. 3rd ed. New York and Oxford: Oxford University Press, 2015. 1061, 1062.

oppressed people. In this famous essay "The Souls of Black Folk," W.E.B. DuBois coins the phrase "double consciousness" to describe the psychological state of oppressed people. This helped me make sense of the terrible conflicts I face looking out on this world. At the same time they struggle to see the world from their own perspective, Blacks also see through the eyes of White people, which means in a negative light. There is this constant struggle for Blacks to establish their own identity in the face of negative White judgments. This is relatable to all of us to some extent, for example, the struggle between each of us finding our identities and others labeling us. But the case is amped up when this is not a temporary but a permanent condition, as it is for people who are oppressed or in my case multiply-oppressed. I struggle with a society that clearly defines two unchangeable genders with my own idea of gender fluidity. I struggle with a society that throws Whiteness on a Black face or thinks of me as less because I have not yet met the criterion of acceptable material wealth. No offense to W.E.B., but I have like a quadruple consciousness. This stuff messes with your head because you never measure up, even though you believe you've done good things. You're the stranger, the outsider, the foreigner being judged, and forced into a mold that is decidedly NOT YOU:

> The history of the American Negro is the history of this strife,—this longing to attain self-conscious manhood, to merge his double self into a better and truer self. In this merging he wishes neither of the older selves to be lost. He would not Africanize America, for America has too much to teach the world and Africa. He would not bleach his Negro soul in a flood of white Americanism, for he knows that Negro blood has a message for the world. He simply wishes to make it possible for a man to be both a Negro and an American, without being cursed and spit upon by his fellows, without having the doors of Opportunity closed roughly in his face. . . .
>
> The Nation has not yet found peace from its sins; the freedman has not yet found in freedom his promised land. Whatever of good may have come in these years of change, the shadow of a deep disappointment rests upon the Negro people,—a disappointment all the more bitter because the unattained ideal was unbounded save by the simple ignorance of a lowly people.
>
> The first decade was merely a prolongation of the vain search for freedom, the boon that seemed ever barely to elude their grasp,—like a tantalizing will-o'-the-wisp, maddening and misleading the headless host. The holocaust of war, the terrors of the Ku-Klux Klan, the lies of carpet-baggers, the disorganization of industry, and the contradictory advice of friends and foes, left the bewildered serf with no new watchword beyond the old cry for freedom. As time flew, however, he began to grasp a new idea. The ideal of liberty demanded for its attainment powerful means, and these the Fifteenth Amendment gave him. The ballot, which before he had looked upon as a visible sign of freedom, he now regarded as the chief means of gaining and perfecting the liberty with which war had partially endowed him. And, why not? Had not votes made war and emancipated millions? Had not votes enfranchised the freedmen? Was anything impossible to a power that had done all this? A million black men started with renewed zeal to vote themselves into the kingdom. So the decade flew away, the revolution of 1876 came, and left the half-free serf weary, wondering, but still inspired. Slowly but steadily, in the following years, a new vision began gradually to replace the dream of political power, a powerful movement, the rise of another ideal to guide the unguided, another pillar of fire by night after a clouded day. It was the ideal of "book-learning": the curiosity, born of compulsory ignorance, to know and test the power of the cabalistic letters of the white man, the longing to know. Here at last seemed to have been discovered the mountain path to Canaan: longer than the highway of Emancipation and law, steep and rugged, but straight, leading to heights enough to overlook life.
>
> Up the new path the advance guard toiled, slowly, heavily, doggedly; only those who have watched and guided the faltering feet, the misty minds, the dull understandings, of the dark pupils of

these schools know how faithfully, how piteously, these people strove to learn. It was weary work. The cold statistician wrote down the inches of progress here and there, noted also where here and there a foot had slipped or someone had fallen. To the tired climbers, the horizon was ever dark, the mists were often cold, the Canaan was always dim and far away. If, however, the vistas disclosed as yet no goal, no resting-place, little but flattery and criticism, the journey at least gave leisure for reflection and self-examination; it changed the child of Emancipation to the youth with dawning self-consciousness, self-realization, and self-respect. In those somber forests of his striving his own soul rose before him, and he saw himself—darkly as through a veil; and yet he saw in himself some faint revelation of his power, of his mission. He began to have a dim feeling that, to attain his place in the world, he must be himself, and not another. For the first time he sought to analyze the burden he bore upon his back that dead-weight of social degradation partially masked behind a half-named Negro problem. He felt his poverty; without a cent, without a home, without land, tools, or savings, he had entered into competition with rich, landed, skilled neighbors. To be a poor man is hard, but to be a poor race in a land of dollars is the very bottom of hardships. He felt the weight of his ignorance—not simply of letters, but of life, of business, of the humanities; the accumulated sloth and shirking and awkwardness of decades and centuries shackled his hands and feet. Nor was his burden all poverty and ignorance. The red stain of bastardy, which two centuries of systematic legal defilement of Negro women had stamped upon his race, meant not only the loss of ancient African chastity, but also the hereditary weight of a mass of corruption from White adulterers, threatening almost the obliteration of the Negro home.

A people thus handicapped ought not to be asked to race with the world but rather allowed to give all its time and thought to its own social problems. But alas! While sociologists gleefully count his bastards and his prostitutes, the very soul of the toiling, sweating Black man is darkened by the shadow of a vast despair. Men call the shadow prejudice and learnedly explain it as the natural defense of culture against barbarism, learning against ignorance, purity against crime, the "higher" against the "lower" races. To which the Negro cries Amen! and swears that to so much of this strange prejudice as is founded on just homage to civilization, culture, righteousness, and progress, he humbly bows and meekly does obeisance. But before that nameless prejudice that leaps beyond all this he stands help-less, dismayed, and well-nigh speechless; before that personal disrespect and mockery, the ridicule and systematic humiliation, the distortion of fact and wanton license of fancy, the cynical ignoring of the better and the boisterous welcoming of the worse, the all-pervading desire to inculcate disdain for ev-erything Black, from Toussaint to the devil,—before this there rises a sickening despair that would dis-arm and discourage any nation save that black host to whom "discouragement" is an unwritten word.

But the facing of so vast a prejudice could not but bring the inevitable self-questioning, self-disparagement, and lowering of ideals which ever accompany repression and breed in an atmo-sphere of contempt and hate. Whisperings and portents came home upon the four winds: Lo! we are diseased and dying, cried the dark hosts; we cannot write, our voting is vain; what need of education, since we must always cook and serve? And the Nation echoed and enforced this self-criticism, saying: Be content to be servants, and nothing more; what need of higher culture for half-men? Away with the black man's ballot, by force or fraud,—and behold the suicide of a race! Nevertheless, out of the evil came something of good,—the more careful adjustment of education to real life, the clearer percep-tion of the Negroes' social responsibilities, and the sobering realization of the meaning of progress.[3]

---

[3] DuBois, W.E.B. *The Souls of Black Folk*. Project Gutenberg. <https://www.gutenberg.org/files/408/408-h/408-h .htm>.

According to these theories, my self-identity is at the mercy of societal forces. Frankly, that didn't suit me too much. As indebted as I am to the ideas of intersectionality, structural oppression, and double-consciousness, I wonder whether is this all I am: a being defined by others. I adjusted to their perspective of me and it fucked me up big time. I then remembered something I read in Dr. King's work that put me on the right track. Dr. King maintains that people should never adjust to immoral or unjust societies. He argues for maladjustment in such cases:

> Now we all should seek to live a well-adjusted life in order to avoid neurotic and schizophrenic personalities. But there are some things within our social order to which I am proud to be maladjusted and to which I call upon you to be maladjusted. I never intend to adjust myself' to segregation and discrimination. I never intend to adjust myself to mob rule. I never intend to adjust myself to the tragic effects of the methods of physical violence and to tragic militarism. I call upon you to be maladjusted to such things. I call upon you to be as maladjusted as Amos who in the midst of the injustices of his day cried out in words that echo across the generation, "Let judgment run down like waters and righteousness like a mighty stream." As maladjusted as Abraham Lincoln who had the vision to see that this nation could not exist half slave and half free. As maladjusted as Jefferson, who in the midst of an age amazingly adjusted to slavery could cry out, "All men are created equal and are endowed by their Creator with certain inalienable rights and that among these are life, liberty and the pursuit of happiness." As maladjusted as Jesus of Nazareth who dreamed a dream of the fatherhood of God and the brotherhood of man, God grant that we will be so maladjusted that we will be able to go out and change our world and our civilization.[4]

But I still felt diminished by the world. And where could I go if the world brought me misery? I yearned for dignity, for freedom. Immanuel Kant's ideas of dignity and freedom awakened me to something deep within me. I am not just in this interaction being crashed into by other people and institutions. I am not a means to an end, but an end in itself. What I took from this is I can define myself differently than I can define a chair. And I can speak up for myself as a dignified being, deserving of rights and respect. Kant distinguishes between price and dignity. Everything in the society is conditioned by other things and has a price in relationship to other things. On the other hand, dignity is beyond price. It is one of a kind, unique. I am a unique being that cannot be judged or labeled by the world. That is what Kant is saying:

> Now I say: man and generally any rational being exists as an end in himself, not merely as a means to be arbitrarily used by this or that will, but in all his actions, whether they concern himself or other rational beings, must be always regarded at the same time as an end. All objects of the inclinations have only a conditional worth, for if the inclinations and the wants founded on them did not exist, then their object would be without value. But the inclinations, themselves being sources of want, are so far from having an absolute worth for which they should be desired that on the contrary it must be the universal wish of every rational being to be wholly free from them. Thus the worth of any object which is to be acquired by our action is always conditional. Beings whose existence depends not on our will but on nature's, have nevertheless, if they are irrational beings, only a relative value as means, and are therefore called things; rational beings, on the contrary, are called persons, because

---

[4] King, Jr., Martin Luther. "The Power of Nonviolence." *The Essential Writings and Speeches of Martin Luther King, Jr.* Ed. James M. Washington. San Francisco: HarperCollins, 1991. 14-15.

their very nature points them out as ends in themselves, that is as something which must not be used merely as means, and so far therefore restricts freedom of action (and is an object of respect). These, therefore, are not merely subjective ends whose existence has a worth for us as an effect of our action, but objective ends, that is, things whose existence is an end in itself; an end moreover for which no other can be substituted, which they should subserve merely as means, for otherwise nothing whatever would possess absolute worth; but if all worth were conditioned and therefore contingent, then there would be no supreme practical principle of reason whatever.

If then there is a supreme practical principle or, in respect of the human will, a categorical imperative, it must be one which, being drawn from the conception of that which is necessarily an end for everyone because it is an end in itself, constitutes an objective principle of will, and can therefore serve as a universal practical law. The foundation of this principle is: rational nature exists as an end in itself. Man necessarily conceives his own existence as being so; so far then this is a subjective principle of human actions. But every other rational being regards its existence similarly, just on the same rational principle that holds for me: so that it is at the same time an objective principle, from which as a supreme practical law all laws of the will must be capable of being deduced. Accordingly the practical imperative will be as follows: So act as to treat humanity, whether in thine own person or in that of any other, in every case as an end withal, never as means only. . . .

In the kingdom of ends everything has either value or dignity. Whatever has a value can be replaced by something else that is equivalent; whatever, on the other hand, is above all value, and therefore admits of no equivalent, has dignity.[5]

Within oppressive intersections, it is hard to grasp one's dignity apart from all the indignities life throws your way. My mind was whirling 100 miles per minute and its soundtrack consisted of voices of diminishment. It occurred to me that such a mind was no fertile ground for dignity, for self-respect. I had to restrain my mind. I learned restraint by doing yoga and reading about the philosophy of yoga in the *Yoga Sutras* by ancient Indian philosopher Patanjali. In this book there are 195 sutras or short verses. Sutras 2, 3, and 4 of Book I say it all for me:

2. The restraint of the modifications of the mind-stuff is Yoga. . . .
3. Then the Seer abides in Its own Nature. . . .
4. At other times, [the Self appears to] assume the forms of the mental modifications.[6]

If we can restrain our minds, we can find our true selves, which are independent of the turbulence we experience in our lives. This doesn't change the oppression in the world, but it does allow us not lose the most part of ourselves, our dignity, because of it. These short verses impacted me, especially after reading Kant. Humans can rise above the world and don't have to be slaves to the identities and labels others put on them.

MILLER
That is powerful stuff. And thanks.

---

[5] Kant, Immanuel. *Fundamental Principles of the Metaphysics of Morals*. Project Gutenberg. <https://www.gutenberg.org/files/5682/5682-h/5682-h.htm>.
[6] Patanjali. *The Yoga Sutras of Patanjali*. Trans. Sri Swami Satchidananda. Buckingham, VA: Integral Yoga Publications, 2012. 3, 6, 7.

JOY-RAY
Anything else before I use the restroom?

MILLER
How did philosophy change you?

JOY-RAY
It gave me the ability to wrap my arms around things. I was walking through this world without having a clue and it wasn't bliss. I was being hurt by the world.

MILLER
And philosophy changed that?

JOY-RAY
It is changing that as we speak. It made me realize my place in the world and how I could change that place.

MILLER
Do you think philosophy is important to the world?

JOY-RAY
People need a wakeup call. It's like they're just going to their jobs and buying things and not caring about the world.

MILLER
They don't care about important things?

JOY-RAY
Most of them don't know they're hurting other people and even themselves. It's like people are living on autopilot and then they die.

MILLER
That bothers you.

JOY-RAY
It doesn't hurt some people when other people are idiots. But it hurts me when they are. Do you understand what I'm saying?

MILLER
I get it. I'm privileged and the stupidity and ignorance of others doesn't affect me as much as it does you.

JOY-RAY
Yeah, so I'm all for people becoming more self-reflective and philosophical.

MILLER
Do you think students should study philosophy?

JOY-RAY

Absolutely. There's so much darkness in the world and philosophy is the light. I'm just not just saying that because I'm trans and don't want the world crapping on me. There has to be more critical thinking going on or else—

MILLER

All of us are screwed.

JOY-RAY

Right. Some people might think something like intersectionality doesn't relate to them. But it does. People my age—all of us—are trying to find out who we are. All people are at intersections where multiple outside forces are impacting them—maybe parents, family, religion, bullies, and social pressures, social media. We often believe we are the impacts made on us instead of the impact we can make by finding our freedom.

MILLER

Even people my age are trying to find out who they are.

JOY-RAY

It feels like I'm getting defined by others all the time and in negative way. Probably everybody feels they're in an intersection and they're getting hit from all sides. We feel labeled. It just feels like everybody has an opinion about us and it just makes us—crazy. Whether it's our parents, our friends, even our lovers, you know.

MILLER

It never ends. People judge. It's what society thinks.

JOY-RAY

Philosophy has taught me to rise above the chatter and the gossip and the judging.

MILLER

Kant's idea of dignity really impacted you?

JOY-RAY

Exactly. Before reading that, I just thought I was the donkey in the pin the tail on the donkey. Your generation played that game, right?

MILLER

Too many times to forget.

JOY-RAY

It's like playing that game and getting all these labels pinned on me and thinking that I had to put up with that crap. But then I realized I am being with dignity and I wasn't going to let other people degrade me.

MILLER

You saw yourself as an end-in-itself.

JOY-RAY

Right. You see then. I wasn't going to be there for people to pin their negative attitudes on.

MILLER

And you experienced freedom in discovering yourself as an end-in-itself.

JOY-RAY

Nobody could touch me. I was somewhere where they couldn't put their bullshit on me. That in itself was worth studying philosophy.

MILLER

I want to thank you, Joy-Ray, for spending time with me—and trusting me.

JOY-RAY

You mean it's over? That was actually fun.

MILLER

I'm glad it wasn't torture.

JOY-RAY

Can I say something before this is officially over?

MILLER

Sure.

JOY-RAY

I know that people think philosophy is like this abstract thing that can't be used in their lives. But if you just try, you'll find out it's the most important thing. It helps you find out who you are. And once you know that, the rest is a lot easier.

MILLER

It's been a pleasure, Joy-Ray.

JOY-RAY

Same here.

Philosophical Creativity

Expressing Oneself Philosophically

I can't really say much about this interview as I would like. It's not as if a gun is pointed at my head, but for the sake of all concerned, especially "Jorge," I am going to keep my mouth shut about particulars. During the tail-end of our conversation, border guards approached "Jorge." We didn't talk politics at all, mainly about how people philosophize differently.

◇◇◇◇

JORGE

Truth if there is truth, it is not easily accessible. It's not like you click and there it is. It's not like you double or even triple click and there it is. It takes philosophical creativity to articulate truth.

MILLER

There are many different philosophical styles.

JORGE

Just like different styles of painting, architecture, music, and clothing. Sometimes philosophy is taught like it's monolithic. It's not people come to it and work within it in different ways. I've personally benefited from knowing those ways and using them at appropriate times when I am philosophizing.

MILLER

What are your favorite philosophical styles?

JORGE

I had a teacher who mentioned four of these and then I added the final two: radical skepticism, moderate skepticism, apology or defense, assumption development, poetry, and anti-systematic.

MILLER

Nice. After you talk about each type of philosophizing, do you have time to chat about what got you into philosophy?

JORGE

Let's do that now because there might not be a "later" for me to chat. People have their eyes on me. I'll make a short story even shorter. I was totally dissatisfied with my education until I stumbled into a lecture hall at the University of Minnesota and heard some jerk talking about the unreality of time and space, and because I had imbibed earlier in the day I shouted at him. He was very nice to me and explained his position. He became my thesis advisor and is working with lawyers to keep me from staying home, and if that happens, I will be forced to drink hemlock.

MILLER

I'll get out of your way then.

JORGE

I'll begin with the radical skeptical approach to philosophy. The radical skeptical approach to philosophy contends that while objects appear to each of us as phenomena, we cannot know things in themselves, their absolute nature. Radical skepticism refuses to say anything about the unknown, what is beyond what appears to us. Nothing has an absolute existence. As Sextus Empiricus, the Roman philosopher explains, when human beings begin to recognize contradictions in their thinking, they grow perplexed instead of realizing *ataraxia* (ἀταραξία) or tranquility. To reach this state of tranquility, each argument cancels its opposite and the result is suspending judgment and having no opinions.

Chapter VI

The Origin of Skepticism.

Skepticism arose in the beginning from the hope of attaining *ataraxia*; for men of the greatest talent were perplexed by the contradiction of things, and being at a loss on what to believe, began to question what things are true, and what false, hoping to attain *ataraxia* as a result of the decision. The fundamental principle of the Skeptical system is especially this, namely, to oppose every argument by one of equal weight, for it seems to us that in this way we finally reach the position where we have no dogmas.

Chapter VII

Does the Skeptic Dogmatize?

We say that the Skeptic does not dogmatize. We do not say this, meaning by the word dogma the popular assent to certain things rather than others (for the Skeptic does assent to feelings that are a necessary result of sensation, as for example, when he is warm or cold, he cannot say that he thinks he is not warm or cold), but we say this, meaning by dogma the acceptance of any opinion with regard to the unknown things investigated by science. For the Pyrrhonean assents to nothing that is unknown. Furthermore, he does not dogmatize even when he utters the Skeptical formulae with regard to things that are unknown, such as "Nothing more," or "I decide nothing," or any of the others about which we shall speak later. For the one who dogmatizes regards the thing about which he is said to dogmatize, as existing in itself; the Skeptic does not however regard these formulae as having an absolute existence, for he assumes that the saying "All is false," includes itself with other things as false, and likewise the saying "Nothing is true"; in the same way "Nothing more," states that together with other things it itself is nothing more, and cancels itself therefore, as well as other things. We say the same also with regard to the other Skeptical expressions. In short, if he who dogmatizes, assumes as existing in itself that about which he dogmatizes, the Skeptic, on the contrary, expresses his sayings in such a way that they are understood to be themselves included, and it cannot be said that he dogmatizes in saying these things. The principal thing in uttering these formulae is that he says what he sees, and communicates his own feelings in an unprejudiced way, without asserting anything with regard to external objects.

Chapter IX

Does the Skeptic Study Natural Science?

We reply similarly also to the question whether the Skeptic should study natural science. For we do not study natural science to express ourselves with confidence regarding any of the dogmas that it teaches, but we take it up to be able to meet every argument by one of equal weight, and also for the sake of *ataraxia*. In the same way we study the logical and ethical part of the so-called philosophy.

Chapter X

Do the Skeptics deny Phenomena?

Those who say that the Skeptics deny phenomena appear to me to be in ignorance of our teachings. For as we said before, we do not deny the sensations that we think we have, and which lead us to assent involuntarily to them, and these are the phenomena. When, however, we ask whether the object is such as it appears to be, while we concede that it appears so and so, we question, not the phenomenon, but with regard to that which is asserted of the phenomenon, and that is different from doubting the phenomenon itself. For example, it appears to us that honey is sweet. This we concede, for we experience sweetness through sensation. We doubt, however, whether it is sweet by reason of its essence, which is not a question of the phenomenon, but of that which is asserted of the phenomenon. Should we, however, argue directly against the phenomena, it is not with the intention of denying their existence, but to show the rashness of the Dogmatics. For if reasoning is such a deceiver that it well-nigh snatches away the phenomena from before your eyes, how should we not distrust it with regard to things that are unknown, so as not to rashly follow it?

objectivity

Chapter XI

The Criterion of Skepticism.

It is evident that we pay careful attention to phenomena from what we say about the criterion of the Skeptical School. The word criterion is used in two ways. First, it is understood as a proof of existence or non-existence, with regard to which we shall speak in the opposing argument. Secondly, when it refers to action, meaning the criterion to which we give heed in life, in doing some things and refraining from doing others, and it is about this that we shall now speak. We say, consequently, that the criterion of the Skeptical School is the phenomenon, and in calling it so, we mean the idea of it. It cannot be doubted, as it is based on susceptibility and involuntary feeling. Hence no one doubts, perhaps, that an object appears so and so, but one questions if it is as it appears. Therefore, as we cannot be entirely inactive as regards the observances of daily life, we live by giving heed to phenomena, and in an unprejudiced way. But this observance of what pertains to daily life, appears to be of four different kinds. Sometimes it is directed by the guidance of nature, sometimes by the necessity of the feelings, sometimes by the tradition of laws and of customs, and sometimes by the teaching of the arts. It is directed by the guidance of nature, for by nature we are capable of sensation and thought; by the necessity of the feelings, for hunger leads us to food, and thirst to drink; by the traditions of laws and customs, for according to them we consider piety a good in daily life, and impiety an evil;

appearance of object vs. reality of appearance

observance of daily life

*1) guidance of nature
2) Necessity of feelings
3) Tradition of law and customs
4) Teaching of arts*

by the teaching of the arts, for we are not inactive in the arts we undertake. We say all these things, however, without expressing a decided opinion.[1]

JORGE

Radical doubt is really a cool weapon to have when you begin philosophizing. It's like a sword that can cut things to ribbons. I especially like to use radical skepticism on obnoxious people in class. But a more moderate kind of skeptical approach offered by the Scottish philosopher David Hume does laser surgery on arguments rather than destroying them. Stick close to everyday life and avoid making claims about things that are outside the bounds of ordinary experience:

129. There is, indeed, a more mitigated skepticism or academical philosophy, which may be both durable and useful, and which may, in part, be the result of this Pyrrhonism, or excessive skepticism, when its undistinguished doubts are, in some measure, corrected by common sense and reflection. The greater part of mankind are naturally apt to be affirmative and dogmatical in their opinions; and while they see objects only on one side, and have no idea of any counterpoising argument, they throw themselves precipitately into the principles, to which they are inclined; nor have they any indulgence for those who entertain opposite sentiments. To hesitate or balance perplexes their understanding, checks their passion, and suspends their action. They are, therefore, impatient till they escape from a state, which to them is so uneasy: and they think, that they could never remove themselves far enough from it, by the violence of their affirmations and obstinacy of their belief. But could such dogmatical reasoners become sensible of the strange infirmities of human understanding, even in its most perfect state, and when most accurate and cautious in its determinations; such a reflection would naturally inspire them with more modesty and reserve, and diminish their fond opinion of themselves, and their prejudice against antagonists. The illiterate may reflect on the disposition of the learned, who, amidst all the advantages of study and reflection, are commonly still diffident in their determinations: and if any of the learned be inclined, from their natural temper, to haughtiness and obstinacy, a small tincture of Pyrrhonism might abate their pride, by showing them, that the few advantages, which they may have attained over their fellows, are but inconsiderable, if compared with the universal perplexity and confusion, which is inherent in human nature. In general, there is a degree of doubt, and caution, and modesty, which, in all kinds of scrutiny and decision, ought for ever to accompany a just reasoner.

130. Another species of mitigated skepticism which may be of advantage to mankind, and which may be the natural result of the Pyrrhonian doubts and scruples, is the limitation of our enquiries to such subjects as are best adapted to the narrow capacity of human understanding. The imagination of man is naturally sublime, delighted with whatever is remote and extraordinary, and running, without control, into the most distant parts of space and time in order to avoid the objects, which custom has rendered too familiar to it. A correct judgment observes a contrary method, and avoiding all distant and high enquiries, confines itself to common life, and to such subjects as fall under daily practice and experience; leaving the more sublime topics to the embellishment of poets and orators, or to the arts of priests and politicians. To bring us to so salutary a determination, nothing can be more serviceable, than to be once thoroughly convinced of the force of the Pyrrhonian doubt, and of the

---

[1] Empiricus, Sextus. "Pyrrhonic Sketches." *Sextus Empricism and Greek Skepticism*. Ed. Mary Wells. Project Gutenberg. <https://www.gutenberg.org/files/17556/17556-h/17556-h.htm>.

impossibility, that anything, but the strong power of natural instinct, could free us from it. Those who have a propensity to philosophy, will still continue their researches; because they reflect, that, besides "the immediate pleasure," of attending to such an occupation, philosophical decisions are nothing but the reflections of common life, methodized and corrected. But they will never be tempted to go beyond common life, so long as they consider the imperfection of those faculties which they employ, their narrow reach, and their inaccurate operations. While we cannot give a satisfactory reason, why we believe, after a thousand experiments, that a stone will fall, or fire burn; can we ever satisfy ourselves concerning any determination, which we may form, with regard to the origin of worlds, and the situation of nature, from, and to eternity? This narrow limitation, indeed, of our enquiries, is, in every respect, so reasonable, that it suffices to make the slightest examination into the natural powers of the human mind and to compare them with their objects, in order to recommend it to us. We shall then find what are the proper subjects of science and enquiry.

131. It seems to me, that the only objects of the abstract science or of demonstration are quantity and number, and that all attempts to extend this more perfect species of knowledge beyond these bounds are mere sophistry and illusion. As the component parts of quantity and number are entirely similar, their relations become intricate and involved; and nothing can be more curious, as well as useful, than to trace, by a variety of mediums, their equality or inequality, through their different appearances. But as all other ideas are clearly distinct and different from each other, we can never advance farther, by our utmost scrutiny, than to observe this diversity, and, by an obvious reflection, pronounce one thing not to be another. Or if there be any difficulty in these decisions, it proceeds entirely from the undeterminate meaning of words, which is corrected by juster definitions. That the square of the hypotenuse is equal to the squares of the other two sides, cannot be known, let the terms be ever so exactly defined, without a train of reasoning and enquiry. But to convince us of this proposition, that where there is no property, there can be no injustice, it is only necessary to define the terms, and explain injustice to be a violation of property. This proposition is, indeed, nothing but a more imperfect definition. It is the same case with all those pretended syllogistical reasonings, which may be found in every other branch of learning, except the sciences of quantity and number; and these may safely, I think, be pronounced the only proper objects of knowledge and demonstration.

132. All other enquiries of men regard only matter of fact and existence; and these are evidently incapable of demonstration. Whatever is may not be. No negation of a fact can involve a contradiction. The non-existence of any being, without exception, is as clear and distinct an idea as its existence. The proposition, which affirms it not to be, however false, is no less conceivable and intelligible, than that which affirms it to be. But the case is different with the sciences. Every proposition, which is not true, is there confused and unintelligible. That the cube root of 64 is equal to the half of 10, is a false proposition, and can never be distinctly conceived. But that Caesar, or the angel Gabriel, or any being never existed, may be a false proposition, but still is perfectly conceivable, and implies no contradiction.

The existence, therefore, of any being can only be proved by arguments for or against its cause or its effect; and these arguments are founded entirely on experience. If we reason a priori, anything may appear to be able to produce anything. The falling of a pebble may, for aught we know, extinguish the sun; or the wish of a man might control the planets in their orbits. It is only experience, which teaches us the nature and bounds of cause and effect, and enables us to infer the existence of one object from that of another. 34. Such is the foundation of moral reasoning, which forms the greater part of human knowledge, and is the source of all human action and behaviour.

Moral reasonings are either concerning particular or general facts. All deliberations in life are attributed to the former; as also all disquisitions in history, chronology, geography, and astronomy.

The sciences, which treat of general facts, are based on general facts are politics, natural philosophy, physics, and chemistry where the qualities, causes, and effects of a whole species of objects are enquired into.

Divinity or theology, as it states the existence of a deity, and the immortality of souls, is composed partly of reasonings concerning particular or general facts. It has a foundation in reason, so far as it is supported by experience. But its best and most solid foundation is faith and divine revelation.

Morals and criticism are not so properly the objectives of understanding as of taste and sentiment. Beauty, whether moral or natural, is felt, more properly than perceived. Or if we reason concerning it, and endeavor to fix its standard, we regard a new fact, to wit, the general tastes of mankind, or some such fact, which may be the object of reasoning and enquiry.

When we run over libraries, persuaded of these principles, what havoc must we make? If we take in our hand any volume, of divinity or school metaphysics, for instance; let us ask, does it contain any abstract reasoning concerning quantity or number? No. Does it contain any experimental reasoning concerning matter of fact and existence? No. Commit it then to the flames: for it can contain nothing but sophistry and illusion.[2]

The staple for most philosophers is to take an argument and defend it. Philosophers can be defenders or apologists for a position, for example, the following argument for the existence of God by Thomas Aquinas:

The first and more manifest way is the argument from motion. It is certain, and evident to our senses, that in the world some things are in motion. Now whatever is in motion is put in motion by another, for nothing can be in motion except it is in potentiality to that towards which it is in motion; whereas a thing moves inasmuch as it is in act. For motion is nothing else than the reduction of something from potentiality to actuality. But nothing can be reduced from potentiality to actuality, except by something in a state of actuality. Thus that which is actually hot, as fire, makes wood, which is potentially hot, to be actually hot, and thereby moves and changes it. Now it is not possible that the same thing should be at once in actuality and potentiality in the same respect, but only in different respects. For what is actually hot cannot simultaneously be potentially hot; but it is simultaneously potentially cold. It is therefore impossible that in the same respect and in the same way a thing should be both mover and moved, i.e. that it should move itself. Therefore, whatever is in motion must be put in motion by another. If that by which it is put in motion be itself put in motion, then this also needs to be put in motion by another, and that by another again. But this cannot go on to infinity, because then there would be no first mover, and, consequently, no other mover; seeing that subsequent movers move only inasmuch as they are put in motion by the first mover; as the staff moves only because it is put in motion by the hand. Therefore it is necessary to arrive at a first mover, put in motion by no other; and this everyone understands to be God.[3]

On the flip side of the defending position, philosophers can make assumptions and just watch where they are, like throwing a ball down the street. In Plato's dialogue *Parmenides*, I learned what I call "see where your assumption goes." Assume something and then just see where it goes. In this passage, the

or "assume and go."

---

[2] Hume, David. *An Enquiry Concerning Human Understanding.* Project Gutenberg. <https://www.gutenberg.org/ebooks/9662>.

[3] Aquinas, Thomas. *Summa Theologica.* Project Gutenberg. <http://www.gutenberg.org/cache/epub/17611/pg17611.html>.

assumption is one and the development of that assumption proves many things that are not anticipated. This kind of inquiry is wide open and is often the most challenging and scary kind of philosophizing:

Parmenides proceeded: 1.a. If one is, he said, the one cannot be many?

Impossible.

Then the one cannot have parts, and cannot be a whole?

Why not?

Because every part is part of a whole; is it not?

Yes.

And what is a whole? Would not that of which no part is wanting to be a whole?

Certainly.

Then, in either case, the one would be made up of parts; both as being a whole, and also as having parts?

To be sure.

And in either case, the one would be many, and not one?

True.

But, surely, it ought to be one and not many?

It ought.

Then, if the one is to remain one, it will not be a whole, and will not have parts?

No.

But if it has no parts, it will have neither beginning, middle, nor end; for these would of course be parts of it.

Right.

"But then, again, a beginning and an end are the limits of everything?

Certainly.

Then the one, having neither beginning nor end, is unlimited?

Yes, unlimited.

And therefore formless; for it cannot partake either of round or straight.

But why?

Why, because the round is that of which all the extreme points are equidistant from the centre?

Yes.

And the straight is that of which the centre intercepts the view of the extremes?

True.

Then the one would have parts and would be many, if it partook either of a straight or of a circular form?

Assuredly.

But having no parts, it will be neither straight nor round?

Right.[4]

---

[4] Plato. *Parmenides*. Project Gutenberg. <https://www.gutenberg.org/ebooks/1687>.

Philosophical creativity is not limited to formal argumentation, but can be expressed poetically, for example, in *De rerum natura* by the Roman philosopher Lucretius:

THE VOID
But yet creation's neither crammed nor blocked
About by body: there's in things a void—
Which to have known will serve thee many a turn,
Nor will not leave thee wandering in doubt,
Forever searching in the sum of all,
And losing faith in these pronouncements mine.
There's place intangible, a void and room.
For were it not, things could in nowise move;
Since body's property to block and check
Would work on all and at all times the same.
Thus naught could evermore push forth and go,
Since naught elsewhere would yield a starting place.
But now through oceans, lands, and heights of heaven,
By diverse causes and in diverse modes,
Before our eyes we mark how much may move,
Which, finding not a void, would fail deprived
Of stir and motion; nay, would then have been
Nowise begot at all, since matter, then,
Had staid at rest, its parts together crammed.
Then too, however solid objects seem,
They yet are formed of matter mixed with void:
In rocks and caves the watery moisture seeps,
And beady drops stand out like plenteous tears;
And food finds way through every frame that lives;
The trees increase and yield the season's fruit
Because their food throughout the whole is poured,
Even from the deepest roots, through trunks and boughs;
And voices pass the solid walls and fly
Reverberant through shut doorways of a house;
And stiffening frost seeps inward to our bones.
Which but for voids for bodies to go through
'Tis clear could happen in nowise at all.
Again, why see we among objects some
Of heavier weight, but of no bulkier size?
Indeed, if in a ball of wool there be
As much of body as in lump of lead,
The two should weigh alike, since body tends
To load things downward, while the void abides,
By contrary nature, the imponderable.
Therefore, an object just as large but lighter
Declares infallibly its more of void;

Even as the heavier more of matter shows,
And how much less of vacant room inside.
That which we're seeking with sagacious quest
Exists, infallibly, commixed with things—
The void, the invisible inane.

Right here
I am compelled a question to expound,
Forestalling something certain folk suppose,
Lest it avail to lead thee off from truth:
Waters (they say) before the shining breed
Of the swift scaly creatures somehow give,
And straightway open sudden liquid paths,
Because the fishes leave behind them room
To which at once the yielding billows stream.
Thus things among themselves can yet be moved,
And change their place, however full the Sum—
Received opinion, wholly false forsooth.
For where can scaly creatures forward dart,
Save where the waters give them room? Again,
Where can the billows yield a way, so long
As ever the fish are powerless to go?
Thus either all bodies of motion are deprived,
Or things contain admixture of a void
Where each thing gets its start in moving on.
Lastly, where after impact two broad bodies
Suddenly spring apart, the air must crowd
The whole new void between those bodies formed;
But air, however it stream with hastening gusts,
Can yet not fill the gap at once—for first
It makes for one place, ere diffused through all.
And then, if haply any think this comes,
When bodies spring apart, because the air
Somehow condenses, wander they from truth:
For then a void is formed, where none before;
And, too, a void is filled which was before.
Nor can air be condensed in such a wise;
Nor, granting it could, without a void, I hold,
It still could not contract upon itself
And draw its parts together into one.
Wherefore, despite demur and counter-speech,
Confess thou must there is a void in things.
And still I might by many an argument
Here scrape together credence for my words.
But for the keen eye these mere footprints serve,

Whereby thou mayest know the rest thyself.
As dogs full oft with noses on the ground,
Find out the silent lairs, though hid in brush,
Of beasts, the mountain-rangers, when but once
They scent the certain footsteps of the way,
Thus thou thyself in themes like these alone
Can hunt from thought to thought, and keenly wind
Along even onward to the secret places
And drag out truth. But, if thou loiter loth
Or veer, however little, from the point,
This I can promise, Memmius, for a fact:
Such copious drafts my singing tongue shall pour
From the large well-springs of my plenished breast
That much I dread slow age will steal and coil
Along our members, and unloose the gates
Of life within us, ere for thee my verse
Hath put within thine ears the stores of proofs
At hand for one soever question broached.

NOTHING EXISTS PER SE EXCEPT ATOMS AND THE VOID

But, now again to weave the tale begun,
All nature, then, as self-sustained, consists
Of twain of things: of bodies and of void
In which they're set, and where they're moved around.
For common instinct of our race declares
That body of itself exists: unless
This primal faith, deep-founded, fail us not,
Naught will there be whereunto to appeal
On things occult when seeking aught to prove
By reasonings of mind. Again, without
That place and room, which we do call the inane,
Nowhere could bodies then be set, nor go
Hither or thither at all—as shown before.
Besides, there's naught of which thou canst declare
It lives disjoined from body, shut from void—
A kind of third in nature. For whatever
Exists must be a somewhat; and the same,
If tangible, however fight and slight,
Will yet increase the count of body's sum,
With its own augmentation big or small;
But, if intangible and powerless ever
To keep a thing from passing through itself
On any side, 'twill be naught else but that
Which we do call the empty, the inane.
Again, whate'er exists, as of itself,

Must either act or suffer action on it,
Or else be that wherein things move and be:
Naught, saving body, acts, is acted on;
Naught but the inane can furnish room. And thus,
Beside the inane and bodies, is no third
Nature amid the number of all things—
Remainder none to fall at any time
Under our senses, nor be seized and seen
By any man through reasonings of mind.
Name o'er creation with what names thou wilt,
Thou'lt find but properties of those first twain,
Or see but accidents those twain produce.
A property is that which not at all
Can be disjoined and severed from a thing
Without a fatal dissolution: such,
Weight to the rocks, heat to the fire, and flow
To the wide waters, touch to corporal things,
Intangibility to the viewless void.
But state of slavery, pauperhood, and wealth,
Freedom, and war, and concord, and all else
Which come and go whilst nature stands the same,
We're wont, and rightly, to call accidents.
Even time exists not of itself; but sense
Reads out of things what happened long ago,
What presses now, and what shall follow after:
No man, we must admit, feels time itself,
Disjoined from motion and repose of things.
Thus, when they say there "is" the ravishment
Of Princess Helen, "is" the siege and sack
Of Trojan Town, look out, they force us not
To admit these acts existent by themselves,
Merely because those races of mankind
(Of whom these acts were accidents) long since
Irrevocable age has borne away:
For all past actions may be said to be
But accidents, in one way, of mankind,—
In other, of some region of the world.
Add, too, had been no matter, and no room
Wherein all things go on, the fire of love
Upblown by that fair form, the glowing coal
Under the Phrygian Alexander's breast,
Had ne'er enkindled that renowned strife
Of savage war, nor had the wooden horse
Involved in flames old Pergama, by a birth
At midnight of a brood of the Hellenes.

And thus thou canst remark that every act
At bottom exists not of itself, nor is
As body is, nor has like name with void;
But rather of sort more fitly to be called
An accident of body, and of place
Wherein all things go on.[5]

Not only do philosophers express themselves in poetry, but in short stories, novels, and plays. Philosophical creativity is broad. There are also philosophers who think it's dishonest to philosophize in a system and are anti-systematic. Rather than pretending to tie together loose ends, the German philosopher Friedrich Nietzsche often scatters in arguments in epigrams and insists that his readers tie them together:

107. A sign of strong character, when once the resolution has been taken, to shut the ear even to the best counter-arguments. Occasionally, therefore, a will to stupidity.

108. There is no such thing as moral phenomena, but only a moral interpretation of phenomena.

109. The criminal is often enough not equal to his deed: he extenuates and maligns it.

110. The advocates of a criminal are seldom artists enough to turn the beautiful terribleness of the deed to the advantage of the doer.

111. Our vanity is most difficult to wound just when our pride has been wounded.

112. To him who feels himself preordained to contemplation and not to belief, all believers are "too noisy and obtrusive; he guards against them.

113. "You want to prepossess him in your favour? Then you must be embarrassed before him."

114. The immense expectation with regard to sexual love, and the coyness in this expectation, spoils all the perspectives of women at the outset.

115. Where there is neither love nor hatred in the game, woman's play is mediocre.

116. The great epochs of our life are at the points when we gain courage to rebaptize our badness as the best in us.

117. The will to overcome an emotion, is ultimately only the will of another, or of several other, emotions.

118. There is an innocence of admiration: it is possessed by him to whom it has not yet occurred that he himself may be admired some day.[6]

This kind of anti-systematic approach does not lead you around by the nose on a specific path. You must fill in the blanks. But the point of any philosophic approach is to lead you to ask questions you never would have imagined asking before.

MILLER
I think maybe we're done here, owing to those people over there. . . .

---

[5] Lucretius. *De rerum natura*. Project Gutenberg. <https://www.gutenberg.org/ebooks/785>.

[6] Nietzsche, Friedrich. *Beyond Good and Evil*. Project Gutenberg. <https://www.gutenberg.org/ebooks/4363>.

Wisdom

What Resonates

I've known Brandon since he was seventeen. I met him at one of those dumb faculty–student events during his freshman year. I don't remember what he was majoring in, but he didn't seem too convinced he was going the right way. He took my Introduction to Philosophy class and I remember me failing him on the first essay. His writing didn't impress me. What did impress me was that he took responsibility for his grade and didn't blame me. Throughout the semester, he laid out his views in class and invited other people to find flaws in his arguments. That really impressed me. By the time he graduated he definitely was one of my best students. When I interviewed Brandon, he had just graduated from law school and was beginning his job as an assistant district attorney. He seemed self-possessed, at ease, and very comfortable in his skin. The furnishings in office befitted a modest person: no awards hanging from the walls or intimidating furniture. Just a single photograph of his wife on top of a glass desk and several simple chairs for guests. He wore a dark suit and looked sleek and sophisticated in it. His lively brown eyes twinkled with excitement and I just knew this interview was going to be great!

◇◇◇◇

BRANDON
Thanks for coming up today. I know it's a hike from the suburbs.

MILLER
This is quite the office, man. You've got quite the view of Lake Michigan.

BRANDON
That's important to some people. How does this go?

MILLER
I would like to ask you about how philosophy impacted your life.

BRANDON
That sounds great. It continues to impact my life.

MILLER
Then let's start there. What is the continuing impact of philosophy on your life?

BRANDON
It can be summed up in one word: Wisdom.

MILLER

It's not the same as knowledge.

BRANDON

Yes. That's one of the most important things philosophy taught me. Knowledge is objective and public. Wisdom is subjective and private. *personal add* —

BRANDON

Like most kids unless you're some kind of genius, I didn't know what the hell I was doing freshman year.

MILLER

Same with me. Same with everybody.

BRANDON

I was brought up very strict, religious schools for twelve years and I thought I knew what wisdom was. It was in the Bible. You'd open the New Testament and memorize what Jesus said. But by the time I got to be about sixteen that stuff didn't resonate anymore. It didn't click. I didn't connect to it. I could not relate. By the time I got to college, I had given up on wisdom. I figured I'd do hardcore science. I wanted facts, I wanted data, I wanted answers, so I gave up on wisdom. But when I took Intro to Philosophy I rediscovered wisdom and realized that without it there was no point in anything I was doing. There was an emptiness in my life that made me look at everything and say WTF?

MILLER

What got you started on this new path?

BRANDON

The essay by the American pragmatist William James called "The Will to Believe" stoked my interest. When I believe something, it is I and no one else who puts my stamp of approval on it. Without my stamp of approval, the belief is lifeless. James distinguishes between live and dead hypotheses. The dead ones don't resonate with us, while the dead ones do not. The idea of material wealth resonates with so many people in this building, but not so much living like a minimalist. James also talks about our choices being momentous or trivial and forced or avoidable:

> Let us give the name of *hypothesis* to anything that may be proposed to our belief; and just as the electricians speak of live and dead wires, let us speak of any hypothesis as either *live* or *dead*. A live hypothesis is one which appeals as a real possibility to him to whom it is proposed. If I ask you to believe in the Mahdi, the notion makes no electric connection with your nature,—it refuses to scintillate with any credibility at all. As an hypothesis it is completely dead. To an Arab, however (even if he be not one of the Mahdi's followers), the hypothesis is among the mind's possibilities: it is alive. This shows that deadness and liveness in an hypothesis are not intrinsic properties, but relations to the individual thinker. They are measured by his willingness to act. The maximum of liveness in an hypothesis means willingness to act irrevocably. Practically, that means belief; but there is some believing tendency wherever there is willingness to act at all.
>
> Next, let us call the decision between two hypotheses an *option*. Options may be of several kinds. They may be—1, *living* or *dead*; 2, *forced* or *avoidable*; 3, *momentous* or *trivial*; and for our purposes we may call an option a *genuine* option when it is of the forced, living, and momentous kind.

1. A living option is one in which both hypotheses are live ones. If I say to you: "Be a theosophist or be a Mohammedan," it is probably a dead option, because for you neither hypothesis is likely to be alive. But if I say: "Be an agnostic or be a Christian," it is otherwise: trained as you are, each hypothesis makes some appeal, however small, to your belief.

2. Next, if I say to you: "Choose between going out with your umbrella or without it," I do not offer you a genuine option, for it is not forced. You can easily avoid it by not going out at all. Similarly, if I say, "Either love me or hate me," "Either call my theory true or call it false," your option is avoidable. You may remain indifferent to me, neither loving nor hating, and you may decline to offer any judgment as to my theory. But if I say, "Either accept this truth or go without it," I put on you a forced option, for there is no standing place outside of the alternative. Every dilemma based on a complete logical disjunction, with no possibility of not choosing, is an option of this forced kind.

3. Finally, if I were Dr. Nansen and proposed to you to join my North Pole expedition, your option would be momentous; for this would probably be your only similar opportunity, and your choice now would either exclude you from the North Pole sort of immortality altogether or put at least the chance of it into your hands. He who refuses to embrace a unique opportunity loses the prize as surely as if he tried and failed. *Per contra*, the option is trivial when the opportunity is not unique, when the stake is insignificant, or when the decision is reversible if it later proves unwise. Such trivial options abound in the scientific life. A chemist finds an hypothesis live enough to spend a year in its verification: he believes in it to that extent. But if his experiments prove inconclusive either way, he is quit for his loss of time, no vital harm being done.[1]

We believe things because we believe what other people have told us. Our teachers, our parents, our priest. James says that we try to be skeptical and suspend belief, but we simply cannot do it:

It is only our already dead hypotheses that our willing nature is unable to bring to life again. But what has made them dead for us is for the most part a previous action of our willing nature of an antagonistic kind. When I say "willing nature," I do not mean only such deliberate volitions as may have set up habits of belief that we cannot now escape from,—I mean all such factors of belief as fear and hope, prejudice and passion, imitation and partisanship, the circumpressure of our caste and set. As a matter of fact we find ourselves believing, we hardly know how or why. Mr. Balfour gives the name of "authority" to all those influences, born of the intellectual climate, that make hypotheses possible or impossible for us, alive or dead. Here in this room, we all of us believe in molecules and the conservation of energy, in democracy and necessary progress, in Protestant Christianity and the duty of fighting for "the doctrine of the immortal Monroe," all for no reasons worthy of the name. We see into these matters with no more inner clearness, and probably with much less, than any disbeliever in them might possess. His unconventionality would probably have some grounds to show for its conclusions; but for us, not insight, but the *prestige* of the opinions, is what makes the spark shoot from them and light up our sleeping magazines of faith. Our reason is quite satisfied, in nine hundred and ninety-nine cases out of every thousands of us, if it can find a few arguments that will do to recite in case our credulity is criticized by someone else. Our faith is faith in someone else's faith, and in the greatest matters this is mostly the case. Our belief in truth itself, for instance, that there is a truth, and that our minds and it are made for each other,—what is it but a passionate affirmation of desire, in which our

---

[1] James, William. "The Will to Believe." *The Will to Believe, and Other Essays in Popular Philosophy*. Project Gutenberg. <https://www.gutenberg.org/ebooks/26659>.

social system backs us up? We want to have a truth; we want to believe that our experiments and studies and discussions must put us in a continually better and better position towards it; and on this line we agree to fight out our thinking lives. But if a pyrrhonistic skeptic asks us *how we know* all this, can our logic find a reply? No! Certainly it cannot. It is just one volition against another,—we willing to go in for life upon a trust or assumption which the other, for his part, does not care to make.

James does not say this, but I think that the more momentous our decisions and the less avoidable they are, the more our beliefs resonate. For myself, the resonance of my beliefs fades unless I am doing something that really charges me, a case that is unique, and in my face, something I can't avoid. When I constantly avoid things and do trivial things, my beliefs fade. While James speaks of the "will to believe," he speaks to a process that is less passive than I see it. Whatever our culture believes to be true, we tend to believe the same. But this is not always the case and often when we attempt to believe what the mainstream believes, it doesn't resonate. According to the Buddha, each one of us furnishes the surroundings of our lives with beliefs and values that if pure lead to enlightenment and if impure lead to delusion:

> Both delusion and enlightenment originate within the mind, and every existence or phenomenon arises from the functions of the mind, just as different things appear from the sleeve of a magician.
>
> The activities of the mind have no limit, they form the surroundings of life. An impure mind surrounds itself with impure things and a pure mind surrounds itself with pure things; hence, surroundings have no more limits than activities of the mind.
>
> Just as a picture is drawn by an artist, surroundings are created by the activities of the mind.[2]

I find a more active idea of resonance in the life work of Socrates, especially in Plato's *Apology*, as Socrates defends himself in court before the Athenian people. I don't get caught up in all the law stuff there, even though you might think I would. My angle is that Socrates's beliefs resonate of how he lived his life: trying to find someone wiser than he was. A goddess proclaims Socrates the wisest of all people, but instead of taking it at face value, he decides to prove the goddess wrong. In that way, Socrates would make this wisdom his own:

> Men of Athens, this reputation of mine has come of a certain sort of wisdom which I possess. If you ask me what kind of wisdom, I reply, wisdom such as may perhaps be attained by man, for to that extent I am inclined to believe that I am wise; whereas the persons of whom I was speaking have a superhuman wisdom which I may fail to describe, because I have it not myself; and he who says that I have, speaks falsely, and is taking away my character. And here, O men of Athens, I must beg you not to interrupt me, even if I seem to say something extravagant. For the word which I will "speak is not mine. I will refer you to a witness who is worthy of credit; that witness shall be the God of Delphi—he will tell you about my wisdom, if I have any, and of what sort it is. You must have known Chaerephon; he was early a friend of mine, and also a friend of yours, for he shared in the recent exile of the people and returned with you. Well, Chaerephon, as you know, was very impetuous in all his doings, and he went to Delphi and boldly asked the oracle to tell him whether—as I was saying, I must beg you not to interrupt—he asked the oracle to tell him whether anyone was wiser than I was, and the Pythian prophetess answered that there was no man wiser. Chaerephon is dead himself; but his brother, who is in court, will confirm the truth of what I am saying.

---

[2] Kyokai, B. D. *The Teachings of Buddha*. Tokyo: Kosaido Printing Co., 1997. 96.

Why do I mention this? Because I am going to explain to you why I have such an evil name. When I heard the answer, I said to myself, What can the god mean? And what is the interpretation of his riddle? for I know that I have no wisdom, small or great. What then can he mean when he says that I am the wisest of men? And yet he is a god, and cannot lie; that would be against his nature. After long consideration, I thought of a method of trying the question. I reflected that if I could only find a man wiser than myself, then I might go to the god with a refutation in my hand. I should say to him, 'Here is a man who is wiser than I am; but you said that I was the wisest.' Accordingly I went to one who had the reputation of wisdom, and observed him—his name I need not mention; he was a politician whom I selected for examination—and the result was as follows: When I began to talk with him, I could not help thinking that he was not really wise, although he was thought wise by many, and still wiser by himself; and thereupon I tried to explain to him that he thought himself wise, but was not really wise, and the consequence was that he hated me, and his enmity was shared by several who were present and heard me. So I left him, saying to myself, as I went away: Well, although I do not suppose that either of us knows anything really beautiful and good, I am better off than he is,—for he knows nothing, and thinks that he knows; I neither know nor think that I know. In the latter, then, I seem to have slightly the advantage of him. Then I went to another who had still higher pretensions to wisdom, and my conclusion was exactly the same. Whereupon I made another enemy of him, and of many others besides him.

Then I went to one man after another, being not unconscious of the enmity which I provoked, and I lamented and feared this: but necessity was laid upon me,—the word of God, I thought, ought to be considered first. And I said to myself, Go I must to all who appear to know, and find out the meaning of the oracle. And I swear to you, Athenians, by the dog I swear!—for I must tell you the truth—the result of my mission was just this: I found that the "men most in repute were all but the most foolish; and that others less esteemed were really wiser and better. I will tell you the tale of my wanderings and of the 'Herculean' labors, as I may call them, which I endured only to find at last the oracle irrefutable. After the politicians, I went to the poets; tragic, dithyrambic, and all sorts. And there, I said to myself, you will be instantly detected; now you will find out that you are more ignorant than they are. Accordingly, I took them some of the most elaborate passages in their own writings, and asked what was the meaning of them—thinking that they would teach me something. Will you believe me? I am almost ashamed to confess the truth, but I must say that there is hardly a person present who would not have talked better about their poetry than they did themselves. Then I knew that not by wisdom do poets write poetry, but by a sort of genius and inspiration; they are like diviners or soothsayers who also say many fine things but do not understand the meaning of them. The poets appeared to me to be much in the same case; and I further observed that upon the strength of their poetry they believed themselves to be the wisest of men in other things in which they were not wise. So I departed, conceiving myself to be superior to them for the same reason that I was superior to the politicians.

At last I went to the artisans. I was conscious that I knew nothing at all, as I may say, and I was sure that they knew many fine things; and here I was not mistaken, for they did know many things of which I was ignorant, and in this they certainly were wiser than I was. But I observed that even the good artisans fell into the same error as the poets;—because they were good workmen they thought that they also knew all sorts of high matters, and this defect in them overshadowed their wisdom; and therefore I asked myself on behalf of the oracle, whether I would like to be as I was, neither having their knowledge nor their ignorance, or like them in both; and I answered to myself and to the oracle that I was better off as I was.

This inquisition has led to my having many enemies of the worst and most dangerous kind, and has given occasion also to many calumnies. And I am called wise, for my hearers always imagine that

I myself possess the wisdom that I find wanting in others: but the truth is, O men of Athens, that God only is wise; and by his answer he intends to show that the wisdom of men is worth little or nothing; he is not speaking of Socrates, he is only using my name by way of illustration, as if he said, He, O men, is the wisest, who, like Socrates, knows that his wisdom is in truth worth nothing. And so I go about the world, obedient to the god, and search and make enquiry into the wisdom of any one, whether citizen or stranger, who appears to be wise; and if he is not wise, then in vindication of the oracle I show him that he is not wise; and my occupation quite absorbs me, and I have no time to give either to any public matter of interest or to any concern of my own, but I am in utter poverty by reason of my devotion to the god.[3]

Socrates proves his point by action and not just acceptance of the proclamation of the goddess. Through his questioning of other people, he learns his wisdom is greater than that of other human beings not by how much of it he has, but how little of it can be gained by any human being. Knowing that he doesn't know is Socrates's supreme wisdom compared to all the other people who claim to know but actually do not. Philosophical resonance emerges in the quest of questioning core beliefs. While for Socrates philosophical resonance occurs through active seeking, for the ancient Chinese philosopher Lao Tzu, such resonance occurs by opening ourselves up to the supreme reality, the Tao. Still our minds and the greatest truths will resonate:

4.1 The Tao is (like) the emptiness of a vessel; and in our employment of it we must be on our guard against all fullness. How deep and unfathomable it is, as if it were the Honored Ancestor of all things!

4.2 We should blunt our sharp points, and unravel the complications of things; we should attemper our brightness, and bring ourselves into agreement with the obscurity of others. How pure and still the Tao is, as if it would ever so continue! . . .

10. 3 (The Tao) produces (all things) and nourishes them; it produces them and does not claim them as its own; it does all, and yet does not boast of it; it presides over all, and yet does not control them. This is what is called 'The mysterious Quality' (of the Tao).

16. 1. The (state of) vacancy should be brought to the utmost degree, and that of stillness guarded with unwearying vigour. All things alike go through their processes of activity, and (then) we see them return (to their original state). When things (in the vegetable world) have displayed their luxuriant growth, we see each of them return to its root. This returning to their root is what we call the state of stillness; and that stillness may be called a reporting that they have fulfilled their appointed end.

2. The report of that fulfilment is the regular, unchanging rule. To know that unchanging rule is to be intelligent; not to know it leads to wild movements and evil issues. The knowledge of that unchanging rule produces a (grand) capacity and forbearance, and that capacity and forbearance lead to a community (of feeling with all things). From this community of feeling comes a kingliness of character; and he who is king-like goes on to be heaven-like. In that likeness to heaven he possesses the Tao. Possessed of the Tao, he endures long; and to the end of his bodily life, is exempt from all dangers of decay. . . .

18. 1. When the Great Tao (Way or Method) ceased to be observed, benevolence and righteousness came into vogue. (Then) appeared wisdom and shrewdness, and there ensued great hypocrisy.

---

[3] Plato. *Apology*. Project Gutenberg. <https://www.gutenberg.org/ebooks/1656>.

20. 2. The multitude of men look satisfied and pleased; as if enjoying a full banquet, as if mounted on a tower in spring. I alone seem listless and still, my desires having as yet given no indication of their presence. I am like an infant which has not yet smiled. I look dejected and forlorn, as if I had no home to go to. The multitude of men all have enough and to spare. I alone seem to have lost everything. My mind is that of a stupid man; I am in a state of chaos.

Ordinary men look bright and intelligent, while I alone seem to be benighted. They look full of discrimination, while I alone am dull and confused. I seem to be carried about as on the sea, drifting as if I had nowhere to rest. All men have their spheres of action, while I alone seem dull and incapable, like a rude borderer. (Thus) I alone am different from other men, but I value the nursing-mother (the Tao). . . .

22. 2. Therefore the sage holds in his embrace the one thing (of humility), and manifests it to all the world. He is free from self-display, and therefore he shines; from self-assertion, and therefore he is distinguished; from self-boasting, and therefore his merit is acknowledged; from self-complacency, and therefore he acquires superiority. It is because he is thus free from striving that therefore no one in the world is able to strive with him. . . .

78. 1. There is nothing in the world more soft and weak than water, and yet for attacking things that are firm and strong there is nothing that can take precedence of it;—for there is nothing (so effectual) for which it can be changed. [4]

I am sure that many things resonate with us because we have been taught they are true. But that is only one type of resonance or connection we have. When we challenge ourselves philosophically, we begin to discern other types of resonations from self-reflection. From Buddha, we learn the mind can be controlled and that we can choose enlightenment over delusion. From Socrates, we learn active seeking and from Lao Tzu, patient waiting. I don't rule out any of these ways for wisdom to resonate.

MILLER
How would you describe wisdom?

BRANDON
You feel wisdom. It's visceral. The deepest truths of the universe and the human condition resonate in and through us. The subjective element is intrinsic to the experience of wisdom.

MILLER
You've gone through a dramatic transformation.

BRANDON
And for the better. I realize I am in control of my belief system. I understand how it functions and that I am responsible for its functioning or malfunctioning. People may agree or disagree with where it has taken me and it might not take them to the same place. But it does it take everybody somewhere.

MILLER
Do other people look at you oddly because of your beliefs?

---

[4] Tzu, Lao. *Tao Te Ching*. Project Gutenberg. <https://www.gutenberg.org/ebooks/23974>.

BRANDON

I'm sure they do because they're stuck on their beliefs and I'm surfing on mine.

MILLER

It does appear to me, an old guy, that there's not too much wisdom in the world.

BRANDON

I share that view. We've been taught to be actors, to give this performance in the classroom rather than seeking something more personal, more private.

MILLER

And far more enriching.

BRANDON

Definitely. But ordinary thinking won't get you there. It takes a strong dose of philosophy, which you gave me.

MILLER

But you have to make it your own.

BRANDON

Philosophy only becomes a magic potion when you learn to make it your own. Create your own way in it.

MILLER

Philosophers sometimes miss out on the creative dimension of philosophy.

BRANDON

I would say without creativity there can't be live hypotheses or wisdom. Wisdom is the way to make your beliefs resonate.

MILLER

I see all the people outside your door waiting for me, so I don't want to take up any more of your assistant attorney time.

BRANDON

I didn't even see them, but yeah, back to work.

MILLER

We'll catch up later.

BRANDON

And thanks for setting me on the journey, man.

MILLER

I was happy to play a small part.

The Environment

Green or Fry

In June 2019, I almost drowned in the Great Barrier Reef 30 miles off the coast of Australia. We were supposed to stay together in groups and I did not and was swept away by the current. One of the marine biologists on our crew swam out and saved my life. After she hoisted me into a motorboat, she ministered to the wounds on my knees, accrued from skinning my knees on the reef close to the surface. She got me out of the panic mode I was in by asking me what I did for a living. When I told her "philosopher," she said she was one, too. In our wetsuits in a little motorboat under the baking sun, we talked shop. She later gave me permission to mention this in the book.

◇◇◇◇

JEDDA
Did you see the white portions on the reef?

MILLER
Yes, when I was not drowning I saw them.

JEDDA
They're dead from climate change. The Great Barrier Reef will be dead in fifteen years.

MILLER
What's the matter with humanity?

JEDDA
It's our ideas. People want to fix the environment, but the real repair work can't happen until we understand the big ideas behind this catastrophe—the philosophical ideas. If you can't identify the big ideas at play, you're playing checkers when the game is chess—and you'll lose.

MILLER
Has environmental philosophy helped you see the ideas driving this crisis?

JEDDA
Definitely. What we're doing now around the edges, like recycling plastic bottles and using energy efficient lightbulbs, is not enough, and scientists say we have like ten years left to get our act together. Practising safe ecology cannot be a hobby: it must a 24/7 responsibility. We're practicing shallow ecology

when we should be practicing deep ecology. Norwegian philosopher Arne Næss articulates the idea of deep ecology in the following seven principles:

1. The shallow ecology movement: Fight against pollution and resource depletion. Central objective: the health and affluence of people in the developed countries.

2. The deep ecology movement:

    (1) Rejection of the man-in-environment image in favor of the relational, total-field image. Organisms as knots in the biospherical net or field of intrinsic relations. An intrinsic relation between two things A and B is such that the relation belongs to the definitions or basic constitutions of A and B, so that without the relation, A and B are no longer the same things. The total-field model dissolves not only the man-in-environment concept, but every compact thing-in-milieu concept-except when talking at a superficial or preliminary level of communication.

    (2) Biospherical egalitarianism—in principle. The 'in principle' clause is inserted because any realistic praxis necessitates some killing, exploitation, and suppression. The ecological field-worker acquires a deep-seated respect, or even veneration, for ways and forms of life. He reaches an understanding from within, a kind of understanding that others reserve for fellowmen and for a narrow section of ways and forms of life. To the ecological field-worker, the equal right to live and blossom is an intuitively clear and obvious value axiom. Its restriction to humans is an anthropocentrism with detrimental effects on the life quality of humans themselves. This quality depends in part on the deep pleasure and satisfaction we receive from close partnership with other forms of life. The attempt to ignore our dependence and to establish a master-slave role has contributed to the alienation of man from himself.

    Ecological egalitarianism implies the reinterpretation of the future research variable, "level of crowding," so that general mammalian crowding and loss of life-equality is taken seriously, not only human crowding. (Research on the high requirements of free space of certain mammals has, incidentally, suggested that theorists of human urbanism have largely underestimated human life–space requirements. Behavioral crowding symptoms [neuroses, aggressiveness, loss of traditions . . .] are largely the same among mammals.)

    (3) Principles of diversity and of symbiosis. Diversity enhances the potentialities of survival, the chances of new modes of life, the richness of forms. And the so-called struggle of life, and survival of the fittest, should be interpreted in the sense of the ability to coexist and cooperate in complex relationships, rather than the ability to kill, exploit, and suppress. "Live and let live" is a more powerful ecological principle than "Either you or me."

    The latter tends to reduce the multiplicity of the forms of life, and also to create destruction within the communities of the same species. Attitudes based on ecology therefore favor diversity in the ways of human life, cultures, occupations, or economies. They support the fight against economic and cultural invasion and domination, as much as the military ones, and they are opposed to the annihilation of seals and whales as much as to that of human tribes or cultures.

    (4) Anti-class posture. The diversity in human ways of life is in part due to (intended or unintended) exploitation and suppression on the part of certain groups. The exploiter lives differently from the exploited, but both are adversely affected in their potentialities of self-realization. The principle of diversity does not cover differences merely due to certain attitudes or behaviors forcibly blocked or restrained. The principles of ecological egalitarianism and of symbiosis support the same anti-class posture. The ecological attitude favors the extension of all three principles to any group conflicts, including those of today between developing and developed

nations. The three principles also favor extreme caution toward any overall plans for the future, except those consistent with wide and widening classless diversity.

(5) Fight against pollution and resource depletion. In this fight ecologists have found powerful supporters, but sometimes to the detriment of their total stand. This happens when attention is focused on pollution and resource depletion rather than on the other points, or when projects are implemented that reduce pollution but increase evils of other kinds. Thus, if prices of life necessities increase because of the installation of anti-pollution devices, class differences increase too. An ethics of responsibility implies that ecologists do not serve the shallow but the deep ecological movement. That is, not only point (5), but all seven points must be considered together.

Ecologists are irreplaceable informants in any society, whatever their political color. If well organized, they have the power to reject jobs in which they submit themselves to institutions or to planners with limited ecological perspectives. As it is now, ecologists sometimes serve masters who deliberately ignore the wider perspectives.

(6) Complexity, not complication. The theory of ecosystems contains an important distinction between what is complicated without any Gestalt or unifying principles—we may think of finding our way through a chaotic city—and what is complex. A multiplicity of more or less lawful, interacting factors may operate together to form a unity, a system. We make a shoe or use a map or integrate a variety of activities into a workaday pattern. Organisms, ways of life, and interactions in the biosphere in general, exhibit complexity of such an astoundingly high level as to color the general outlook of ecologists. Such complexity makes thinking in terms of vast systems inevitable. It also makes for a keen, steady perception of the profound human ignorance of biospherical relationships and therefore of the effect of disturbances.

Applied to humans, the complexity-not-complication principle favors division of labor, not fragmentation of labor. It favors integrated actions in which the whole person is active, not mere reactions. It favors complex economies, an integrated variety of means of living. (Combinations of industrial and agricultural activity, of intellectual and manual work, of specialized and nonspecialized occupations, urban and non-urban activity, of work in city and recreation in nature with recreation in city and work in nature . . .)

It favors a soft technique and 'soft future-research', less prognosis, and more clarification of possibilities: more sensitivity toward continuity and live traditions, and—most importantly—toward our state of ignorance.

The implementation of ecologically responsible policies requires in this century an exponential growth of technical skill and invention—but in new directions, directions that, today, are not consistently and liberally supported by the research policy organs of our nation–states.

(7) Local autonomy and decentralization. The vulnerability of a form of life is roughly proportional to the weight of influences from afar, from outside the local region in which that form has obtained an ecological equilibrium. This lends support to our efforts to strengthen local self-government and material and mental self-sufficiency. But these efforts presuppose an impetus toward decentralization. Pollution problems, including those of thermal pollution and recirculation of materials, also lead us in this direction, because increased local autonomy, if we are able to keep other factors constant, reduces energy consumption. (Compare an approximately self-sufficient locality with one requiring the importation of foodstuff, materials for house construction, fuel, and skilled labor from other continents. The former may use only 5 percent of the energy used by the latter.) Local autonomy is strengthened by a reduction in the number of links in the hierarchical chains Q£ decision. (For example, a chain consisting of a local board, municipal council, highest sub-national decision-maker, a state-wide institution in a state federation, a

federal national government institution, a coalition of nations, and of institutions, e.g., E.E.C. top levels, and a global institution, can be reduced to one made up of a local board, nation-wide institution, and global institution.) Even if a decision follows majority rules at each step, many local interests may be dropped along the line, if it is too long.

Summing up, then, it should, first of all, be borne in mind that the norms and tendencies of the deep ecology movement are not derived from ecology by logic or induction. Ecological knowledge and the life-style of the ecological field-worker have suggested, inspired, and fortified the perspectives of the deep ecology movement. Many of the formulations in the above seven-point survey are rather vague generalizations, only tenable if they are made more precise in certain directions. But all over the world the inspiration from ecology has shown remarkable convergencies. The survey does not pretend to be more than one of the possible condensed codifications of these convergencies.

Secondly, it should be fully appreciated that the significant tenets of the deep ecology movement are clearly and forcefully normative. They express a value priority system only in part based on results (or lack of results, cf. point [6]) of scientific research. Today, ecologists try to influence policy-making bodies largely through threats, through predictions concerning pollutants and resource depletion, knowing that policy-makers accept at least certain minimum norms concerning health and just distribution. But it is clear that there is a vast number of people in all countries, and even a considerable number of people in power, who accept as valid the wider norms and values characteristic of the deep ecology movement. There are political potentials in this movement that should not be overlooked and which have little to do with pollution and resource depletion. In plotting possible futures, the norms should be freely used and elaborated.

Thirdly, in so far as ecology movements deserve our attention, they are *ecophilosophical* rather than ecological. Ecology is a limited science which makes use of scientific methods. Philosophy is the most general forum of debate on fundamentals, descriptive as well as prescriptive, and political philosophy is one of its subsections. By an *ecosophy* I mean a philosophy of ecological harmony or equilibrium. A philosophy as a kind of *sofia* wisdom, is openly normative, it contains both norms, rules, postulates, value priority announcements *and* hypotheses concerning the state of affairs in our universe. Wisdom is policy wisdom, prescription, not only scientific description and prediction.

These seven principles are great, but could stand some clarification, which is what I'm doing in my research:[1]

1. All beings, living and non-living, have intrinsic value. Humans are not in the world with some kind of more value than other beings. ~~Humans are of the world~~ (principle of intrinsic value).
2. All beings, living and non-living, are equal. Except in extreme cases of self-defense, humans cannot exploit other beings (principle of equality).
3. Diversity extends to all living and non-living beings (principle of deep and ubiquitous diversity). In this web of deep and ubiquitous diversity, living and non-living beings are interdependent (principle of interdependence). Coexistence and cooperation are valued over killing, subjugating, and suppressing. This applies as much to how humans treat each other as it does to how humans treat other species and the environment.

[1] *From* Inquiry: An Interdisciplinary Journal of Philosophy, *Vol. 16, 1973 by Arne Næss. Copyright © 1973 by Taylor & Francis. Reprinted by permission.*

4. Diversity cannot come at the expense of humans oppressing each other and creating a human class system. The goal is classless diversity (principle of anti-classism).
5. Deep ecology should not bring about social inequalities, for example, green practices should not put people out of work.
6. Humans need to understand the complex web of relationships between living and non-living beings and look at the big picture: the biosphere (principle of big picture).
7. Take the power of greening the planet away from energy companies and put it in the hands of local communities (principle of decentralization and community power).

When I think about deep ecology, I think "Yeah, cool." But I realize that to truly grasp deep ecology, they're going to evolve into a different kind of spirituality. The models for this are out there. We just don't teach them. Like Saint Francis of Assisi. He sees consciousness in all beings; thus all beings are respected and cared for: *humans recognizing a democratize the biosphere*

> The key to an understanding of Francis is his belief in the virtue of humility—not merely for the individual but for humans as a species. Francis tried to depose humans from their monarchy over creation and set up a democracy of all God's creatures. With him the ant is no longer simply a homily for the lazy, flames a sign of the thrust of the soul toward union with God; now they are Brother Ant and Sister Fire, praising the Creator in their own ways as Brother Man does in his.

> Later commentators have said that Francis preached to the birds as a rebuke to people who would not listen. The records do not read so: he urged the little birds to praise God, and in spiritual ecstasy they flapped their wings and chirped rejoicing. Legends of saints, especially the Irish saints, had long told of their dealings with animals but always, I believe, to show their human dominance over creatures. With Francis it is different. The land around Gubbio in the Apennines was ravaged by a fierce wolf. Saint Francis, says the legend, talked to the wolf and persuaded him of the error of his ways. The wolf repented, died in the odor of sanctity, and was buried in consecrated ground. *Missing* *Footnote*

Saint Francis espouses a profound humility to all of creation rather than an arrogance that leads us to exploit the environment. This arrogance stemming from our so-called superiority translates into ideas and practices of dominance. A transformation from religious, psychological, and cultural ideas into justifying dominance into a more egalitarian relationship with all beings is insurmountable without changing at our deepest spiritual core. Until we master ourselves, we will be prone to act out aggressively on the world at a time when this could spell the end of the world. I enjoy this little chart from the Buddhist philosopher Georg Feuerstein concerning two paths we can take: *Chart here*

Destruction of the human race and the environment comes from a desire to conquer nature, while individual and collective wholeness (and presumably saving both humans and the environment) comes from mastering oneself. Mastery of self helps us reach a spiritual plane beyond our self-destructive impulses. Most of our species are seriously screwed up, you know, and want to feed their fat faces at the expense of destroying everything else. We practise the kind of egoism Plato describes in *The Republic*:

> Because you fancy that the shepherd or neatherd fattens or tends the sheep or oxen with a view to their own good and not to the good of himself or his master; and you further imagine that the rulers of states, if they are true rulers, never think of their subjects as sheep, and that they are not studying their own advantage day and night. Oh, no; and so entirely astray are you in your ideas about the just and unjust as not even to know that justice and the just are in reality another's good; that is to say, the interest of

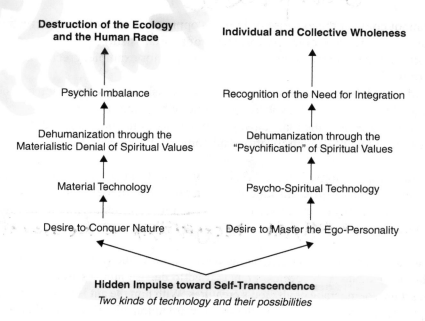

Destruction of the Ecology and the Human Race

Individual and Collective Wholeness

Psychic Imbalance

Recognition of the Need for Integration

Dehumanization through the Materialistic Denial of Spiritual Values

Dehumanization through the "Psychification" of Spiritual Values

Material Technology

Psycho-Spiritual Technology

Desire to Conquer Nature

Desire to Master the Ego-Personality

Hidden Impulse toward Self-Transcendence
Two kinds of technology and their possibilities

the ruler and stronger, and the loss of the subject and servant; and injustice the opposite; for the unjust is lord over the truly simple and just: he is the stronger, and his subjects do what is for his interest, and minister to his happiness, which is very far from being their own. Consider further, most foolish Socrates, that the just is always a loser in comparison with the unjust. First of all, in private contracts: wherever the unjust is the partner of the just you will find that, when the partnership is dissolved, the unjust man has always more and the just less. Secondly, in their dealings with the State: when there is an income-tax, the just man will pay more and the unjust less on the same amount of income; and when there is anything to be received the one gains nothing and the other much. Especially when pursued on a great scale. Observe also what happens when they take an office; there is the just man neglecting his affairs and perhaps suffering other losses, and getting nothing out of the public, because he is just; moreover he is hated by his friends and acquaintance for refusing to serve them in unlawful ways. But all this is reversed in the case of the unjust man. I am speaking, as before, of injustice on a large scale in which the advantage of the unjust is most apparent; and my meaning will be most clearly seen if we turn to that highest form of injustice in which the criminal is the happiest of men, and the sufferers or those who refuse to do injustice are the most miserable—that is to say tyranny, which by fraud and force takes away the property of others, not little by little but wholesale; comprehending in one, things sacred as well as profane, private, and public; for which acts of wrong, if he were detected perpetrating any one of them singly, he would be punished and incur great disgrace—they who do such wrong in particular cases are called robbers of temples, and man-stealers and burglars and swindlers and thieves. But when a man besides taking away the money of the citizens has made slaves of them, then, instead of these names of reproach, he is termed happy and blessed, not only by the citizens but by all who hear of his having achieved the consummation of injustice. For mankind censures injustice fearing that they may be the victims of it and not because they shrink from committing it. And thus, as I have shown, Socrates, injustice, when on a sufficient scale, has more strength and freedom and mastery than justice; and, as I said at first, justice is the interest of the stronger, whereas injustice is a man's own profit and interest.[2]

---

[2] Plato. *The Republic*. Project Guttenberg. <https://www.gutenberg.org/ebooks/55201>.

People usually only think of themselves. They're not thinking about the environment when they support a consumerist culture that mega-produces garbage and pollution. They can get away with it and since they can get away with it, they'll do it over and over again. When it occurs to them that the resources are scarce, they have no problem, sacrificing others so that they can continue to like their same pollutive lifestyle. When I read about lifeboat ethics, I immediately think about the kind of selfishness that doesn't mind putting other people in peril and refusing to share resources with them. What the people in the lifeboat don't realize is that they're eventually going to be thrown off as resources become even more scarce. Finally, when all the resources are depleted, who cares who owns the boat? Creating a Commons that works for all species—a habitat healed from the effects of climate change is the best way to ensure the survival of the human race and all life on this planet. According to Garrett Hardin, since the world has limited resources, trying to save every human being will cause the death of all of us. To drive home his point, Hardin proposes a thought experiment. Imagine a lifeboat that can accommodate 50 people. More than that and everybody's life is jeopardized. Do we allow our humanitarian impulses to lead us and allow the extra passengers on the boat? Or do we take a hard and calculated view and keep them off the boat? When society adopts this perspective, then people look to save their own skins, but in the process lose sight of the interconnectedness of all things and end up destroying the habitat that sustains all life.[3]

I find equally disturbing the views of Milton Friedman, who asserts that corporations have no social responsibility other than to increase profits:

I have called it a "fundamentally subversive doctrine" in a free society, and have said that in such a society, "there is one and only one social responsibility of business—to use its resources and engage in activities designed to increase its profits so long as it stays within the rules of the game, which is to say, engages in open and free competition without deception or fraud."[4]

As long as they follow the laws, corporations are good to go. However, because of money in politics and control of the mass media, laws that are created by brown energy monsters (oil and coal) favor the perpetuation of the use of coal and oil that is CO_2-ing the planet into a death spiral. The view that business and people in general can do whatever the hell they want to and that will make everyone richer and the world better is crystalized in "The Fable of the Bees":

A spacious hive well stock'd with bees,
That liv'd in luxury and ease;
And yet as fam'd for laws and arms,
As yielding large and early swarms;
Was counted the great nursery
Of sciences and industry.
No bees had better government,
More fickleness, or less content:
They were not slaves to tyranny.
Nor rul'd by wild democracy;

[3] Hardin, Garrett. 1974. "Living on a lifeboat" *Bioscience* 24 (10), 561–568.
[4] Friedman, Milton. "A Friedman Doctrine." *The New York Times Archive.* <https://www.nytimes.com/1970/09/13/archives/a-friedman-doctrine-the-social-responsibility-of-business-is-to.html>.

But kings, that could not wrong, because
Their power was circumscrib'd by laws.
    These insects liv'd like men, and all
Our actions they performed in small:
They did whatever's done in town,
And what belongs to sword or gown:
Though th' artful works, by nimble slight
Of minute limbs, 'scap'd human sight;
Yet we've no engines, labourers,
Ships, castles, arms, artificers,
Craft, science, shop, or instrument,
But they had an equivalent:
Which, since their language is unknown,
Must be call'd, as we do our own.
As grant, that among other things,
They wanted dice, yet they had kings;
And those had guards; from whence we may
Justly conclude, they had some play;
Unless a regiment be shown
Of soldiers, that make use of none.
Vast numbers throng'd the fruitful hive;
Yet those vast numbers made 'em thrive;
Millions endeavouring to supply
Each other's lust and vanity;
While other millions were employ'd,
To see their handy-works destroy'd;
They furnish'd half the universe;
Yet had more work than labourers.
Some with vast flocks, and little pains,
Jump'd into business of great gains;
And some were damn'd to scythes and spades,
And all those hard laborious trades;
Where willing wretches daily sweat,
And wear out strength and limbs to eat:
While others follow'd mysteries,
To which few folks binds 'prentices;
That want no stock, but that of brass,
And may set up without a cross;
As sharpers, parasites, pimps, players,
Pickpockets, coiners, quacks, soothsayers,
And all those, that in enmity,
With downright working, cunningly
Convert to their own use the labour
Of their good-natur'd heedless neighbour.
These were call'd Knaves, but bar the name,

The grave industrious were the same:
All trades and places knew some cheat,
No calling was without deceit.

The lawyers, of whose art the basis
Was raising feuds and splitting cases,
Oppos'd all registers, that cheats
Might make more work with dipt estates;
As were't unlawful, that one's own,
Without a law-suit, should be known.
They kept off hearings wilfully,
To finger the refreshing fee;
And to defend a wicked cause,
Examin'd and survey'd the laws,
As burglar's shops and houses do,
To find out where they'd best break through.

Physicians valu'd fame and wealth
Above the drooping patient's health,
Or their own skill: the greatest part
Study'd, instead of rules of art,
Grave pensive looks and dull behaviour,
To gain th' apothecary's favour;
The praise of midwives, priests, and all
That serv'd at birth or funeral.
To bear with th' ever-talking tribe,
And hear my lady's aunt prescribe;
With formal smile, and kind how d'ye,
To fawn on all the family;
And, which of all the greatest curse is,
T' endure th' impertinence of nurses.

Among the many priests of Jove,
Hir'd to draw blessings from above,
Some few were learn'd and eloquent,
But thousands hot and ignorant:
Yet all pass'd muster that could hide
Their sloth, lust, avarice and pride;
For which they were as fam'd as tailors
For cabbage, or for brandy sailors,
Some, meagre-look'd, and meanly clad,
Would mystically pray for bread,
Meaning by that an ample store,
Yet lit'rally received no more;
And, while these holy drudges starv'd,
The lazy ones, for which they serv'd,
Indulg'd their ease, with all the graces
Of health and plenty in their faces.

The soldiers, that were forc'd to fight,
If they surviv'd, got honour by't;
Though some, that shunn'd the bloody fray,
Had limbs shot off, that ran away:
Some valiant gen'rals fought the foe;
Others took bribes to let them go:
Some ventur'd always where 'twas warm,
Lost now a leg, and then an arm;
Till quite disabled, and put by,
They liv'd on half their salary;
While others never came in play,
And staid at home for double pay.

Their kings were serv'd, but knavishly,
Cheated by their own ministry;
Many, that for their welfare slaved,
Robbing the very crown they saved:
Pensions were small, and they liv'd high,
Yet boasted of their honesty.
Calling, whene'er they strain'd their right,
The slipp'ry trick a perquisite;
And when folks understood their cant,
They chang'd that for emolument;
Unwilling to be short or plain,
In any thing concerning gain;
For there was not a bee but would
Get more, I won't say, than he should;
But than he dar'd to let them know,
That pay'd for't; as your gamesters do,
That, though at fair play, ne'er will own
Before the losers that they've won.

But who can all their frauds repeat?
The very stuff which in the street
They sold for dirt t' enrich the ground,
Was often by the buyers found
Sophisticated with a quarter
Of good-for-nothing stones and mortar;
Though Flail had little cause to mutter.
Who sold the other salt for butter.

Justice herself, fam'd for fair dealing,
By blindness had not lost her feeling;
Her left hand, which the scales should hold,
Had often dropt 'em, brib'd with gold;
And, though she seem'd impartial,
Where punishment was corporal,
Pretended to a reg'lar course,

In murder, and all crimes of force;
Though some first pillory'd for cheating,
Were hang'd in hemp of their own beating;
Yet, it was thought, the sword she bore
Check'd but the desp'rate and the poor;
That, urg'd by mere necessity,
Were ty'd up to the wretched tree
For crimes, which not deserv'd that fate,
But to secure the rich and great.
    Thus every part was full of vice,
Yet the whole mass a paradise;
Flatter'd in peace, and fear'd in wars
They were th' esteem of foreigners,
And lavish of their wealth and lives,
The balance of all other hives.
Such were the blessings of that state;
Their crimes conspir'd to make them great:
And virtue, who from politics
Has learn'd a thousand cunning tricks,
Was, by their happy influence,
Made friends with vice: And ever since,
The worst of all the multitude
Did something for the common good.
    This was the state's craft, that maintain'd
The whole of which each part complain'd:
This, as in music harmony
Made jarrings in the main agree,
Parties directly opposite,
Assist each other, as 'twere for spite;
And temp'rance with sobriety,
Serve drunkenness and gluttony.
    The root of evil, avarice,
That damn'd ill-natur'd baneful vice,
Was slave to prodigality,
That noble sin; whilst luxury
Employ'd a million of the poor,
And odious pride a million more:
Envy itself, and vanity,
Were ministers of industry;
Their darling folly, fickleness,
In diet, furniture, and dress,
That strange ridic'lous vice, was made
The very wheel that turn'd the trade.
Their laws and clothes were equally
Objects of mutability!

For, what was well done for a time,
In half a year became a crime;
Yet while they altered thus their laws,
Still finding and correcting flaws,
They mended by inconstancy
Faults, which no prudence could foresee.
    Thus vice nurs'd ingenuity,
Which join'd the time and industry,
Had carry'd life's conveniences,

}

Its real pleasures, comforts, ease,
To such a height, the very poor
Liv'd better than the rich before.
And nothing could be added more.
    How vain is mortal happiness!
Had they but known the bounds of bliss;
And that perfection here below
Is more than gods can well bestow;
The grumbling brutes had been content
With ministers and government.
But they, at every ill success,
Like creatures lost without redress,
Curs'd politicians, armies, fleets;
While everyone cry'd, damn the cheats,
And would, though conscious of his own,
In others barb'rously bear none.
    One, that had got a princely store,
By cheating master, king, and poor,
Dar'd cry aloud, the land must sink
For all its fraud; and whom d'ye think
The sermonizing rascal child?
A glover that sold lamb for kid.
    The least thing was not done amiss,
Or cross'd the public business;
But all the rogues cry'd brazenly,
Good gods, had we but honesty!
Merc'ry smil'd at th' impudence,
And others call'd it want of sense,
Always to rail at what they lov'd:
But Jove with indignation mov'd,
At last in anger swore, he'd rid
The bawling hive of fraud; and did.

The very moment it departs,
And honesty fills all their hearts;
There shows 'em, like th' instructive tree,
Those crimes which they're asham'd to see;
Which now in silence they confess,
By blushing at their ugliness:
Like children, that would hide their faults,
And by their colour own their thoughts:
Imag'ning, when they're look'd upon,
That others see what they have done.
    But, O ye gods! what consternation,
How vast and sudden was th' alteration!
In half an hour, the nation round,
Meat fell a penny in the pound.
The mask hypocrisy's sitting down,
From the great statesman to the clown:
And in some borrow'd looks well known,
Appear'd like strangers in their own.
The bar was silent from that day;
For now the willing debtors pay,
Ev'n what's by creditors forgot;
Who quitted them that had it not.
Those that were in the wrong, stood mute,
And dropt the patch'd vexatious suit:
On which since nothing else can thrive,
Than lawyers in an honest hive,
All, except those that got enough,
With inkhorns by their sides troop'd off.
    Justice hang'd some, set others free;
And after gaol delivery,
Her presence being no more requir'd,
With all her train and pomp retir'd.
First march'd some smiths with locks and grates,
Fetters, and doors with iron plates:
Next gaolers, turnkeys and assistants:
Before the goddess, at some distance,
Her chief and faithful minister,
'Squire Catch, the law's great finisher,
Bore not th' imaginary sword,
But his own tools, an ax and cord:
Then on a cloud the hood-wink'd fair,
Justice herself was push'd by air:
About her chariot, and behind,
Were serjeants, bums of every kind,
Tip-staffs, and all those officers,

That squeeze a living out of tears.
    Though physic liv'd, while folks were ill,
None would prescribe, but bees of skill,
Which through the hive dispers'd so wide,
That none of them had need to ride;
Wav'd vain disputes, and strove to free
The patients of their misery;
Left drugs in cheating countries grown,
And us'd the product of their own;
Knowing the gods sent no disease,
To nations without remedies.
    Their clergy rous'd from laziness,
Laid not their charge on journey-bees;
But serv'd themselves, exempt from vice,
The gods with pray'r and sacrifice;
All those, that were unfit, or knew,
Their service might be spar'd, withdrew:
Nor was their business for so many,
(If th' honest stand in need of any,)
Few only with the high-priest staid,
To whom the rest obedience paid:
Himself employ'd in holy cares;
Resign'd to others state-affairs.
He chas'd no starv'ling from his door,
Nor pinch'd the wages of the poor:

But at his house the hungry's fed,
The hireling finds unmeasur'd bread,
The needy trav'ller board and bed.
    Among the king's great ministers,
And all th' inferior officers,
The change was great; for frugally
They now liv'd on their salary:
That a poor bee should ten times come
To ask his due, a trifling sum,
And by some well-hir'd clerk be made
To give a crown, or ne'er be paid,
Would now be call'd a downright cheat,
Though formerly a perquisite.
All places manag'd first by three,
Who watch'd each other's knavery
And often for a fellow-feeling,

Promoted one another's stealing,
Are happily supply'd by one,
By which some thousands more are gone.
 No honour now could be content,
To live and owe for what was spent;
Liv'ries in brokers shops are hung,
They part with coaches for a song;
Sell stately horses by whole sets;
And country-houses, to pay debts.
 Vain cost is shunn'd as much as fraud;
They have no forces kept abroad;
Laugh at th' esteem of foreigners,
And empty glory got by wars;
They fight but for their country's sake,
When right or liberty's at stake.
 Now mind the glorious hive, and see
How honesty and trade agree.
The show is gone, it thins apace;
And looks with quite another face.
For 'twas not only that they went,
By whom vast sums were yearly spent;
But multitudes that liv'd on them,
Were daily forc'd to do the same.
In vain to other trades they'd fly;
All were o'er-stock'd accordingly.
 The price of land and houses falls;
Mirac'lous palaces, whose walls,
Like those of Thebes, were rais'd by play,
Are to be let; while the once gay,
Well-seated household gods would be
More pleas'd to expire in flames, than see
The mean inscription on the door
Smile at the lofty ones they bore.
The building trade is quite destroy'd,
Artificers are not employ'd;
No limner for his art is fam'd,
Stone-cutters, carvers are not nam'd.
 Those, that remain'd, grown temp'rate, strive,
Not how to spend, but how to live;
And, when they paid their tavern score,
Resolv'd to enter it no more:
No vintner's jilt in all the hive
Could wear now cloth of gold, and thrive;
Nor Torcol such vast sums advance,
For Burgundy and Ortolans;

The courtier's gone that with his miss
Supp'd at his house on Christmas peas;
Spending as much in two hours stay,
As keeps a troop of horse a day.
    The haughty Chloe, to live great,
Had made her husband rob the state:
But now she sells her furniture,
Which th' Indies had been ransack'd for;
Contracts the expensive bill of fare,
And wears her strong suit a whole year:
The slight and fickle age is past;
And clothes, as well as fashions, last.
Weavers, that join'd rich silk with plate,
And all the trades subordinate,
Are gone; still peace and plenty reign,
And everything is cheap, though plain:
Kind nature, free from gard'ners force,
Allows all fruits in her own course;
But rarities cannot be had,
Where pains to get them are not paid.
    As pride and luxury decrease,
So by degrees they leave the seas.
Not merchants now, but companies
Remove whole manufactories.
All arts and crafts neglected lie;
Content, the bane of industry,
Makes 'em admire their homely store,
And neither seek nor covet more.
    So few in the vast hive remain,
The hundredth part they can't maintain
Against th' insults of numerous foes;
Whom yet they valiantly oppose:
'Till some well fenc'd retreat is found,
And here they die or stand their ground.
No hireling in their army's known;
But bravely fighting for their own,
Their courage and integrity
At last were crown'd with victory.
    They triumph'd not without their cost,
For many thousand bees were lost.
Harden'd with toils and exercise,
They counted ease itself a vice;
Which so improv'd their temperance;
That, to avoid extravagance,
They flew into a hollow tree,
Blest with content and honesty.

THE MORAL.

Then leave complaints: fools only strive
To make a great and honest hive.
T' enjoy the world's conveniences,
Be fam'd in war, yet live in ease,
Without great vices, is a vain
Eutopia seated in the brain.
Fraud, luxury, and pride must live,
While we the benefits receive:
Hunger's a dreadful plague, no doubt,
Yet who digests or thrives without?
Do we not owe the growth of wine
To the dry shabby crooked vine?
Which, while its shoots neglected stood,
Chok'd other plants, and ran to wood;
But blest us with its noble fruit,
As soon as it was ty'd and cut:
So vice is beneficial found,
When it's by justice lopp'd and bound;

Nay, where the people would be great,
As necessary to the state,
As hunger is to make 'em eat.
Bare virtue can't make nations live
In splendor; they, that would revive
A golden age, must be as free
For acorns as for honesty.[5]

Following this philosophy of greed means millions of people overconsume and perpetually pollute a planet whose knees are buckling.

MILLER
You're extremely broad thinker, Jedda.

JEDDA
It goes with the territory of philosophy.

MILLER
What got you interested in philosophy?

---

[5] Mandeville, Bernard. *The Fable of the Bees; Or, Private Vices, Public Benefits*. Project Gutenberg. <https://www.gutenberg.org/ebooks/57260>.

JEDDA

Philosophy is how I am going to save First Nation Persons—our people and our culture. It is also the way to make it clear to everybody what is going on and hopefully make the earth perpetually habitable. By the way, we're coming up to our ship now.

MILLER

One final question. Should students study philosophy?

JEDDA

Yea. If we want to live.

Mideducation
Why Students Hate Learning

Herbert is an old-fashioned name and I expected to find an old-fashioned kind of person when I met him at an undisclosed location near the southern border of the United States. A long-time colleague of mine—we had gone to grad school together—often brought up Herbert in his small list of exceptional students, one who had gotten more out of philosophy than he had ever known. I expected a pocket watch and a weary-eyed person without a jawline, stooped, and wearing a cardigan. Instead I found this vigilant young man who spoke with confidence without being uncivil. A tinge of gray glinted in his flaxen hair as we walked briskly in the blazing summer heat outside the detention centers.

<><><>

MILLER
What got you into philosophy?

HERBERT
There was a part of me that I could get at. It was like a diamond in the mine I knew was there, but somehow escaped me. I had so many majors before philosophy: English, theatre, sociology, psychology, and others I just can't remember. Nothing made an impact. I didn't know it, but I was looking for a deep relationship with my education, but nothing seemed to work—until I took Dr. Mason's Philosophy of Education course, which I took only because I needed a course on Monday, Wednesday, and Friday.

MILLER
Which philosophical ideas have had the most impact on you?

HERBERT
Education. Once I began reading stuff by Whitehead, Dewey, Freire, Gardiner, Mill, and Bloom, I encountered that it changed me at the core. I learned the value of education to me and began to see how miseducated I had been. For me, this was a revelation. It's like you've been trying to do this thing that just didn't work and being miserable because of it.

MILLER
How did your ideas change?

HERBERT
I always felt yucky leaving school. Like I was leaving with stinky clothes and bad breath. It didn't sit well with me. I always noticed people leaving the classroom like they had just attended a funeral.

49

Philosophy pointed me in the direction of understanding why. I would be like my friends "I'm paying for this course, it better be good." But good in what way? Is it good because I get a high grade or good because it deepens me, grounds me? My education is the most important thing to me. Without it, I stay in one spot. Philosophy taught me the power of education. It was a horrible high school. How I got from high school to college is one of those mysteries of the universe.

MILLER
Why don't you take me through some of those Philosophy of Education texts that impacted you?

HERBERT
Alfred North Whitehead, also known for hardcore work on logic and mathematics, opened up to the notion that education is not about this subject or that, but "life in its all manifestations." The unity in education is not an artificial curriculum, but life. That really opened my eyes. Analyzing, reflecting, and testing ideas is the driving force of human existence and that driving force needs to drive education. Whitehead talks about how inert ideas—ideas that are given to students but never analyzed or tested by students—kill the spirit of learning. Teachers play a huge role in creating an environment where students use ideas instead of being used by ideas.

> In training a child to activity of thought, above all things we must beware of what I will call "inert ideas"—that is to say, ideas that are merely received into the mind without being utilised, or tested, or thrown into fresh combinations. In the history of education, the most striking phenomenon is that schools of learning, which at one epoch are alive with a ferment of genius, in a succeeding generation exhibit merely pedantry and routine. The reason is, that they are overladen with inert ideas. Education with inert ideas is not only useless: it is, above all things, harmful—*Corruptio optimi, pessima.* Except at rare intervals of intellectual ferment, education in the past has been radically infected with inert ideas. . . .
>
> The solution which I am urging, is to eradicate the fatal disconnection of subjects which kills the vitality of our modern curriculum. There is only one subject-matter for education, and that is Life in all its manifestations. Instead of this single unity, we offer children—Algebra, from which nothing follows; Geometry, from which nothing follows; Science, from which nothing follows; History, from which nothing follows; a Couple of Languages, never mastered; and lastly, most dreary of all, Literature, represented by plays of Shakespeare, with philological notes and short analyses of plot and character to be in substance committed to memory. Can such a list be said to represent Life, as it is known in the midst of the living of it?[1]

What I derived from Whitehead's ideas became even clearer to me when I read a section on individuality in *On Liberty* by John Stuart Mill, famous for, among many things, for his outstanding book on utilitarianism and his efforts to gain equal rights for women, which was pretty remarkable for a guy living in the 1800s. Mill's society and our society want everyone to conform and does whatever it can do for that. In the courses I've taken, for example, everything is tied to a rigid syllabus and assessed according to rubrics that students basically follow like orders in the army. There's little thought. It's like checking off boxes of a customer service survey rather than learning. What Mill offers and what appeals deeply to me is the idea that individuality is a good thing. The individualistic I become the better my life is and

---

[1] Whitehead, Alfred North. *The Aims of Education and Other Essays.* New York: The Free Press, 1957. 1–2, 6–7.

the better the lives of my fellow citizens. Embrace individuality, Mill argues, and you open up the door for genius. Geniuses are not to be feared, but are role models for others to seek their genius. We have to think of ourselves as having that spark of genius to really make our education valuable to each of us. Mill contends that the people who don't like genius and originality are the people who have never cultivated it in themselves and therefore don't see it in others. The reason I am going to school to get my doctorate in philosophy is to take my place among educators and save the students from uniformity that is frankly killing them:

It is not by wearing down into uniformity all that is individual in themselves, but by cultivating it and calling it forth, within the limits imposed by the rights and interests of others, that human beings become a noble and beautiful object of contemplation; and as the works partake the character of those who do them, by the same process human life also becomes rich, diversified, and animating, furnishing more abundant aliment to high thoughts and elevating feelings, and strengthening the tie which binds every individual to the race, by making the race infinitely better worth belonging to. In proportion to the development of his individuality, each person becomes more valuable to himself, and is therefore capable of being more valuable to others. There is a greater fullness of life about his own existence, and when there is more life in the units there is more in the mass which is composed of them. As much compression as is necessary to prevent the stronger specimens of human nature from encroaching on the rights of others, cannot be dispensed with; but for this there is ample compensation even in the point of view of human development. The means of development which the individual loses by being prevented from gratifying his inclinations to the injury of others, are chiefly obtained at the expense of the development of other people. And even to himself there is a full equivalent in the better development of the social part of his nature, rendered possible by the restraint put upon the selfish part. To be held to rigid rules of justice for the sake of others, develops the feelings and capacities which have the good of others for their object. But to be restrained in things not affecting their good, by their mere displeasure, develops nothing valuable, except such force of character as may unfold itself in resisting the restraint. If acquiesced in, it dulls and blunts the whole nature. To give any fair-play to the nature of each, it is essential that different persons should be allowed to lead different lives. In proportion as this latitude has been exercised in any age, has that age been noteworthy to posterity. Even despotism does not produce its worst effects, so long as individuality exists under it; and whatever crushes individuality is despotism, by whatever name it may be called, and whether it professes to be enforcing the will of God or the injunctions of men.

Having said that individuality is the same thing as development, and that it is only the cultivation of individuality which produces, or can produce, well-developed human beings, I might here close the argument: for what more or better can be said of any condition of human affairs, than that it brings human beings themselves nearer to the best thing they can be? or what worse can be said of any obstruction to good, than that it prevents this? Doubtless, however, these considerations will not suffice to convince those who most need convincing; and it is necessary further to show, that these developed human beings are of some use to the undeveloped—to point out to those who do not desire liberty, and would not avail themselves of it, that they may be in some intelligible manner rewarded for allowing other people to make use of it without hindrance.

In the first place, then, I would suggest that they might possibly learn something from them. It will not be denied by anybody, that originality is a valuable element in human affairs. There is always need for persons not only to discover new truths, and point out when what were once truths are true no longer, but also to commence new practices, and set the example of more enlightened conduct, and better taste and sense in human life. This cannot well be gainsaid by anybody who does not believe that the world has already attained perfection in all its ways and practices. It is true that this benefit is not capable of being rendered by everybody alike: there are but few persons, in comparison with the whole of mankind, whose experiments, if adopted by others, would be likely to be any improvement on established practice. But these few are the salt of the earth; without them, human life would become a stagnant pool. Not only is it they who introduce good things which did not before exist; it is they who keep the life in those which already existed. If there were nothing new to be done, would human intellect cease to be necessary? Would it be a reason why those who do the old things should forget why they are done, and do them like cattle, not like human beings? There is only too great a tendency in the best beliefs and practices to degenerate into the mechanical; and unless there were a succession of persons whose ever-recurring originality prevents the grounds of those beliefs and practices from becoming merely traditional, such dead matter would not resist the smallest shock from anything really alive, and there would be no reason why civilisation should not die out, as in the Byzantine Empire. Persons of genius, it is true, are, and are always likely to be, a small minority; but in order to have them, it is necessary to preserve the soil in which they grow. Genius can only breathe freely in an atmosphere of freedom. Persons of genius are, *ex vi termini*, more individual than any other people—less capable, consequently, of fitting themselves, without hurtful compression, into any of the small number of moulds which society provides in order to save its members the trouble of forming their own character. If from timidity they consent to be forced into one of these moulds, and to let all that part of themselves which cannot expand under the pressure remain unexpanded, society will be little the better for their genius. If they are of a strong character, and break their fetters, they become a mark for the society which has not succeeded in reducing them to commonplace, to point at with solemn warning as "wild," "erratic," and the like; much as if one should complain of the Niagara river for not flowing smoothly between its banks like a Dutch canal.

I insist thus emphatically on the importance of genius, and the necessity of allowing it to unfold itself freely both in thought and in practice, being well aware that no one will deny the position in theory, but knowing also that almost every one, in reality, is totally indifferent to it. People think genius a fine thing if it enables a man to write an exciting poem, or paint a picture. But in its true sense, that of originality in thought and action, though no one says that it is not a thing to be admired, nearly all, at heart, think that they can do very well without it. Unhappily this is too natural to be wondered at. Originality is the one thing which unoriginal minds cannot feel the use of. They cannot see what it is to do for them: how should they? If they could see what it would do for them, it would not be originality. The first service which originality has to render them, is that of opening their eyes: which being once fully done, they would have a chance of being themselves original. Meanwhile, recollecting that nothing was ever yet done which some one was not the first to do, and that all good things which exist are the fruits of originality, let them be modest enough to believe that there is something still left for it to accomplish, and assure themselves that they are more in need of originality, the less they are conscious of the want.[2]

Howard Gardner's views on multiple intelligences, I believe, would definitely help bring about a resurgence in schooling. People are not intelligent, as if "intelligence" is a single block. Rather, human beings have different kinds of intelligences in the same way they have different skin colors, tastes, and attitudes. We're not going to get individuality and genius in schooling if we make everyone conform to

---

[2] Mill, John Stuart. *On Liberty*. Project Gutenberg. <https://www.gutenberg.org/ebooks/34901>.

same standards. The scientist has a different kind of intelligence than the dancer, who has different type of intelligence than the politician, who has a different kind of intelligence than the musician. Einstein has a different kind of intelligence than Lebron James; Lebron James has a different kind of intelligence from Beethoven; Beethoven has a different kind of intelligence than Donald Trump.

In fact, however, nearly every cultural role of any degree of sophistication requires a combination of intelligences. Thus, even an apparently straightforward role, like playing the violin, transcends a reliance on musical intelligence. To become a successful violinist requires bodily-kinesthetic dexterity and the interpersonal skills of relating to an audience and, in a different way, choosing a manager; quite possibly it involves an intrapersonal intelligence as well. Dance requires skills in bodily-kinesthetic, musical, interpersonal, and spatial intelligences in varying degrees. Politics requires an interpersonal skill, a linguistic facility, and perhaps some logical aptitude.

Inasmuch as nearly every cultural role requires several intelligences, it becomes important to consider individuals as a collection of aptitudes rather than as having a singular problem-solving faculty that can be measured directly through pencil-and-paper tests. Even given a relatively small number of such intelligences, the diversity of human ability is created through the differences in these profiles. In fact, it may well be that the "total is greater than the sum of the parts." An individual may not be particularly gifted in any intelligence; and yet, because of a particular combination or blend of skills, he or she may be able to fill some niche uniquely well. Thus it is of paramount importance to assess the particular combination of skills that may earmark an individual for a certain vocational or avocational niche.

In brief, MI theory leads to three conclusions:

1. All of us have the full range of intelligences; that is what makes us human beings, cognitively speaking.
2. No two individuals—not even identical twins—have exactly the same intellectual profile. That is because, even when the genetic material is identical, individuals have different experiences; and those who are identical twins are often highly motivated to distinguish themselves from one another.
3. Having a strong intelligence does not mean that one necessarily acts intelligently. A person with high mathematical intelligence might use her abilities to carry out important experiments in physics or create powerful new geometric proofs; but she might waste these abilities in playing the lottery all day or multiplying ten-digit numbers in her head.[3]

When education is so obsessed with finding people jobs, they fail to develop the whole spectrum of human abilities. That is a tragedy for individuals and for society as a whole. Perhaps the most influential and greatest American in Philosophy of Education, John Dewey, understands that we become fully human by fully participating in our society and by revitalizing our spiritual lives through poetry, art, and religion.

How can philosophic change seriously affect social philosophy? As far as fundamentals are concerned, every view and combination appears to have been formulated already. Society is composed of individuals: this obvious and basic fact no philosophy, whatever its pretensions to novelty, can question or alter. Hence these three alternatives: Society must exist for the sake of individuals; or individuals must have their ends and ways of living set for them by society; or else society and individuals are correlative, organic, to one another, society requiring the service and subordination of

---

[3] Gardiner, Howard. *In a Nutshell.* <https://howardgardner.com/>.

individuals and at the same time existing to serve them. Beyond these three views, none seems to be logically conceivable. Moreover, while each of the three types includes many subspecies and variations within itself, yet the changes seem to have been so thoroughly rung that at most only minor variations are now possible.

Especially would it seem true that the "organic" conception meets all the objections to the extreme individualistic and extreme socialistic theories, avoiding the errors alike of Plato and Bentham. Just because society is composed of individuals, it would seem that individuals and the associative relations that hold them together must be of coequal importance. Without strong and competent individuals, the bonds and ties that form society have nothing to lay hold on. Apart from associations with one another, individuals are isolated from one another and fade and wither; or are opposed to one another and their conflicts injure individual development. Law, state, church, family, friendship, industrial association, these and other institutions and arrangements are necessary in order that individuals may grow and find their specific capacities and functions. Without their aid and support human life is, as Hobbes said, brutish, solitary, nasty.

We plunge into the heart of the matter, by asserting that these various theories suffer from a common defect. They are all committed to the logic of general notions under which specific situations are to be brought. What we want light upon is this or that group of individuals, this or that concrete human being, this or that special institution or social arrangement. For such a logic of inquiry, the traditionally accepted logic substitutes discussion of the meaning of concepts and their dialectical relationship to one another. The discussion goes on in terms of the state, the individual; the nature of institutions as such, society in general.

We need guidance in dealing with particular perplexities in domestic life, and are met by dissertations on the Family or by assertions of the sacredness of individual Personality. We want to know about the worth of the institution of private property as it operates under given conditions of definite time and place. We meet with the reply of Proudhon that property generally is theft, or with that of Hegel that the realization of will is the end of all institutions, and that private ownership as the expression of mastery of personality over physical nature is a necessary element in such realization. Both answers may have a certain suggestiveness in connection with specific situations. But the conceptions are not proffered for what they may be worth in connection with special historic phenomena. They are general answers supposed to have a universal meaning that covers and dominates all particulars. Hence they do not assist inquiry. They close it. They are not instrumentalities to be employed and tested in clarifying concrete social difficulties. They are ready-made principles to be imposed upon particulars in order to determine their nature. They tell us about the state when we want to know about some state. But the implication is that what is said about the state applies to any state that we happen to wish to know about.

In transferring the issue from concrete situations to definitions and conceptual deductions, the effect, especially of the organic theory, is to supply the apparatus for intellectual justification of the established order. Those most interested in practical social progress and the emancipation of groups from oppression have turned a cold shoulder to the organic theory. The effect, if not the intention, of German idealism as applied in social philosophy was to provide a bulwark for the maintenance of the political status quo against the tide of radical ideas coming from revolutionary France. Although Hegel asserted in explicit form that the end of states and institutions is to further the realization of the freedom of all, his effect was to consecrate the Prussian State and to enshrine bureaucratic absolutism. Was this apologetic tendency accidental, or did it spring from something in the logic of the notions that were employed?

Surely the latter. If we talk about the state and the individual, rather than about this or that political organization and this or that group of needy and suffering human beings, the tendency is to throw the glamor and prestige, the meaning and value attached to the general notion, over the concrete situation and thereby to cover up the defects of the latter and disguise the need of serious reforms. The meanings which are found in the general notions are injected into the particulars that come under them. Quite properly so if we once grant the logic of rigid universals under which the concrete cases have to be subsumed in order to be understood and explained.

Again, the tendency of the organic point of view is to minimize the significance of specific conflicts. Since the individual and the state or social institution are but two sides of the same reality, since they are already reconciled in principle and conception, the conflict in any particular case can be but apparent. Since in theory the individual and the state are reciprocally necessary and helpful to one another, why pay much attention to the fact that in this state a whole group of individuals are suffering from oppressive conditions? In "reality" their interests cannot be in conflict with those of the state to which they belong; the opposition is only superficial and casual. Capital and labor cannot "really" conflict because each is an organic necessity to the other, and both to the organized community as a whole. There cannot "really" be any sex-problem because men and women are indispensable both to one another and to the state. In his day, Aristotle could easily employ the logic of general concepts superior to individuals to show that the institution of slavery was in the interests both of the state and of the slave class. Even if the intention is not to justify the existing order the effect is to divert attention from special situations. Rationalistic logic formerly made men careless in observation of the concrete in physical philosophy. It now operates to depress and retard observation in specific social phenomena. The social philosopher, dwelling in the region of his concepts, "solves" problems by showing the relationship of ideas, instead of helping men solve problems in the concrete by supplying them hypotheses to be used and tested in projects of reform.

Meanwhile, of course, the concrete troubles and evils remain. They are not magically waived out of existence because in theory society is organic. The region of concrete difficulties, where the assistance of intelligent method for tentative plans for experimentation is urgently needed, is precisely where intelligence fails to operate. In this region of the specific and concrete, men are thrown back upon the crudest empiricism, upon short-sighted opportunism and the matching of brute forces. In theory, the particulars are all neatly disposed of; they come under their appropriate heading and category; they are labelled and go into an orderly pigeon-hole in a systematic filing cabinet, labelled political science or sociology. But in empirical fact they remain as perplexing, confused and unorganized as they were before. So they are dealt with not by even an endeavor at scientific method but by blind rule of thumb, citation of precedents, considerations of immediate advantage, smoothing things over, use of coercive force and the clash of personal ambitions. The world still survives; it has therefore got on somehow—so much cannot be denied. The method of trial and error and competition of selfishnesses has somehow wrought out many improvements. But social theory nevertheless exists as an idle luxury rather than as a guiding method of inquiry and planning. In the question of methods concerned with reconstruction of special situations rather than in any refinements in the general concepts of institution, individuality, state, freedom, law, order, progress, etc., lies the true impact of philosophical reconstruction.

Consider the conception of the individual self. The individualistic school of England and France in the eighteenth and nineteenth centuries was empirical in intent. It based its individualism, philosophically speaking, upon the belief that individuals are alone real, that classes and organizations are secondary and derived. They are artificial, while individuals are natural. In what way then can individualism be said to come under the animadversions that have been passed? To say the defect was that this school overlooked those connections with other persons which are a part of the constitution of every individual is true as far as it goes; but unfortunately it rarely goes beyond the point of just that wholesale justification of institutions which has been criticized.

The real difficulty is that the individual is regarded as something given, something already there. Consequently, he can only be something to be catered to, something whose pleasures are to be magnified and possessions multiplied. When the individual is taken as something given already, anything that can be done to him or for him it can only be by way of external impressions and belongings: sensations of pleasure and pain, comforts, securities. Now it is true that social arrangements, laws, institutions are made for man, rather than that man is made for them; that they are means and agencies of human welfare and progress. But they are not means for obtaining something for individuals, not even happiness. They are means of creating individuals. Only in the physical sense of physical bodies that to the senses are separate is individuality an original datum. Individuality in a social and moral sense is something to be wrought out. It means initiative, inventiveness, varied resourcefulness, assumption of responsibility in choice of belief and conduct. These are not gifts, but achievements. As achievements, they are not absolute but relative to the use that is to be made of them. And this use varies with the environment.

The import of this conception comes out in considering the fortunes of the idea of self-interest. All members of the empirical school emphasized this idea. It was the sole motive of mankind. Virtue was to be attained by making benevolent action profitable to the individual; social arrangements were to be reformed so that egoism and altruistic consideration of others would be identified. Moralists of the opposite school were not backward in pointing out the evils of any theory that reduced both morals and political science to means of calculating self-interest. Consequently they threw the whole idea of interest overboard as obnoxious to morals. The effect of this reaction was to strengthen the cause of authority and political obscurantism. When the play of interest is eliminated, what remains? What concrete moving forces can be found? Those who identified the self with something ready-made and its interest with acquisition of pleasure and profit took the most effective means possible to reinstate the logic of abstract conceptions of law, justice, sovereignty, freedom, etc.—all of those vague general ideas that for all their seeming rigidity can be manipulated by any clever politician to cover up his designs and to make the worse seem the better cause. Interests are specific and dynamic; they are the natural terms of any concrete social thinking. But they are damned beyond recovery when they are identified with the things of a petty selfishness. They can be employed as vital terms only when the self is seen to be in process, and interest to be a name for whatever is concerned in furthering its movement.

The same logic applies to the old dispute of whether reform should start with the individual or with institutions. When the self is regarded as something complete within itself, then it is readily argued that only internal moralistic changes are of importance in general reform. Institutional changes are said to be merely external. They may add conveniences and comforts to life, but they cannot effect moral improvements. The result is to throw the burden for social improvement upon free-will in its most impossible form. Moreover, social and economic passivity are encouraged. Individuals are led to concentrate in moral introspection upon their own vices and virtues, and to neglect the character of the environment. Morals withdraw from active concern with detailed economic and political conditions. Let us perfect ourselves within, and in due season changes in society will come of themselves is the teaching. And while saints are engaged in introspection, burly sinners run the world. But when self-hood is perceived to be an active process it is also seen that social modifications are the only means of the creation of changed personalities. Institutions are viewed in their educative effect:—with reference to the types of individuals they foster. The interest in individual moral improvement and the social interest in objective reform of economic and political conditions are identified. And inquiry into the meaning of social arrangements gets definite point and direction. We are led to ask what the specific stimulating, fostering and nurturing power of each specific social arrangement may be. The old-time separation between politics and morals is abolished at its root.

Consequently we cannot be satisfied with the general statement that society and the state is organic to the individual. The question is one of specific causations. Just what response does this social arrangement, political or economic, evoke, and what effect does it have upon the disposition of those who engage in it? Does it release capacity? If so, how widely? Among a few, with a corresponding depression in others, or in an extensive and equitable way? Is the capacity which is set free also directed in some coherent way, so that it becomes a power, or its manifestation spasmodic and capricious? Since responses are of an indefinite diversity of kind, these inquiries have to be detailed and specific. Are men's senses rendered more delicately sensitive and appreciative, or are they blunted and dulled by this and that form of social organization? Are their minds trained so that the hands are more deft and cunning? Is curiosity awakened or blunted? What is its quality: is it merely esthetic, dwelling on the forms and surfaces of things or is it also an intellectual searching into their meaning? Such questions as these (as well as the more obvious ones about the qualities conventionally labelled moral), become the starting-points of inquiries about every institution of the community when it is recognized that individuality is not originally given but is created under the influences of associated life. Like utilitarianism, the theory subjects every form of organization to continual scrutiny and criticism. But instead of leading us to ask what it does in the way of causing pains and pleasures to individuals already in existence, it inquires what is done to release specific capacities and co-ordinate them into working powers. What sort of individuals are created?

The waste of mental energy due to conducting discussion of social affairs in terms of conceptual generalities is astonishing. How far would the biologist and the physician progress if when the subject of respiration is under consideration, discussion confined itself to bandying back and forth the concepts of organ and organism:—If for example one school thought respiration could be known and understood by insisting upon the fact that it occurs in an individual body and therefore is an "individual" phenomenon, while an opposite school insisted that it is simply one function in organic interaction with others and can be known or understood therefore only by reference to other functions taken in an equally general or wholesale way? Each proposition is equally true and equally futile. What is needed is specific inquiries into a multitude of specific structures and interactions. Not only does the solemn reiteration of categories of individual and organic or social whole not further these definite and detailed inquiries, but it checks them. It detains thought within pompous and sonorous generalities wherein controversy is as inevitable as it is incapable of solution. It is true enough that if cells were not in vital interaction with one another, they could neither conflict nor co-operate. But the fact of the existence of an "organic" social group, instead of answering any questions merely marks the fact that questions exist: Just what conflicts and what co-operations occur, and what are their specific causes and consequences? But because of the persistence within social philosophy of the order of ideas that has been expelled from natural philosophy, even sociologists take conflict or co-operation as general categories upon which to base their science, and condescend to empirical facts only for illustrations. As a rule, their chief "problem" is a purely dialectical one, covered up by a thick quilt of empirical anthropological and historical citations: How do individuals unite to form society? How are individuals socially controlled? And the problem is justly called dialectical because it springs from antecedent conceptions of "individual" and "social."

"free experimentation and power of choice of the individual"

Just as "individual" is not one thing, but is a blanket term for the immense variety of specific reactions, habits, dispositions and powers of human nature that are evoked, and confirmed under the influences of associated life, so with the term "social." Society is one word, but infinitely many things. It covers all the ways in which by associating together men share their experiences, and build up common interests and aims; street gangs, schools for burglary, clans, social cliques, trades unions, joint stock corporations, villages and international alliances. The new method takes effect in substituting inquiry into these specific, changing and relative facts (relative to problems and purposes, not metaphysically relative) for solemn manipulation of general notions. . . .

It signifies an active process, that of release of capacity from whatever hems it in. But since society can develop only as new resources are put at its disposal, it is absurd to suppose that freedom has positive significance for individuality but negative meaning for social interests. Society is strong, forceful, stable against accident only when all its members can function to the limit of their capacity. Such functioning cannot be achieved without allowing a leeway of experimentation beyond the limits of established and sanctioned custom. A certain amount of overt confusion and irregularity is likely to accompany the granting of the margin of liberty without which capacity cannot find itself. But socially as well as scientifically the great thing is not to avoid mistakes but to have them take place under conditions such that they can be utilized to increase intelligence in the future.

If British liberal social philosophy tended, true to the spirit of its atomistic empiricism, to make freedom and the exercise of rights ends in themselves, the remedy is not to be found in recourse to a philosophy of fixed obligations and authoritative law such as characterized German political thinking. The latter, as events have demonstrated, is dangerous because of its implicit menace to the free self-determination of other social groups. But it is also weak internally when put to the final test. In its hostility to the free experimentation and power of choice of the individual in determining social affairs, it limits the capacity of many or most individuals to share effectively in social operations, and thereby deprives society of the full contribution of all its members. The best guarantee of collective efficiency and power is liberation and use of the diversity of individual capacities in initiative, planning, foresight, vigor and endurance. Personality must be educated, and personality cannot be educated by confining its operations to technical and specialized things, or to the less important relationships of life. Full education comes only when there is a responsible share on the part of each person, in proportion to capacity, in shaping the aims and policies of the social groups to which he belongs. This fact fixes the significance of democracy. It cannot be conceived as a sectarian or racial thing nor as a consecration of some form of government which has already attained constitutional sanction. It is but a name for the fact that human nature is developed only when its elements take part in directing things which are common, things for the sake of which men and women form groups—families, industrial companies, governments, churches, scientific associations and so on. The principle holds as much of one form of association, say in industry and commerce, as it does in government. The identification of democracy with political democracy which is responsible for most of its failures is, however, based upon the traditional ideas which make the individual and the state ready-made entities in themselves.

As the new ideas find adequate expression in social life, they will be absorbed into a moral background, and will the ideas and beliefs themselves be deepened and be unconsciously transmitted and sustained. They will color the imagination and temper the desires and affections. They will not form a set of ideas to be expounded, reasoned out and argumentatively supported, but will be a spontaneous way of envisaging life. Then they will take on religious value. The religious spirit will be revivified because it will be in harmony with men's unquestioned scientific beliefs and their ordinary

spontaneous way of envisaging life   *"shaping aims and policies of social groups"*

All spirituality is connected to life and ready action

day-by-day social activities. It will not be obliged to lead a timid, half-concealed and half-apologetic life because tied to scientific ideas and social creeds that are continuously eaten into and broken down. But especially will the ideas and beliefs themselves be deepened and intensified because spontaneously fed by emotion and translated into imaginative vision and fine art, while they are now maintained by more or less conscious effort, by deliberate reflection, by taking thought. They are technical and abstract just because they are not as yet carried as matter of course by imagination and feelings.

We began by pointing out that European philosophy arose when intellectual methods and scientific results moved away from social traditions which had consolidated and embodied the fruits of spontaneous desire and fancy. It was pointed out that philosophy had ever since had the problem of adjusting the dry, thin and meagre scientific standpoint with the obstinately persisting body of warm and abounding imaginative beliefs. Conceptions of possibility, progress, free movement and infinitely diversified opportunity have been suggested by modern science. But until they have displaced from imagination the heritage of the immutable and the once-for-all ordered and systematized, the ideas of mechanism and matter will lie like a dead weight upon the emotions, paralyzing religion and distorting art. When the liberation of capacity no longer seems a menace to organization and established institutions, something that cannot be avoided practically and yet something that is a threat to conservation of the most precious values of the past, when the liberating of human capacity operates as a socially creative force, art will not be a luxury, a stranger to the daily occupations of making a living. Making a living economically speaking, will be at one with making a life that is worth living. And when the emotional force, the mystic force one might say, of communication, of the miracle of shared life and shared experience is spontaneously felt, the hardness and crudeness of contemporary life will be bathed in the light that never was on land or sea.

Poetry, art, religion are precious things. They cannot be maintained by lingering in the past and futilely wishing to restore what the movement of events in science, industry and politics has destroyed. They are an out-flowering of thought and desires that unconsciously converge into a disposition of imagination as a result of thousands and thousands of daily episodes and contact. They cannot be willed into existence or coerced into being. The wind of the spirit bloweth where it listeth and the kingdom of God in such things does not come with observation. But while it is impossible to retain and recover by deliberate volition old sources of religion and art that have been discredited, it is possible to expedite the development of the vital sources of a religion and art that are yet to be. Not indeed by action directly aimed at their production, but by substituting faith in the active tendencies of the day for dread and dislike of them, and by the courage of intelligence to follow whither social and scientific changes direct us. We are weak today in ideal matters because intelligence is divorced from aspiration. The bare force of circumstance compels us onwards in the daily detail of our beliefs and acts, but our deeper thoughts and desires turn backwards. When philosophy shall have co-operated with the course of events and made clear and coherent the meaning of the daily detail, science and emotion will interpenetrate, practice and imagination will embrace. Poetry and religious feeling will be the unforced flowers of life. To further this articulation and revelation of the meanings of the current course of events is the task and problem of philosophy in days of transition.[4]

---

[4] Dewey, John. *Reconstruction in Philosophy*. Project Gutenberg. <http://www.gutenberg.org/cache/epub/40089/pg40089.txt>.

human nature is developed only when directed to things that are common prudent

Even though I find many things in *The Closing of the American Mind* to be objectionable, especially Allan Bloom's embracing of elitism and his rejection of multiculturalism, he fastened on to this idea of teachers helping students to discover their souls—their inner workings, their ultimate drives, the ideas that push them out of bed every day and keep them going through the hard times:

> Although much effort has been expended in trying to prove that the teacher is always the agent of such [social] forces, in fact he is, willy-nilly, guided by the awareness, or the divination, that there is a human nature, and that assisting its fulfillment is his task. He does not come to this by way of abstractions or complicated reasoning. He sees it in the eyes of his students. Those students are only potential, but potential points beyond itself; and this is the source of the hope, almost always disappointed but ever renascent, that man is not just a creature of accident, chained to and formed by the particular cave in which he is born. . . . No real teacher can doubt that his task is to assist his pupil to fulfill human nature against all the deforming forces of convention and prejudice. The vision of what that nature is may be clouded, the teacher may be more or less limited, but his activity is solicited by something beyond him that at the same time provides him with a standard for judging his students' capacity and achievement. Moreover there is no real teacher who in practice does not believe in the existence of the soul, or in a magic that acts on it through speech.[5]

MILLER
What big lesson have you learned from your study of Philosophy of Education?

HERBERT
People who hate learning hate themselves.

MILLER
That is a bold statement. Why?

HERBERT
Because they have allowed the genius and greatness in themselves to wither and eventually die. What's there to look forward to in life when you are dead inside?

MILLER
Are you going to do something to rectify that situation?

HERBERT
I'll teach in a way that allows the genius to flow from everybody. When I teach a course, it will be for the souls of students, to help them give birth to their greatness.

MILLER
Any suggestions for your peers?

HERBERT
Find your genius and greatness and don't let anybody take it from you.

~~19-20.~~   *delete*

---

[5] Bloom, Allan. *The Closing of the American Mind*. New York: Simon & Schuster, Inc., 1987. 19-20.

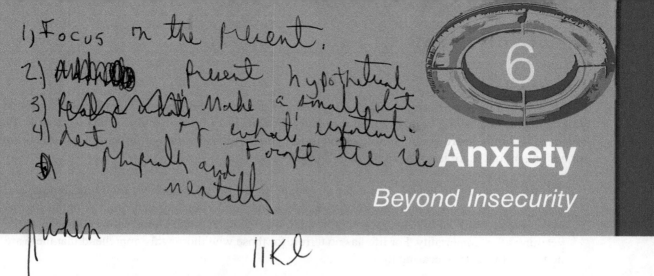

Carolyn is a stay-at-home mom in a small town on the Illinois–Wisconsin border. I found her on Facebook while trolling philosophy groups. I just liked her attitude right from the beginning—out there and honest, especially with her challenges with anxiety. We meet at a large grocery store. She's says she's relaxed, she's shopping, and I'd get a better interview than if it were just her and me at her kitchen table. She's a person of size, but is immensely graceful and fluid in her movements, almost like a ballerina. She wears khakis and a corduroy shirt.

◇◇◇◇

CAROLYN
I am so glad you met me here. I've got a full schedule today. The kids are in school and I have carved out four hours today to write the final chapter of my dissertation.

MILLER
What is your topic?

CAROLYN
Anxiety.

MILLER
Of course. I should have known. I would guess that your experience with anxiety drew you into philosophy.

CAROLYN
That's accurate enough to say. I struggled putting my finger on what was happening to me. Anxiety paralyzed me. I couldn't do anything. I couldn't make the most basic decisions like what to eat or what clothes to wear. I ate myself up to 600 lbs. I'm half that now. Anxiety ruined my marriage and I almost lost the kids because of it. But once I understood what anxiety really was—not what Dr. Phil said it was or any of those other folks—I got a handle on it and my life back. I can't say enough about the value of philosophy—it got me my life back.

MILLER
I'd love to hear what philosophers influenced you.

61

CAROLYN

It started with a passage from the Greek philosopher Epicurus and deepened when I really started to get into Patanjali, Nietzsche, Frankl, and surprisingly, Pascal. I say "surprisingly" when it came to Pascal because I had only heard about his wager and didn't know much about anything else. Epicurus is known for hedonism, but there is so much more to that guy than that.

> Accustom yourself to believe that death is nothing to us, for good and evil imply awareness, and death is the privation of all awareness; therefore a right understanding that death is nothing to us makes the mortality of life enjoyable, not by adding to life an unlimited time, but by taking away the yearning after immortality. For life has no terror; for those who thoroughly apprehend that there are no terrors for them in ceasing to live.[1]

Death always scared me, but if you think about it like Epicurus does, we never meet death. While we live death is absent. When we are absent, death is present. Also, while we might have some control of the future, but we don't own it. The future could come out in ways we neither plan for nor desire. Those few words steered me in another direction and made my life, believe it or not, easier.

Sure, I was anxious about the future, but also about the past, the things I had done, the regrets I had by doing this thing and not something. The past is an hornet's nest of anxiety for me. Memories of the past and anticipations of the future were competitors for the present and I could never enjoy life unless these competitors could be eliminated with high spirits. However, there were deeper aspects to anxiety that I had not yet faced until I understood what the Indian philosopher Patanjali maintains: pain is caused by "the anxiety and fear over losing what is gained" and even the wise "cling to life."[2] I tried way too hard to keep things rather than letting them go. This applied not only to my possessions, but to my beliefs as well. I needed to put things into bigger picture where the true values of things became clearer to me and that's where the Stoic philosopher Epictetus comes in:

> There are things which are within our power, and there are things which are beyond our power. Within our power are opinion, aim, desire, aversion, and, in one word, whatever affairs are our own. Beyond our power are body, property, reputation, office, and, in one word, whatever are not properly our own affairs.
>
> Now the things within our power are by nature free, unrestricted, unhindered; but those beyond our power are weak, dependent, restricted, alien. Remember, then, that if you attribute freedom to things that are by nature dependent and take what belongs to others for your own, you will be hindered, you will lament, you will be disturbed, you will find fault both with gods and men. But if you take for your own only that which is your own and view what belongs to others just as it really is, then no one will ever compel you, no one will restrict you; you will find fault with no one, you will accuse no one, you will do nothing against your will; no one will hurt you, you will not have an enemy, nor will you suffer any harm.

---

[1] Epicurus. *Letter to Menoeceus*. The Internet Classics Archives. <http://classics.mit.edu/Epicurus/menoec.html>.
[2] Patanjali. *The Yoga Sutras of Patanjali*. Trans. Sri Swami Satchidannanda. Buckingham, VA: Integral Yoga Productions, 2015. 94, 86.

Aiming, therefore, at such great things, remember that you must not allow yourself any inclination, however slight, toward the attainment of the others, but that you must entirely quit some of them, and for the present postpone the rest. But if you would have these, and possess power and wealth likewise, you may miss the latter in seeking the former; and you will certainly fail of that by which alone happiness and freedom are procured.

Seek at once, therefore, to be able to say to every unpleasing semblance, "You are but a semblance and by no means the real thing." And then examine it by those rules which you have; and first and chiefly by this: whether it concerns the things which are within our own power or those which are not; and if it concerns anything beyond our power, be prepared to say that it is nothing to you.

II

Remember that desire demands the attainment of that of which you are desirous; and aversion demands the avoidance of that to which you are averse; that he who fails of the object of his desires is disappointed; and he who incurs the object of his aversion is wretched. If, then, you shun only those undesirable things which you can control, you will never incur anything which you shun; but if you shun sickness, or death, or poverty, you will run the risk of wretchedness. Remove [the habit of] aversion, then, from all things that are not within our power, and apply it to things undesirable which are within our power. But for the present, altogether restrain desire; for if you desire any of the things not within our own power, you must necessarily be disappointed; and you are not yet secure of those which are within our power, and so are legitimate objects of desire. Where it is practically necessary for you to pursue or avoid anything, do even this with discretion and gentleness and moderation.

III

With regard to whatever objects either delight the mind or contribute to use or are tenderly beloved, remind yourself of what nature they are, beginning with the merest trifles: if you have a favorite cup, that it is but a cup of which you are fond of—for thus, if it is broken, you can bear it; if you embrace your child or your wife, that you embrace a mortal—and thus, if either of them dies, you can bear it.

IV

When you set about any action, remind yourself of what nature the action is. If you are going to bathe, represent to yourself the incidents usual in the bath—some persons pouring out, others pushing in, others scolding, others pilfering. And thus you will more safely go about this action if you say to yourself, "I will now go to bathe and keep my own will in harmony with nature." And so with regard to every other action.[3]

Yet I still needed to deepen my inquiry into anxiety if I would be able to seek its full scope. In my existentialism course, we read a strange and wild book by the God is dead guy Nietzsche. There was so much more in that book than that. Nietzsche talks about how humans can create new values: by shouldering the old values, then destroying them, and the creating new values. This idea inspired me: I had the power inside to author my existence. My existence did not have to be authored by other people. I would have my own belief system! I had shouldered theirs—from my parents, from my friends, from society—and

---

[3] Epictetus. *Enchiridion*. Project Gutenberg. <https://www.gutenberg.org/ebooks/45109>.

But I learned to destroy
smash their values

it made me anxious because I could meet their standards. What a pain and how anxious it made me feel
not live to up the expectations of other people. *destroy their values and*
create values of my own

I. The Three Metamorphoses

Three metamorphoses of the spirit do I designate to you: how the spirit becometh a camel, the
camel a lion, and the lion at last a child.

Many heavy things are there for the spirit, the strong load-bearing spirit in which reverence
dwelleth: for the heavy and the heaviest longeth its strength.

What is heavy? so asketh the load-bearing spirit; then kneeleth it down like the camel, and wan-
teth to be well laden.

What is the heaviest thing, ye heroes? asketh the load-bearing spirit, that I may take it upon me
and rejoice in my strength.

Is it not this: To humiliate oneself in order to mortify one's pride? To exhibit one's folly in order
to mock at one's wisdom?

Or is it this: To desert our cause when it celebrateth its triumph? To ascend high mountains to
tempt the tempter?

Or is it this: To feed on the acorns and grass of knowledge, and for the sake of truth to suffer
hunger of soul?

Or is it this: To be sick and dismiss comforters, and make friends of the deaf, who never hear thy
requests?

Or is it this: To go into foul water when it is the water of truth, and not disclaim cold frogs and
hot toads?

Or is it this: To love those who despise us, and give one's hand to the phantom when it is going
to frighten us?

All these heaviest things the load-bearing spirit taketh upon itself: and like the camel, which,
when laden, hasteneth into the wilderness, so hasteneth the spirit into its wilderness.

But in the loneliest wilderness happeneth the second metamorphosis: here the spirit becometh a lion;
freedom will it capture, and lordship in its own wilderness.]

Its last Lord it here seeketh: hostile will it be to him, and to its last God; for victory will it struggle
with the great dragon.

What is the great dragon which the spirit is no longer inclined to call Lord and God? "Thou-shalt,"
is the great dragon called. But the spirit of the lion saith, "I will."

"Thou-shalt," lieth in its path, sparkling with gold—a scale-covered beast; and on every scale
glittereth golden, "Thou shalt!"

The values of a thousand years glitter on those scales, and thus speaketh the mightiest of all
dragons: "All the values of things—glitter on me.

All values have already been created, and all created values—do I represent. Verily, there shall
be no 'I will' any more. Thus speaketh the dragon.

My brethren, wherefore is there need of the lion in the spirit? Why sufficeth not the beast of
burden, which renounceth and is reverent?

To create new values—that, even the lion cannot yet accomplish: but to create itself freedom for
new creating—that can the might of the lion do.

To create itself freedom, and give a holy Nay even unto duty: for that, my brethren, there is need of the lion.

To assume the right to new values—that is the most formidable assumption for a load-bearing and reverent spirit. Verily, unto such a spirit it is preying, and the work of a beast of prey.

As its holiest, it once loved "Thou-shalt": now is it forced to find illusion and arbitrariness even in the holiest things, that it may capture freedom from its love: the lion is needed for this capture.

But tell me, my brethren, what the child can do, which even the lion could not do? Why hath the preying lion still to become a child?

Innocence is the child, and forgetfulness, a new beginning, a game, a self-rolling wheel, a first movement, a holy Yea.

Aye, for the game of creating, my brethren, there is needed a holy Yea unto life: ITS OWN will, willeth now the spirit; HIS OWN world winneth the world's outcast.

Three metamorphoses of the spirit have I designated to you: how the spirit became a camel, the camel a lion, and the lion at last a child.[4]

I must always balance my power with the recognition that I am not God. Too many times I thought myself God: I could control the future and every aspect of my life. My anxiety peaked when I took that view. Blaise Pascal, in his *Penses* (*Thoughts*) brought me back to earth after reading Nietzsche.

Man's disproportion. –[This is where our innate knowledge leads us. If it be not true, there is no truth in man; and if it be true, he finds therein great cause for humiliation, being compelled to abase himself in one way or another. And since he cannot exist without this knowledge, I wish that, before entering on deeper researches into nature, he would consider her both seriously and at leisure, that he would reflect upon himself also, and knowing what proportion there is. . . .] Let man then contemplate the whole of nature in her full and grand majesty, and turn his vision from the low objects which surround him. Let him gaze on that brilliant light, set like an eternal lamp to illumine the universe; let the earth appear to him a point in comparison with the vast circle described by the sun; and let him wonder at the fact that this vast circle is itself but a very fine point in comparison with that described by the stars in their revolution round the firmament. But if our view be arrested there, let our imagination pass beyond; it will sooner exhaust the power of conception than nature that of supplying material for conception. The whole visible world is only an imperceptible atom in the ample bosom of nature. No idea approaches it. We may enlarge our conceptions beyond all imaginable space; we only produce atoms in comparison with the reality of things. It is an infinite sphere, the centre of which is everywhere, the circumference nowhere.[30] In short it is the greatest sensible mark of the almighty power of God, that imagination loses itself in that thought.

Returning to himself, let man consider what he is in comparison with all existence; let him regard himself as lost in this remote corner of nature; and from the little cell in which he finds himself lodged, I mean the universe, let him estimate at their true value the earth, kingdoms, cities, and himself. What is a man in the Infinite?

But to show him another prodigy equally astonishing, let him examine the most delicate things he knows. Let a mite be given him, with its minute body and parts incomparably more minute, limbs with their joints, veins in the limbs, blood in the veins, humours in the blood, drops in the humours, vapours in the drops. Dividing these last things again, let him exhaust his powers of conception, and

---

[4] Nietzsche, Friedrich. *Thus Spoke Zarathustra*. Project Gutenberg. <https://www.gutenberg.org/ebooks/1998>.

what we see is only an atom compared to the rest of the universe. Even what we imagine is only an atom compared to the rest of the universe.

let the last object at which he can arrive be now that of our discourse. Perhaps he will think that here is the smallest point in nature. I will let him see therein a new abyss.

I will paint for him not only the visible universe, but all that he can conceive of nature's immensity in the womb of this abridged atom. Let him see therein an infinity of universes, each of which has its firmament, its planets, its earth, in the same proportion as in the visible world; in each earth animals, and in the last mites, in which he will find again all that the first had, finding still in these others the same thing without end and without cessation. Let him lose himself in wonders as amazing in their littleness as the others in their vastness. For who will not be astounded at the fact that our body, which a little while ago was imperceptible in the universe, itself imperceptible in the bosom of the whole, is now a colossus, a world, or rather a whole, in respect of the nothingness which we cannot reach? He who regards himself in this light will be afraid of himself, and observing himself sustained in the body given him by nature between those two abysses of the Infinite and Nothing, will tremble at the sight of these marvels; and I think that, as his curiosity changes into admiration, he will be more disposed to contemplate them in silence than to examine them with presumption.

For in fact what is man in nature? A Nothing in comparison with the Infinite, an All in comparison with the Nothing, a mean between nothing and everything. Since he is infinitely removed from comprehending the extremes, the end of things and their beginning are hopelessly hidden from him in an impenetrable secret, he is equally incapable of seeing the Nothing from which he was made, and the Infinite in which he is swallowed up.

What will he do then, but perceive the appearance of the middle of things, in an eternal despair of knowing either their beginning or their end. All things proceed from the Nothing, and are borne towards the Infinite. Who will follow these marvellous processes? The Author of these wonders understands them. None other can do so.

Through failure to contemplate these Infinites, men have rashly rushed into the examination of nature, as though they bore some proportion to her. It is strange that they have wished to understand the beginnings of things, and thence to arrive at the knowledge of the whole, with a presumption as infinite as their object. For surely this design cannot be formed without presumption or without a capacity infinite like nature.

If we are well informed, we understand that, as nature has graven her image and that of her Author on all things, they almost all partake of her double infinity. Thus we see that all the sciences are infinite in the extent of their researches. For who doubts that geometry, for instance, has an infinite infinity of problems to solve? They are also infinite in the multitude and fineness of their premises; for it is clear that those which are put forward as ultimate are not self-supporting, but are based on others which, again having others for their support, do not permit of finality. But we represent some as ultimate for reason, in the same way as in regard to material objects we call that an indivisible point beyond which our senses can no longer perceive anything, although by its nature it is infinitely divisible.

Of these two Infinites of science, that of greatness is the most palpable, and hence a few persons have pretended to know all things. "I will speak of the whole,"[31] said Democritus.

But the infinitely little is the least obvious. Philosophers have much oftener claimed to have reached it, and it is here they have all stumbled. This has given rise to such common titles as First Principles, Principles of Philosophy,[32] and the like, as ostentatious in fact, though not in appearance, as that one which blinds us, *De omni scibili*.[33]

We naturally believe ourselves far more capable of reaching the centre of things than of embracing their circumference. The visible extent of the world visibly exceeds us; but as we exceed little things, we think ourselves more capable of knowing them. And yet we need no less capacity for attaining the Nothing than the All. Infinite capacity is required for both, and it seems to me that whoever shall have understood the ultimate principles of being might also attain the knowledge of the Infinite. The one depends on the other, and one leads to the other. These extremes meet and reunite by force of distance, and find each other in God, and in God alone.

Let us then take our compass; we are something, and we are not everything. The nature of our existence hides from us the knowledge of first beginnings which are born of the Nothing; and the littleness of our being conceals from us the sight of the Infinite.

Our intellect holds the same position in the world of thought as our body occupies in the expanse of nature.

Limited as we are in every way, this state which holds the mean between two extremes is present in all our impotence. Our senses perceive no extreme. Too much sound deafens us; too much light dazzles us; too great distance or proximity hinders our view. Too great length and too great brevity of discourse tend to obscurity; too much truth is paralysing (I know some who cannot understand that to take four from nothing leaves nothing). First principles are too self-evident for us; too much pleasure disagrees with us. Too many concords are annoying in music; too many benefits irritate us; we wish to have the wherewithal to over-pay our debts. *Beneficia eo usque læta sunt dum videntur exsolvi posse; ubi multum antevenere, pro gratia odium redditur.* [34] We feel neither extreme heat nor extreme cold. Excessive qualities are prejudicial to us and not perceptible by the senses; we do not feel but suffer them. Extreme youth and extreme age hinder the mind, as also too much and too little education. In short, extremes are for us as though they were not, and we are not within their notice. They escape us, or we them.

This is our true state; this is what makes us incapable of certain knowledge and of absolute ignorance. We sail within a vast sphere, ever drifting in uncertainty, driven from end to end. When we think to attach ourselves to any point and to fasten to it, it wavers and leaves us; and if we follow it, it eludes our grasp, slips past us, and vanishes forever. Nothing stays for us. This is our natural condition, and yet most contrary to our inclination; we burn with desire to find solid ground and an ultimate sure foundation whereon to build a tower reaching to the Infinite. But our whole groundwork cracks, and the earth opens to abysses.

Let us therefore not look for certainty and stability. Our reason is always deceived by fickle shadows; nothing can fix the finite between the two Infinites, which both enclose and fly from it.

If this be well understood, I think that we shall remain at rest, each in the state wherein nature has placed him. As this sphere which has fallen to us as our lot is always distant from either extreme, what matters is that man should have a little more knowledge of the universe? If he has it, he but gets a little higher. Is he not always infinitely removed from the end, and is not the duration of our life equally removed from eternity, even if it lasts ten years longer?

In comparison with these Infinites all finites are equal, and I see no reason for fixing our imagination on one more than on another. The only comparison which we make of ourselves to the finite is painful to us.

If man made himself the first object of study, he would see how incapable he is of going further. How can a part know the whole? But he may perhaps aspire to know at least the parts to which he bears some proportion. But the parts of the world are all so related and linked to one another, that I believe it is impossible to know one without the other and without the whole.

Man, for instance, is related to all he knows. He needs a place wherein to abide, time through which to live, motion in order to live, elements to compose him, warmth and food to nourish him, air to breathe. He sees light; he feels bodies; in short, he is in a dependent alliance with everything. To know man, then, it is necessary to know how it happens that he needs air to live, and, to know the air, we must know how it is thus related to the life of man, etc. Flame cannot exist without air; therefore to understand the one, we must understand the other.

Since everything then is cause and effect, dependent and supporting, mediate and immediate, and all is held together by a natural though imperceptible chain, which binds together things most distant and most different, I hold it equally impossible to know the parts without knowing the whole, and to know the whole without knowing the parts in detail.

[The eternity of things in itself or in God must also astonish our brief duration. The fixed and constant immobility of nature, in comparison with the continual change which goes on within us, must have the same effect.]

And what completes our incapability of knowing things, is the fact that they are simple, and that we are composed of two opposite natures, different in kind, soul and body. For it is impossible that our rational part should be other than spiritual; and if any one maintains that we are simply corporeal, this would far more exclude us from the knowledge of things, there being nothing so inconceivable as to say that matter knows itself. It is impossible to imagine how it should know itself.

So if we are simply material, we can know nothing at all; and if we are composed of mind and matter, we cannot know perfectly things which are simple, whether spiritual or corporeal. Hence it comes that almost all philosophers have confused ideas of things, and speak of material things in spiritual terms, and of spiritual things in material terms. For they say boldly that bodies have a tendency to fall, that they seek after their centre, that they fly from destruction, that they fear the void, that they have inclinations, sympathies, antipathies, all of which attributes pertain only to mind. And in speaking of minds, they consider them as in a place, and attribute to them movement from one place to another; and these are qualities which belong only to bodies.

Instead of receiving the ideas of these things in their purity, we colour them with our own qualities, and stamp with our composite being all the simple things which we contemplate.

Who would not think, seeing us compose all things of mind and body, but that this mixture would be quite intelligible to us? Yet it is the very thing we least understand. Man is to himself the most wonderful object in nature; for he cannot conceive what the body is, still less what the mind is, and least of all how a body should be united to a mind. This is the consummation of his difficulties, and yet it is his very being. *Modus quo corporibus adhærent spiritus comprehendi ab hominibus non potest, et hoc tamen homo est.* Finally, to complete the proof of our weakness, I shall conclude with these two considerations. . . .[5]

Everything was stressing me out and I was not doing well. But I held the trump card: I could create positive value in the meaning. I could let anxiety beat me up or make it disappear.

MILLER
I like the way your philosophical thinking evolved: from something rather simplistic to rather refined.

CAROLYN
And I can finally do my own food shopping without driving myself crazy. Yea!

MILLER
Yea!

---

[5] Pascal, Blaise. *Pensées*. Project Gutenberg. <https://www.gutenberg.org/ebooks/18269>

Human Relationships

Can't We Just Get Along?

yet

Gentry looks a little older than most of the people I've interviewed. His face looks like it's gone through the wars and he walks with a slight limp. Yet he is tall and his manner his evolved, pleasant, polite, and polished. While interviewing him, I ~~got~~ the sense he was damaged and because of that he had a pessimistic view, especially when it came to human relationships. But the more I thought about what he said, the more I understood that he was schooling me—someone who should have known better—the obstacles of getting close to another human being and forging a relationship. Gentry works as a VP at an arboretum and it is an early Saturday in July when we connect while walking around a manmade pond.

◇◇◇◇

MILLER
What aroused your interest in philosophy?

GENTRY
That's a great way to put it. A great-looking undergrad teacher aroused me if I could be blunt.

MILLER
Be blunt, be frank.

GENTRY
You know, a crush. We never hooked up or anything, but I never missed his class on human nature. He mainly did phenomenology and his focus was human relationships—why they didn't usually work. This became a problem for me. I had a lot of relationships, but for whatever reason they just fell apart. I wasn't abusive, but it never clicked for me. Yet I wanted one of them to work. Philosophically, I wanted to prove a different point than my handsome professor had: that human relations did not often work because people failed to understand each other. Once we figured that problem, relationships would be possible.

MILLER
It's so personal what philosophical issues become problems for certain individuals, which for others are side issues.

GENTRY
That's true. I had a colleague in grad school obsessed with pre-Socratic philosophy, which never piqued my interest, even though I taught in class on it.

MILLER

What thinkers influenced you in this area of philosophy so compelling?

GENTRY

They can be influences even when you hate them?

MILLER

Of course.

GENTRY

The French existentialist Jean-Paul Sartre argues that when two people encounter each other, one is always a slave, and the other is a master. And Max Scheler, the German phenomenologist, who shows us that *ressentiment* is the result of this constant bullying.

MILLER

What about positive influences?

GENTRY

Aristotle. He writes about three kinds of friends: those we use, those we have fun with, and those whose good is foremost on our minds. The last kind of friendship is the type of relationship offers me hope that people can be decent to and care about each other. In his moral essays, Joseph Butler argues that not all acts are selfish. Butler makes me believe that human desire has been misunderstood and that calculated self-interest is not as common as we would like. I also like the Buddhist notion of compassion that The Dalai Lama talks about.

First, to the negative views. Sartre describes what happens when a person believes she is seen by another person. Being-seen means to be at the mercy of the other person, a bulls-eye, completely defined by this other person. When we feel embarrassed, for example, we see ourselves through the eyes of the other person. Either I define you or you define me and there's nothing in between. Human encounters are not equal and are in the character of master–slave or in the language of today, the bully and bullied:

> As a spatial-temporal object in the world, as an essential structure of a temporal-spatial situation in the world, I offer myself to the Other's appraisal. This also I apprehend by the pure existence of the *cogito*. To be looked at is apprehend oneself as the unknown object of unknowable appraisals—in particular, of value judgments. But at the same time that in shame and or pride I recognize the justice of these appraisals, I do not cease to take them for what they are—a free surpassing of the given toward possibilities. A judgment is the transcendental act of a free being. Thus being-seen constitutes me as a defenseless being for a freedom which is not my freedom. It is in this sense that we appear to the Other. But this slavery is not a historical result—not capable of being surmounted—of a *life* in the abstract form of consciousness. I am a slave to the degree that my being in dependent at the center of a freedom which is not mine and which is the very condition of my being. In so far as I am an object of values which come to qualify me without my being able to act on this qualification or even know it, I am enslaved. By the same token in so far as I am the instrument of possibilities which are not my possibilities.[1]

---

[1] Sartre, Jean-Paul. *Being and Nothingness*. Trans. Hazel E. Barnes. New York: Washington Square Press, 1956. 358.

It's easier to have relationships with trees than human beings—the trees don't talk back. I really think imprecise expectations about other people contribute to the absence of healthy relationships. People expect way too much from each other and sometimes we all should wear signs that say "BEWARE OF THE HUMAN." Intimacy with another person is a special place and maybe most don't get to that point in a relationship. But that doesn't mean we can't love or have healthy relationships. I didn't understand that human beings do not come into relationships unblemished. They're like boxes that have been mishandled by the post office, even though they say FRAGILE on them. Everybody's insecure, traumatized, sensitive, and has an agenda. I don't know too many whole people. Even in the most advanced societies, people are insensitive, cruel, and even brutal to each other. They can just go off, but the scarier thing is when you know they're pissed and they hold in, but it still comes out in creepy ways, as Max Scheler explains:

> Revenge, envy, the impulse to detract, spite, Schadenfreude, and malice lead to *ressentiment* only if there occurs neither a moral self-conquest (such as genuine forgiveness in the case of revenge) nor an act or some other adequate expression of emotion (such as verbal abuse or shaking one's fist), and if this restraint is caused by a pronounced awareness of impotence. There will be no *ressentiment* if he who thirsts for revenge really acts and avenges himself, if he who is consumed by hatred harms his enemy, gives him "a piece of his mind," or even merely vents his spleen in the presence of others. Nor will the envious fall under the dominion of *ressentiment* if he seeks to acquire the envied possession by means of work, barter, crime, or violence. *Ressentiment* can only arise if these emotions are particularly powerful and yet must be suppressed because they are coupled with the feeling that one is unable to act them out—either because of weakness, physical or mental, or because of fear. . . . *Ressentiment* can only arise if these emotions are particularly powerful and yet must be suppressed because they are coupled with the feeling that one is unable to act them out—either because of weakness, physical or mental, or because of fear. Through its very origin, *ressentiment* is therefore chiefly confined to those who serve and are dominated at the moment.[2]

Sartre and Scheler bum me out, but Aristotle gives me hope. For Aristotle, there are "friends" who take advantage of us, but then there are friends who are about what's best for us:

II

Our view will soon be cleared on these points when we have ascertained what is properly the object-matter of Friendship: for it is thought that not everything indiscriminately, but some peculiar matter alone, is the object of this affection; that is to say, what is good, or pleasurable, or useful. Now it would seem that that is useful through which accrues any good or pleasure, and so the objects of Friendship, as absolute Ends, are the good and the pleasurable.

    A question here arises; whether it is good absolutely or that which is good to the individuals, for which men feel Friendship (these two being sometimes distinct): and similarly in respect of the pleasurable. It seems then that each individual feels it towards that which is good to himself, and that abstractedly it is the real good which is the object of Friendship, and to each individual that which is good to each. It comes then to this; that each individual feels Friendship not for what is but

---

[2] Scheler, Max. *Ressentiment.* Trans. Louis A. Cosar. <https://hscif.org/wp-content/uploads/2018/04/Max-Scheler-Ressentiment.pdf>.

for that which conveys to his mind the impression of being good to himself. But this will make no real difference, because that which is truly the object of Friendship will also convey this impression to the mind.

There are then three causes from which men feel Friendship: but the term is not applied to the case of fondness for things inanimate because there is no requital of the affection nor desire for the good of those objects: it certainly savours of the ridiculous to say that a man fond of wine wishes well to it: the only sense in which it is true being that he wishes it to be kept safe and sound for his own use and benefit. But to the friend they say one should wish all good for his sake. And when men do thus wish good to another (he not *[Sidenote: 1156a] reciprocating the feeling), people call them Kindly; because Friendship they describe as being "Kindliness between persons who reciprocate it." But must they not add that the feeling must be mutually known? for many men are kindly disposed towards those whom they have never seen but whom they conceive to be amiable or useful: and this notion amounts to the same thing as a real feeling between them.

Well, these are plainly Kindly-disposed towards one another: but how can one call them friends while their mutual feelings are unknown to one another? to complete the idea of Friendship, then, it is requisite that they have kindly feelings towards one another, and wish one another good from one of the aforementioned causes, and that these kindly feelings should be mutually known.

III

As the motives to Friendship differ in kind so do the respective feelings and Friendships. The species then of Friendship are three, in number equal to the objects of it, since in the line of each there may be "mutual affection mutually known."

Now they who have Friendship for one another desire one another's good according to the motive of their Friendship; accordingly they whose motive is utility have no Friendship for one another really, but only in so far as some good arises to them from one another.

And they whose motive is pleasure are in like case: I mean, they have Friendship for men of easy pleasantry, not because they are of a given character but because they are pleasant to themselves. So then they whose motive to Friendship is utility love their friends for what is good to themselves; they whose motive is pleasure do so for what is pleasurable to themselves; that is to say, not in so far as the friend beloved is but in so far as he is useful or pleasurable. These Friendships then are a matter of result: since the object is not beloved in that he is the man he is but in that he furnishes advantage or pleasure as the case may be. Such Friendships are of course very liable to dissolution if the parties do not continue alike: I mean, that the others cease to have any Friendship for them when they are no longer pleasurable or useful. Now it is the nature of utility not to be permanent but constantly varying: so, of course, when the motive which made them friends is vanished, the Friendship likewise dissolves; since it existed only relatively to those circumstances.

Friendship of this kind is thought to exist principally among the old (because men at that time of life pursue not what is pleasurable but what is profitable); and in such, of men in their prime and of the young, as are given to the pursuit of profit. They that are such have no intimate intercourse with one another; for sometimes they are not even pleasurable to one another; nor, in fact, do they desire such intercourse unless their friends are profitable to them, because they are pleasurable only in so far as they have hopes of advantage. With these Friendships is commonly ranked that of hospitality.

But the Friendship of the young is thought to be based on the motive of pleasure: because they live at the beck and call of passion and generally pursue what is pleasurable to themselves and the object of the present moment: and as their age changes so likewise do their pleasures.

This is the reason why they form and dissolve Friendships rapidly: since the Friendship changes with the pleasurable object and such pleasure changes quickly.

The young are also much given up to Love; this passion being, in great measure, a matter of impulse and based on pleasure: for which cause they conceive Friendships and quickly drop them, changing often in the same day: but these wish for society and intimate intercourse with their friends, since they thus attain the object of their Friendship.

That then is perfect Friendship which subsists between those who are good and whose similarity consists in their goodness: for these men wish one another's good in similar ways; in so far as they are good (and good they are in themselves); and those are specially friends who wish good to their friends for their sakes, because they feel thus towards them on their own account and not as a mere matter of result; so the Friendship between these men continues to subsist so long as they are good; and goodness, we know, has in it a principle of permanence.

Moreover, each party is good abstractedly and also relatively to his friend, for all good men are not only abstractedly good but also useful to one another. Such friends are also mutually pleasurable because all good men are so abstractedly, and also relatively to one another, inasmuch as to each individual those actions are pleasurable which correspond to his nature, and all such as are like them. Now when men are good these will be always the same, or at least similar.

Friendship then under these circumstances is permanent, as we should reasonably expect, since it combines in itself all the requisite qualifications of friends. I mean, that Friendship of whatever kind is based upon good or pleasure (either abstractedly or relatively to the person entertaining the sentiment of Friendship), and results from a similarity of some sort; and to this kind belong all the aforementioned requisites in the parties themselves, because in this the parties are similar, and so on: moreover, in it there is the abstractedly good and the abstractedly pleasant, and as these are specially the object-matter of Friendship so the feeling and the state of Friendship is found most intense and most excellent in men thus qualified.

Rare it is probable Friendships of this kind will be, because men of this kind are rare. Besides, all requisite qualifications being presupposed, there is further required time and intimacy: for, as the proverb says, men cannot know one another "till they have eaten the requisite quantity of salt together;" nor can they in fact admit one another to intimacy, much less be friends, till each has appeared to the other and been proved to be a fit object of Friendship. They who speedily commence an interchange of friendly actions may be said to wish to be friends, but they are not so unless they are also proper objects of Friendship and mutually known to be such: that is to say, a desire for Friendship may arise quickly but not Friendship itself.

IV

Well, this Friendship is perfect both in respect of the time and in all other points; and exactly the same and similar results accrue to each party from the other; which ought to be the case between friends.

The friendship based upon the pleasurable is, so to say, a copy of this, since the good are sources of pleasure to one another: and that based on utility likewise, the good being also useful to one another. Between men thus connected Friendships are most permanent when the same result accrues to both from one another, pleasure, for instance; and not merely so but from the same source, as in the case of two men of easy pleasantry; and not as it is in that of a lover and the object of his affection, these not deriving their pleasure from the same causes, but the former from seeing the latter and the latter from receiving the attentions of the former: and when the bloom of youth fades the Friendship sometimes ceases also, because then the lover derives no pleasure from seeing and the object of his affection ceases to receive the attentions which were paid before: in many cases, however, people so connected continue friends, if being of similar tempers they have come from custom to like one another's disposition.

Where people do not interchange pleasure but profit in matters of Love, the Friendship is both less intense in degree and also less permanent: in fact, they who are friends because of advantage commonly part when the advantage ceases; for, in reality, they never were friends of one another but of the advantage.

So then it appears that from motives of pleasure or profit bad men may be friends to one another, or good men to bad men or men of neutral character to one of any character whatever: but disinterestedly, for the sake of one another, plainly the good alone can be friends; because bad men have no pleasure even in themselves unless in so far as some advantage arises.

And further, the Friendship of the good is alone superior to calumny; it not being easy for men to believe a third person respecting one whom they have long tried and proved: there is between good men mutual confidence, and the feeling that one's friend would never have done one wrong, and all other such things as are expected in Friendship really worthy the name; but in the other kinds there is nothing to prevent all such suspicions.

I call them Friendships, because since men commonly give the name of friends to those who are connected from motives of profit (which is justified by political language, for alliances between states are thought to be contracted with a view to advantage), and to those who are attached to one another by the motive of pleasure (as children are), we may perhaps also be allowed to call such persons friends, and say there are several species of Friendship; primarily and specially that of the good, in that they are good, and the rest only in the way of resemblance: I mean, people connected otherwise are friends in that way in which there arises to them somewhat good and some mutual resemblance (because, we must remember the pleasurable is good to those who are fond of it).

These secondary Friendships, however, do not combine very well; that is to say, the same persons do not become friends by reason of advantage and by reason of the pleasurable, for these matters of result are not often combined. And Friendship having been divided into these kinds, bad men will be friends by reason of pleasure or profit, this being their point of resemblance; while the good are friends for one another's sake, that is, in so far as they are good.[3]

Ressentiment is hard to get around in human relationships, but so is basic selfishness. I then surmised that if we are naturally selfish, then love, loyalty, and respect are basically fake and just ruses we use to get stuff from others. Butler demonstrates that people can do things for themselves, but also do things entirely for others. Self-love demands a cool calculation of the world and strategies to excise what we want from others. Obviously and frequently, we don't act from such cool calculation and we act in such ways, for example, from revenge or lust, that are focused on objects in the world and not on our own self-interest. If we actually live only according to self-interest, in our attempt to funnel everything back to us, we value ourselves more than the things to be experienced, thus miss out on the experience, and

[3] Aristotle. *The Ethics of Aristotle.* Project Gutenberg. <https://www.gutenberg.org/ebooks/8438>

thus defeat self-love in the first place. This argument opens up the possibility of doing good for good's sake and not out of selfish motives:

It is commonly observed that there is a disposition in men to complain of the viciousness and corruption of the age in which they live as greater than that of former ones; which is usually followed with this further observation, that mankind has been in that respect much the same in all times. Now, not to determine whether this last be not contradicted by the accounts of history; thus much can scarce be doubted, that vice and folly takes different turns, and some particular kinds of it are more open and avowed in some ages than in others; and, I suppose, it may be spoken of as very much the distinction of the present to profess a contracted spirit, and greater regards to self-interest, than appears to have been done formerly. Upon this account it seems worthwhile to inquire whether private interest is likely to be promoted in proportion to the degree in which self-love engrosses us, and prevails over all other principles; or whether the contracted affection may not possibly be so prevalent as to disappoint itself, and even contradict its own and private good.

And since, further, there is generally thought to be some peculiar kind of contrariety between self-love and the love of our neighbour, between the pursuit of public and of private good; insomuch that when you are recommending one of these, you are supposed to be speaking against the other; and from hence arises a secret prejudice against, and frequently open scorn of, all talk of public spirit and real good-will to our fellow-creatures; it will be necessary to inquire what respect benevolence hath to self-love_, _and the pursuit of private interest to the pursuit of public: or whether there be anything of that peculiar inconsistence and contrariety between them over and above what there is between self-love and other passions and particular affections, and their respective pursuits.

These inquiries, it is hoped, may be favourably attended to; for there shall be all possible concessions made to the favourite passion, which hath so much allowed to it, and whose cause is so universally pleaded: it shall be treated with the utmost tenderness and concern for its interests.

In order to do this, as well as to determine the forementioned questions, it will be necessary to consider the nature, the object, and end of that self-love, as distinguished from other principles or affections in the mind, and their respective objects.

Every man hath a general desire of his own happiness; and likewise a variety of particular affections, passions, and appetites to particular external objects. The former proceeds from, or is, self-love; and seems inseparable from all sensible creatures, who can reflect upon themselves and their own interest or happiness so as to have that interest an object to their minds; what is to be said of the latter is, that they proceed from or together make up that particular nature, according to which man is made. The object the former pursues is somewhat internal—our own happiness, enjoyment, satisfaction; whether we have, or have not, a distinct particular perception what it is, or wherein it consists: the objects of the latter are this or that particular external thing, which the affections tend towards, and of which it hath always a particular idea or perception. The principle we call self-love never seeks anything external for the sake of the thing, but only as a means of happiness or good: particular affections rest in the external things themselves. One belongs to man as a reasonable creature reflecting upon his own interest or happiness. The other, though quite distinct from reason, are as much a part of human nature.

That all particular appetites and passions are towards external things themselves, distinct from the pleasure arising from them, is manifested from hence; that there could not be this pleasure, were it not for that prior suitableness between the object and the passion: there could be no enjoyment or delight from one thing more than another, from eating food more than from swallowing a stone, if there were not an affection or appetite to one thing more than another.

Every particular affection, even the love of our neighbour, is as really our own affection as self-love; and the pleasure arising from its gratification is as much my own pleasure as the pleasure self-love would have from knowing I myself should be happy some time hence would be my own pleasure. And if, because every particular affection is a man's own, and the pleasure arising from its gratification his own pleasure, or pleasure to himself, such particular affection must be called self-love; according to this way of speaking, no creature whatever can possibly act but merely from self-love; and every action and every affection whatever is to be resolved up into this one principle. But then this is not the language of mankind; or if it were, we should want words to express the difference between the principle of an action, proceeding from cool consideration that it will be to my own advantage; and an action, suppose of revenge or of friendship, by which a man runs upon certain ruin, to do evil or good to another. It is manifest the principles of these actions are totally different, and so want different words to be distinguished by; all that they agree in is that they both proceed from, and are done to gratify, an inclination in a man's self. But the principle or inclination in one case is self-love; in the other, hatred or love of another. There is then a distinction between the cool principle of self-love, or general desire of our own happiness, as one part of our nature, and one principle of action; and the particular affections towards particular external objects, as another part of our nature, and another principle of action. How much soever therefore is to be allowed to self-love, yet it cannot be allowed to be the whole of our inward constitution; because, you see, there are other parts or principles which come into it.

Further, private happiness or good is all which self-love can make us desire, or be concerned about: in having this consists its gratification: it is an affection to ourselves; a regard to our own interest, happiness, and private good: and in the proportion a man hath this, he is interested, or a lover of himself. Let this be kept in mind; because there is commonly, as I shall presently have occasion to observe, another sense put upon these words. On the other hand, particular affections tend towards particular external things: these are their objects: having these is their end: in this consists their gratification: no matter whether it be, or be not, upon the whole, our interest or happiness. An action done from the former of these principles is called an interested action. An action proceeding from any of the latter has its denomination of passionate, ambitious, friendly, revengeful, or any other, from the particular appetite or affection from which it proceeds. Thus self-love as one part of human nature, and the several particular principles as the other part, are, themselves, their objects and ends, stated and shown.

From hence it will be easy to see how far, and in what ways, each of these can contribute and be subservient to the private good of the individual. Happiness does not consist in self-love. The desire of happiness is no more the thing itself than the desire of riches is the possession or enjoyment of them. People might love themselves with the most entire and unbounded affection, and yet be extremely miserable. Neither can self-love any way help them out, but by setting them on work to get rid of the causes of their misery, to gain or make use of those objects which are by nature adapted to afford satisfaction. Happiness or satisfaction consists only in the enjoyment of those objects which are by nature suited to our several particular appetites, passions, and affections. So that if self-love wholly engrosses us, and leaves no room for any other principle, there can be absolutely no such thing at all as happiness or enjoyment of any kind whatever; since happiness consists in the gratification of particular passions, which supposes the having of them. Self-love then does not constitute this or that to be our interest or good; but, our interest or good being constituted by nature and supposed, self-love only puts us upon obtaining and securing it. Therefore, if it be possible that self-love may prevail and exert itself in a degree or manner which is not subservient to this end; then it will not follow that our interest will be promoted in proportion to the degree in which that principle engrosses us, and prevails over others. Nay, further, the private and contracted affection, when it is not subservient to this end, private good may, for anything that appears, have a direct contrary tendency and effect. And if we will consider the matter, we shall see that it often really has. Disengagement is absolutely necessary to enjoyment; and a person may have so steady and fixed an eye upon his own interest, whatever he places it in, as may hinder him from attending to many gratifications within his reach, which others have their minds free and open to. Over-fondness for a child is not generally thought to be for its advantage; and, if there be any guess to be made from appearances, surely that character we call selfish is not the most promising for happiness. Such a temper may plainly be, and exert itself in a degree and manner which may give unnecessary and useless solicitude and anxiety, in a degree and manner which may prevent obtaining the means and materials of enjoyment, as well as the making use of them. Immoderate self-love does very ill consult its own interest: and, how much soever a paradox it may appear, it is certainly true that even from self-love we should endeavour to get over all inordinate regard to and consideration of ourselves. Every one of our passions and affections hath its natural stint and bound, which may easily be exceeded; whereas our enjoyments can possibly be but in a determinate measure and degree. Therefore such excess of the affection, since it cannot procure any enjoyment, must in all cases be useless; but is generally attended with inconveniences, and often is downright pain and misery. This holds as much with regard to self-love as to all other affections. The natural degree of it, so far as it sets us on work to gain and make use of the materials of satisfaction, may be to our real advantage; but beyond or besides this, it is in several respects an inconvenience and disadvantage. Thus it appears that private interest is so far from being likely to be promoted in proportion to the degree in which self-love engrosses us, and prevails over all other principles, that the contracted affection may be so prevalent as to disappoint itself, and even contradict its own and private good.

"But who, except the most sordidly covetous, ever thought there was any rivalship between the love of greatness, honour, power, or between sensual appetites and self-love? No, there is a perfect harmony between them. It is by means of these particular appetites and affections that self-love is gratified in enjoyment, happiness, and satisfaction. The competition and rivalship is between self-love and the love of our neighbour: that affection which leads us out of ourselves, makes us regardless of our own interest, and substitute that of another in its stead." Whether, then, there be any peculiar competition and contrariety in this case shall now be considered.

Self-love and interestedness was stated to consist in or be an affection to ourselves, a regard to our own private good: it is therefore distinct from benevolence, which is an affection to the good of our fellow-creatures. But that benevolence is distinct from, that is, not the same thing with self-love, is no reason for its being looked upon with any peculiar suspicion; because every principle whatever, by means of which self-love is gratified, is distinct from it; and all things which are distinct from each other are equally so. A man has an affection or aversion to another: that one of these tends to, and is gratified by, doing good, that the other tends to, and is gratified by, doing harm, does not in the least alter the respect which either one or the other of these inward feelings has to self-love. We use the word property so as to exclude any other persons having an interest in that of which we say a particular man has the property. And we often use the word selfish so as to exclude in the same manner all regards to the good of others. But the cases are not parallel: for though that exclusion is really part of the idea of property; yet such positive exclusion, or bringing this peculiar disregard to the good of others into the idea of self-love, is in reality adding to the idea, or changing it from what it was before stated to consist in, namely, in an affection to ourselves. This being the whole idea of self-love, it can no otherwise exclude good-will or love of others, than merely by not including it, no otherwise, than it excludes love of arts or reputation, or of anything else. Neither on the other hand does benevolence, any more than love of arts or of reputation exclude self-love. Love of our neighbour, then, has just the same respect to, is no more distant from, self-love, than hatred of our neighbour, or than love or hatred of anything else. Thus the principles, from which men rush upon certain ruin for the destruction of an enemy, and for the preservation of a friend, have the same respect to the private affection, and are equally interested, or equally disinterested; and it is of no avail whether they are said to be one or the other. Therefore to those who are shocked to hear virtue spoken of as disinterested, it may be allowed that it is indeed absurd to speak thus of it; unless hatred, several particular instances of vice, and all the common affections and aversions in mankind, are acknowledged to be disinterested too. Is there any less inconsistence between the love of inanimate things, or of creatures merely sensitive, and self-love, than between self-love and the love of our neighbour? Is desire of and delight in the happiness of another any more a diminution of self-love than desire of and delight in the esteem of another? They are both equally desire of and delight in somewhat external to ourselves; either both or neither are so. The object of self-love is expressed in the term self; and every appetite of sense, and every particular affection of the heart, are equally interested or disinterested, because the objects of them all are equally self or somewhat else. Whatever ridicule therefore the mention of a disinterested principle or action may be supposed to lie open to, must, upon the matter being thus stated, relate to ambition, and every appetite and particular affection as much as to benevolence. And indeed all the ridicule, and all the grave perplexity, of which this subject hath had its full share, is merely from words. The most intelligible way of speaking of it seems to be this: that self-love and the actions done in consequence of it (for these will presently appear to be the same as to this question) are interested; that particular affections towards external objects, and the actions done in consequence of those affections are not so. But every one is at liberty to use words as he pleases. All that is here insisted upon is that ambition, revenge, benevolence, all particular passions whatever, and the actions they produce, are equally interested or disinterested.

Thus it appears that there is no peculiar contrariety between self-love and benevolence; no greater competition between these than between any other particular affections and self-love. This relates to the affections themselves. Let us now see whether there be any peculiar contrariety between the respective courses of life which these affections lead to; whether there be any greater competition between the pursuit of private and of public good, than between any other particular pursuits and that of private good.

There seems no other reason to suspect that there is any such peculiar contrariety, but only that the course of action which benevolence leads to has a more direct tendency to promote the good of others, than that course of action which love of reputation suppose, or any other particular affection leads to. But that any affection tends to the happiness of another does not hinder its tending to one's own happiness too. That others enjoy the benefit of the air and the light of the sun does not hinder but that these are as much one's own private advantage now as they would be if we had the property of them exclusive of all others. So a pursuit which tends to promote the good of another, yet may have as great tendency to promote private interest, as a pursuit which does not tend to the good of another at all, or which is mischievous to him. All particular affections whatever, resentment, benevolence, love of arts, equally lead to a course of action for their own gratification; i.e., the gratification of ourselves; and the gratification of each gives delight: so far, then, it is manifest they have all the same respect to private interest. Now take into consideration, further, concerning these three pursuits, that the end of the first is the harm, of the second, the good of another, of the last, somewhat indifferent; and is there any necessity that these additional considerations should alter the respect, which we before saw these three pursuits had to private interest, or render any one of them less conducive to it, than any other? Thus one man's affection is to honour as his end; in order to obtain which he thinks no pains too great. Suppose another, with such a singularity of mind, as to have the same affection to public good as his end, which he endeavours with the same labour to obtain. In case of success, surely the man of benevolence hath as great enjoyment as the man of ambition; they both equally having the end their affections, in the same degree, tended to; but in case of disappointment, the benevolent man has clearly the advantage; since endeavouring to do good, considered as a virtuous pursuit, is gratified by its own consciousness, i.e., is in a degree its own reward.

And as to these two, or benevolence and any other particular passions whatever, considered in a further view, as forming a general temper, which more or less disposes us for enjoyment of all the common blessings of life, distinct from their own gratification, is benevolence less the temper of tranquillity and freedom than ambition or covetousness? Does the benevolent man appear less easy with himself from his love to his neighbour? Does he less relish his being? Is there any peculiar gloom seated on his face? Is his mind less open to entertainment, to any particular gratification? Nothing is more manifest than that being in good humour, which is benevolence whilst it lasts, is itself the temper of satisfaction and enjoyment.

Suppose then, a man sitting down to consider how he might become most easy to himself, and attain the greatest pleasure he could, all that which is his real natural happiness. This can only consist in the enjoyment of those objects which are by nature adapted to our several faculties. These particular enjoyments make up the sum total of our happiness, and they are supposed to arise from riches, honours, and the gratification of sensual appetites. Be it so; yet none profess themselves so completely happy in these enjoyments, but that there is room left in the mind for others, if they were presented to them: nay, these, as much as they engage us, are not thought so high, but that human nature is capable even of greater. Now there have been persons in all ages who have professed that they found satisfaction in the exercise of charity, in the love of their neighbour, in endeavouring to promote the happiness of all they had to do with, and in the pursuit of what is just and right and good as the general bent of their mind and end of their life; and that doing an action of baseness or cruelty would be as great violence to their self, as much breaking in upon their nature, as any external force. Persons of this character would add, if they might be heard, that they consider themselves as acting in the view of an Infinite Being, who is in a much higher sense the object of reverence and of love, than all the world besides; and therefore they could have no more enjoyment from a wicked action done under His eye than the persons to whom they are making their apology could if all mankind were the spectators of it; and that the satisfaction of approving themselves to his unerring judgment, to whom they thus refer all their actions, is a more continued settled satisfaction than any this world can afford; as also that they have, no less than others, a mind free and open to all the common innocent gratifications of it, such as they are. And if we go no further, does there appear any absurdity in this? Will any one take upon him to say that a man cannot find his account in this general course of life as much as in the most unbounded ambition, and the excesses of pleasure? Or that such a person has not consulted so well for himself, for the satisfaction and peace of his own mind, as the ambitious or dissolute man? And though the consideration that God himself will in the end justify their taste, and support their cause, is not formally to be insisted upon here, yet thus much comes in, that all enjoyments whatever are much more clear and unmixed from the assurance that they will end well. Is it certain, then, that there is nothing in these pretensions to happiness? especially when there are not wanting persons who have supported themselves with satisfactions of this kind in sickness, poverty, disgrace, and in the very pangs of death; whereas it is manifest all other enjoyments fail in these circumstances. This surely looks suspicions of having somewhat in it. Self-love, methinks, should be alarmed. May she not possibly pass over greater pleasures than those she is so wholly taken up with?

The short of the matter is no more than this. Happiness consists in the gratification of certain affections, appetites, passions, with objects which are by nature adapted to them. Self-love may indeed set us on work to gratify these, but happiness or enjoyment has no immediate connection with self-love, but arises from such gratification alone. Love of our neighbour is one of those affections. This, considered as a virtuous principle, is gratified by a consciousness of endeavouring to promote the good of others, but considered as a natural affection, its gratification consists in the actual accomplishment of this endeavour. Now indulgence or gratification of this affection, whether in that consciousness or this accomplishment, has the same respect to interest as indulgence of any other affection; they equally proceed from or do not proceed from self-love, they equally include or equally exclude this principle. Thus it appears, that _benevolence and the pursuit of public good hath at least as great respect to self-love and the pursuit of private good as any other particular passions, and their respective pursuits.

Neither is covetousness, whether as a temper or pursuit, any exception to this. For if by covetousness is meant the desire and pursuit of riches for their own sake, without any regard to, or consideration of, the uses of them, this hath as little to do with self-love as benevolence hath. But by this word is usually meant, not such madness and total distraction of mind, but immoderate affection to and pursuit of riches as possessions in order to some further end, namely, satisfaction, interest, or good. This, therefore, is not a particular affection or particular pursuit, but it is the general principle of self-love, and the general pursuit of our own interest, for which reason the word selfish is by every one appropriated to this temper and pursuit. Now as it is ridiculous to assert that self-love and the love of our neighbour are the same, so neither is it asserted that following these different affections hath the same tendency and respect to our own interest. The comparison is not between self-love and the love of our neighbour, between pursuit of our own interest and the interest of others, but between the several particular affections in human nature towards external objects, as one part of the comparison, and the one particular affection to the good of our neighbour as the other part of it: and it has been shown that all these have the same respect to self-love and private interest.

There is indeed frequently an inconsistence or interfering between self-love or private interest and the several particular appetites, passions, affections, or the pursuits they lead to. But this competition or interfering is merely accidental, and happens much oftener between pride, revenge, sensual gratifications, and private interest, than between private interest and benevolence. For nothing is more common than to see men give themselves up to a passion or an affection to their known prejudice and ruin, and in direct contradiction to manifest and real interest, and the loudest calls of self-love: whereas the seeming competitions and interfering, between benevolence and private interest, relate much more to the materials or means of enjoyment than to enjoyment itself. There is often an interfering in the former when there is none in the latter. Thus as to riches: so much money as a man gives away, so much less will remain in his possession. Here is a real interfering. But though a man cannot possibly give without lessening his fortune, yet there are multitudes might give without lessening their own enjoyment, because they may have more than they can turn to any real use or advantage to themselves. Thus the more thought and time any one employs about the interests and good of others, he must necessarily have less to attend his own: but he may have so ready and large a supply of his own wants, that such thought might be really useless to himself, though of great service and assistance to others.

The general mistake, that there is some greater inconsistence between endeavouring to promote the good of another and self-interest, than between self-interest and pursuing anything else, seems, as hath already been hinted, to arise from our notions of property, and to be carried on by this property's being supposed to be itself our happiness or good. People are so very much taken up with this one subject, that they seem from it to have formed a general way of thinking, which they apply to other things that they have nothing to do with. Hence in a confused and slight way it might well be taken for granted that another's having no interest in an affection (i.e., his good not being the object of it) renders, as one may speak, the proprietor's interest in it greater; and that if another had an interest in it this would render his less, or occasion that such affection could not be so friendly to self-love, or conducive to private good, as an affection or pursuit which has not a regard to the good of another. This, I say, might be taken for granted, whilst it was not attended to, that the object of every particular affection is equally somewhat external to ourselves, and whether it be the good of another person, or whether it be any other external thing, makes no alteration with regard to its being one's own affection, and the gratification of it one's own private enjoyment. And so far as it is taken for granted that barely having the means and materials of enjoyment is what constitutes interest and happiness; that our interest or good consists in possessions themselves, in having the property of riches, houses, lands, gardens, not in the enjoyment of them; so far it will even more strongly be taken for granted, in the way already explained, that an affection's conducing to the good of another must even necessarily occasion it to conduce less to private good, if not to be positively detrimental to it. For, if property and happiness are one and the same thing, as by increasing the property of another you lessen your own property, so by promoting the happiness of another you must lessen your own happiness. But whatever occasioned the mistake, I hope it has been fully proved to be one, as it has been proved, that there is no peculiar rivalship or competition between self-love and benevolence: that as there may be a competition between these two, so there many also between any particular affection whatever and self-love; that every particular affection, benevolence among the rest, is subservient to self-love by being the instrument of private enjoyment; and that in one respect benevolence contributes more to private interest, i.e., enjoyment or satisfaction, than any other of the particular common affections, as it is in a degree its own gratification.[4]

And if Butler is right about transcending selfishness, then other things are possible as well, including compassion. I remember someone telling me that love affairs begin with passion but are sustained by compassion. Compassion can be cultivated so that it can extend to all beings as The Dalai Lama explains:

> Actually, genuine compassion and attachment are contradictory. According to Buddhist practice, to develop genuine compassion you must first practice the meditation of equalization and equanimity, detaching oneself from those people who are very close to you. Then, you must remove negative feelings towards your enemies. All sentient beings should be looked on as equal. On that basis, you can gradually develop genuine compassion for all of them. It must not be said that genuine compassion is not like pity or a feeling that others are somewhat lower than yourself. Rather, with genuine compassion you view others as more important than you.[5]

---

[4] Butler, Joseph. *Human Nature, and Other Essays*. Project Gutenberg. <https://www.gutenberg.org/ebooks/3150>.
[5] The Dalai Lama. *The Power of Compassion*. Trans. Gesche Thupten Jinpa. London: Thorsens, 2001. 64.

If we're going to get along, we can't jam our agendas down each other's throats. We must exercise a fair amount of compassion. But we can't look at each other like we're harmless creatures, either. We have fangs and claws. We feel threatened and insecure and distrustful. But we can never overplay the negative side and downplay the positive side. Both have to be carefully measured. Selfishness is real and you'd be a fool to ignore it. But compassion is underrated. It's there but needs to be cultivated.

MILLER
That was awesome! Anything else?

GENTRY
I didn't let you get a word in edgewise. I apologize.

MILLER
No reason to.

at Fermi Lab

Margaret is a scientist with a "sensitive role" at Fermi Lab. She never reveals what her job is and I can't seem to get her to open up too much. She prefers for us not to meet in her office, but in a barn on campus at where Sunday square dance is held. I have to go through almost two hours of dancing with many experienced but impatient partners before we sat down for Cokes at a table just out of earshot of the music. She is completely drenched from dancing. Her brown hair is a pulled back bun and lithe brown face alternates between severity and sereneness. I notice a big bump on her arm and wonder whether she's on some secret project and has been doused by radiation. Margaret notices my not-so-subtle glances at her arm and smiles.

MARGARET
This bump is not from being exposed to extraterrestrials or some secret government project.

MILLER
Is it job related?

MARGARET
Next question, please.

MILLER
Okay, then. When did you catch the philosophy bug?

MARGARET
In grade school, middle school, and high school, I was looked upon as a science goddess. I won all the science fairs. I worshipped hard sciences, you know, material things, objects that could be sensed. I looked down at people who weren't doing real science, but were kind of playing at it. When I took my first philosophy course, metaphysics, I was attracted to views that supported my perspective. My first crush in philosophy was A.J. Ayer. Whatever is true, Ayer argues, is verifiable. The statement "We are standing in a barn" can be verified by experience. This is what Ayer calls practical verifiability. It can be verified by immediate experience and is verifiability in the strong sense. In other cases, something other than immediate experience brings about verifiability. This what Ayer calls "verifiability in principle" and is verifiability in the weak sense. I'll change his example from the moon to a civilization in a distant part of the universe, unknown to us at this point in time. While actual observation is not possible in this, we can say that if and when we are in the position to observe, we can then verify. Such a situation would be theoretically conceivable. It is not theoretically conceivable to verify the existence of God or statements that are emotionally significant to me "The Mona Lisa is beautiful" or "I love you." Only the literally significant is verifiable:

The criterion which we use to test the genuineness of apparent statements of fact is the criterion of verifiability. We say that a sentence is factually significant to any given person, if, and only if, he knows how to verify the proposition which it purports to express—that is, if he knows what observations would lead him, under certain conditions, to accept the proposition as being true, or reject it as being false. If, on the other hand, the putative proposition is of such a character that the assumption of its truth, or falsehood, is consistent with any assumption whatsoever concerning the nature of his future experience, then, as far as he is concerned, it is, if not a tautology, a mere pseudo-proposition. The sentence expressing it may be emotionally significant to him; but it is not literally significant. And with regard to questions the procedure is the same. We inquire in every case what observations would lead us to answer the question, one way or the other; and, if none can be discovered, we must conclude that the sentence under consideration does not, as far as we are concerned, express a genuine question, however strongly its grammatical appearance may suggest that it does.[1]

Ayer was simple and straightforward and I thought obviously correct. Whatever is true can be confirmed by experience. This point made even clearer when I read the Scottish philosopher David Hume and his distinction between impressions and ideas. These ideas made me think hard and led me to the phenomenalism of David Hume, who basically sees things in terms of sensations. Again, I was attracted to something quite simple: the distinction between ideas and impressions. Impressions are immediate perceptions, for example, sun in my eyes or a stomachache. Ideas are copies of ideas. I grasp the distinction between the two because impressions are livelier or more vivacious than ideas. If we cannot trace our ideas to impressions, then that idea has no basis in reality. A gold mountain I can conceive by combining gold and mountain, but that object does not reside in my immediate experience or impressions and is not real. The idea of God I can conceive by taking the impressions of wisdom, goodness, and intelligence and multiplying them to infinity. Yet I do not experience God in my impressions.

11. Every one will readily allow, that there is a considerable difference between the perceptions of the mind, when a man feels the pain of excessive heat, or the pleasure of moderate warmth, and when he afterwards recalls to his memory this sensation, or anticipates it by his imagination. These faculties may mimic or copy the perceptions of the senses; but they never can entirely reach the force and vivacity of the original sentiment. The utmost we say of them, even when they operate with greatest vigour, is, that they represent their object in so lively a manner, that we could almost say we feel or see it: But, except the mind be disordered by disease or madness, they never can arrive at such a pitch of vivacity, as to render these perceptions altogether undistinguishable. All the colours of poetry, however splendid, can never paint natural objects in such a manner as to make the description be taken for a real landscape. The most lively thought is still inferior to the dullest sensation.

We may observe a like distinction to run through all the other perceptions of the mind. A man in a fit of anger, is actuated in a very different manner from one who only thinks of that emotion. If you tell me, that any person is in love, I easily understand your meaning, and form a just conception of his situation; but never can mistake that conception for the real disorders and agitations of the passion. When we reflect on our past sentiments and affections, our thought is a faithful mirror, and copies its objects truly; but the colours which it employs are faint and dull, in comparison of those in which our original perceptions were clothed. It requires no nice discernment or metaphysical head to mark the distinction between them.

---

[1] Ayer, A. J. *Language, Truth and Logic*. New York: Penguin. 16.

12. Here therefore we may divide all the perceptions of the mind into two classes or species, which are distinguished by their different degrees of force and vivacity. The less forcible and lively are commonly denominated *thoughts* or *ideas*. The other species want a name in our language, and in most others, I suppose, because it was not requisite for any, but philosophical purposes, to rank them under a general term or appellation. Let us, therefore, use a little freedom, and call them *impressions,* employing that word in a sense somewhat different from the usual. By the term impression, then, I mean all our more lively perceptions, when we hear, or see, or feel, or love, or hate, or desire, or will. And impressions are distinguished from ideas, which are the less lively perceptions, of which we are conscious, when we reflect on any of those sensations or movements above mentioned.

13. Nothing, at first view, may seem more unbounded than the thought of man, which not only escapes all human power and authority, but is not even restrained within the limits of nature and reality. To form monsters, and join incongruous shapes and appearances, costs the imagination no more trouble than to conceive the most natural and familiar objects. And while the body is confined to one planet, along which it creeps with pain and difficulty; the thought can in an instant transport us into the most distant regions of the universe; or even beyond the universe, into the unbounded chaos, where nature is supposed to lie in total confusion. What never was seen, or heard of, may yet be conceived; nor is anything beyond the power of thought, except what implies an absolute contradiction.

But though our thought seems to possess this unbounded liberty, we shall find, upon a nearer examination, that it is really confined within very narrow limits, and that all this creative power of the mind amounts to no more than the faculty of compounding, transposing, augmenting, or diminishing the materials afforded us by the senses and experience. When we think of a golden mountain, we only join two consistent ideas, gold, and mountain, with which we were formerly acquainted. A virtuous horse we can conceive; because, from our own feeling, we can conceive virtue; and this we may unite to the figure and shape of a horse, which is an animal familiar to us. In short, all the materials of thinking are derived either from our outward or inward sentiment: the mixture and composition of these belongs alone to the mind and will. Or, to express myself in philosophical language, all our ideas or more feeble perceptions are copies of our impressions or more lively ones.

14. To prove this, the two following arguments will, I hope, be sufficient. First, when we analyze our thoughts or ideas, however compounded or sublime, we always find that they resolve themselves into such simple ideas as were copied from a precedent feeling or sentiment. Even those ideas, which, at first view, seem the most wide of this origin, are found, upon a nearer scrutiny, to be derived from it. The idea of God, as meaning an infinitely intelligent, wise, and good Being, arises from reflecting on the operations of our own mind, and augmenting, without limit, those qualities of goodness and wisdom. We may prosecute this enquiry to what length we please; where we shall always find, that every idea which we examine is copied from a similar impression. Those who would assert that this position is not universally true nor without exception, have only one, and that an easy method of refuting it; by producing that idea, which, in their opinion, is not derived from this source. It will then be incumbent on us, if we would maintain our doctrine, to produce the impression, or lively perception, which corresponds to it.

15. Secondly, if it happens from a defect of the organ, that a man is not susceptible to any species of sensation, we always find that he is as little susceptible to the correspondent ideas. A blind man can form no notion of colours and a deaf man, of sounds. Restore either of them that sense in which he is deficient; by opening this new inlet for his sensations, you also open an inlet for the ideas; and he finds no difficulty in conceiving these objects. The case is the same, if the object, proper for exciting any sensation, has never been applied to the organ. A Laplander or Negro has no notion of the relish of wine. And though there are few or no instances of a like deficiency in the mind, where a person has

never felt or is wholly incapable of a sentiment or passion that belongs to his species; yet we find the same observation to take place in a less degree. A man of mild manners can form no idea of inveterate revenge or cruelty; nor can a selfish heart easily conceive the heights of friendship and generosity. It is readily allowed, that other beings may possess many senses of which we can have no conception; because the ideas of them have never been introduced to us in the only manner by which an idea can have access to the mind, to wit, by the actual feeling and sensation.

16. There is, however, one contradictory phenomenon, which may prove that it is not absolutely impossible for ideas to arise, independent of their correspondent impressions. I believe it will readily be allowed, that the several distinct ideas of colour, which enter by the eye, or those of sound, which are conveyed by the ear, are really different from each other; though, at the same time, resembling. Now if this be true of different colours, it must be no less so of the different shades of the same co-lour; and each shade produces a distinct idea, independent of the rest. For if this should be denied, it is possible, by the continual gradation of shades, to run a colour insensibly into what is most remote from it; and if you will not allow any of the means to be different, you cannot, without absurdity, deny the extremes to be the same. Suppose, therefore, a person to have enjoyed his sight for thirty years, and to have become perfectly acquainted with colours of all kinds except one particular shade of blue, for instance, which it never has been his fortune to meet with. Let all the different shades of that colour, except that single one, be placed before him, descending gradually from the deepest to the lightest; it is plain that he will perceive a blank, where that shade is wanting, and will be sensible that there is a greater distance in that place between the contiguous colours than in any other. Now I ask, whether it be possible for him, from his own imagination, to supply this deficiency, and raise up to himself the idea of that particular shade, though it had never been conveyed to him by his senses? I believe there are few but will be of the opinion that he can: and this may serve as a proof that the simple ideas are not always, in every instance, derived from the correspondent impressions; though this instance is so singular, that it is scarcely worth our observation, and does not merit that for it alone we should alter our general maxim.

17. Here, therefore, is a proposition, which not only seems, in itself, simple and intelligible; but, if a proper use were made of it, might render every dispute equally intelligible, and banish all that jar-gon, which has so long taken possession of metaphysical reasoning, and drawn disgrace upon them. All ideas, especially abstract ones, are naturally faint and obscure: the mind has but a slender hold of them: they are apt to be confounded with other resembling ideas; and when we have often employed any term, though without a distinct meaning, we are apt to imagine it has a determinate idea annexed to it. On the contrary, all impressions, that is, all sensations, either outward or inward, are strong and vivid: the limits between them are more exactly determined: nor is it easy to fall into any error or mistake with regard to them. When we entertain, therefore, any suspicion that a philosophical term is employed without any meaning or idea (as is but too frequent), we need but enquire, from what impression is that supposed idea derived? And if it be impossible to assign any, this will serve to confirm our suspicion. By bringing ideas into so clear a light we may reasonably hope to remove all dispute, which may arise, concerning their nature and reality.[2]

With Ayer and Hume on my side, I'm thinking: that's the end of the story. Which worked for a while I ran into a buzz saw named Karl Popper. Popper taught me taught that anything can very verified. You can pick and choose what facts confirm your theory and ignore the rest. A vague theory can be verified

---

[2] Hume, David. *An Inquiry Concerning Human Understanding*. Project Gutenberg. <https://www.gutenberg.org/ebooks/9662>.

by any number of observations. Observations can be cherry-picked to fit the theory. It wasn't so simple to verify a proposition by matching it with an experience. One-to-one correlation is simplistic. If an astrologer says that tomorrow some interesting opportunities are going to come your way, what exactly is an "interesting opportunity?" This is so general and vague that practically anything will confirm it. A person dedicated to a certain idea, a conspiracy theorist, for example, is going to find conspiracy in everything. Our agendas allow us to look at any situation and find the facts we want to find there. I could say that country X has dangerous weapons and go to war against on the flimsiest evidence—perhaps a photograph of silo. Maybe there's only one photograph and perhaps the photograph is old—no matter. It's verifiable and rationale for war. If you go to a therapist who believes in medicating you, for whatever behavior you exhibit, medication will be the solution. Hard science, I learned from Popper, cannot be based on easy confirmation, but by risky predictions. You need to put yourself out there and allow your theory to be battered by every conceivable objection. Figure what every conceivable way a theory can be falsified. Be suspicious when observations refute a theory but the theory is reinterpreted to fit the facts. Hard science wins the day when it is stipulated what proves the theory wrong. Otherwise, the goal posts can be changed and any fact whatsoever can confirm the theory. This is distinction between actual empiricism and science and myth and non-science.

1. It is easy to obtain confirmations, or verifications, for nearly every theory—if we look for confirmations.
2. Confirmations should count only if they are a result of risky predictions; that is to say, if, unenlightened by the theory in question, we should have expected an event which is incompatible with the theory—an event which would have refuted the theory.
3. Every "good" scientific theory is a prohibition: it forbids certain things to happen. The more a theory forbids, the better it is.
4. A theory which is not refutable by any conceivable event is non-scientific. Irrefutability is not a virtue of a theory . . . but a vice.
5. Every genuine test of a theory is an attempt to falsify it, or to refute it. Testability is falsifiability; but there are degrees of testability. Some theories are more testable, more exposed to refutation, than others; they take, as it were, greater risks.
6. Confirming evidence should not count except when it is the result of a genuine test of the theory; and this means that it can be presented as a serious but unsuccessful attempt to falsify the theory. . . .
7. Some genuinely testable theories, when to be false, are still upheld by admirers—for example, by introducing *ad hoc* some arbitrary assumption, or by reinterpreting the theory *ad hoc* in such a way that it escapes refutation. . . .

[T]he criterion of the scientific status of a theory is its falsifiability, or refutability, or testability.[3]

I found Popper's distinction between science and pseudo-science depended upon falsifiability, genuine tests to refute the theory. Yet what constitutes a "genuine" test? What defines it? When do we say: "Enough testing—this theory is true." That kind of question leads me directly into the house of the pragmatists, who were not interested in destroying theories, but seeing how they fit together. For William James, along with John Dewey and Charles Sanders Pierce, the pillars of American pragmatism, theorizing is not so simple as Ayer and Popper would have us believe. Pragmatism looks directly at experience

---

[3] Popper, Karl. "Science: Conjectures and Refutations." *Scientific Knowledge: Basic Issues in the Philosophy of Science.* Ed. Janet A. Kourany. Belmont, CA: Wadsworth, 1987. 141-42.

for answers and leaves issues open-ended rather than coming to any final truth. Theories are instruments that help us open the universe, just like a can opener is an instrument that opens up a can. Instead of looking at theories and first principles, the focus of pragmatism is results. Ideas become true only when they relate "satisfactorily" with other parts of our experience.

> Pragmatism, on the other hand, asks its usual question. "Grant an idea or belief to be true," it says, "what concrete difference will its being true make in anyone's actual life? How will the truth be realized? What experiences will be different from those which would obtain if the belief were false? What, in short, is the truth's cash-value in experiential terms?"

The moment pragmatism asks this question, it sees the answer: TRUE IDEAS ARE THOSE THAT WE CAN ASSIMILATE, VALIDATE, CORROBORATE AND VERIFY. FALSE IDEAS ARE THOSE THAT WE CANNOT. That is the practical difference it makes to us to have true ideas; that, therefore, is the meaning of truth, for it is all that truth is known-as.

This thesis is what I have to defend. The truth of an idea is not a stagnant property inherent in it. Truth HAPPENS to an idea. It BECOMES true, is MADE true by events. Its verity is in fact an event, a process: the process namely of its verifying itself, its veri-FICATION. Its validity is the process of its valid-ATION.

But what do the words verification and validation themselves pragmatically mean? They again signify certain practical consequences of the verified and validated idea. It is hard to find any one phrase that characterizes these consequences better than the ordinary agreement-formula—just such consequences being what we have in mind whenever we say that our ideas 'agree' with reality. They lead us, namely, through the acts and other ideas which they instigate, into or up to, or towards, other parts of experience with which we feel all the while such feeling being among our potentialities—that the original ideas remain in agreement. The connexions and transitions come to us from point to point as being progressive, harmonious, satisfactory. This function of agreeable leading is what we mean by an idea's verification. Such an account is vague and it sounds at first quite trivial, but it has results which it will take the rest of my hour to explain.

Let me begin by reminding you of the fact that the possession of true thoughts means everywhere the possession of invaluable instruments of action; and that our duty to gain truth, so far from being a blank command from out of the blue, or a 'stunt' self-imposed by our intellect, can account for itself by excellent practical reasons.

The importance to human life of having true beliefs about matters of fact is a thing too notorious. We live in a world of realities that can be infinitely useful or infinitely harmful. Ideas that tell us which of them to expect count as the true ideas in all this primary sphere of verification, and the pursuit of such ideas is a primary human duty. The possession of truth, so far from being here an end in itself, is only a preliminary means towards other vital satisfactions. If I am lost in the woods and starved, and find what looks like a cow-path, it is of the utmost importance that I should think of a human habitation at the end of it, for if I do so and follow it, I save myself. The true thought is useful here because the house which is its object is useful. The practical value of true ideas is thus primarily derived from the practical importance of their objects to us. Their objects are, indeed, not important at all times. I may on another occasion have no use for the house; and then my idea of it, however verifiable, will be practically irrelevant, and had better remain latent. Yet since almost any object may some day become temporarily important, the advantage of having a general stock of extra truths, of ideas that shall be true of merely possible situations, is obvious. We store such extra truths away in our memories, and with the overflow we fill our books of reference. Whenever such an extra truth becomes practically relevant to one of our emergencies, it passes from cold-storage to do work in the world, and our belief in it grows active. You can say of it then either that 'it is useful because it is true' or that 'it is true because it is useful.' Both these phrases mean exactly the same thing, namely that here is an idea that gets fulfilled and can be verified. True is the name for whatever idea starts the verification-process, useful is the name for its completed function in experience. True ideas would never have been singled out as such, would never have acquired a class-name, least of all a name suggesting value, unless they had been useful from the outset in this way.

From this simple cue pragmatism gets her general notion of truth as something essentially bound up with the way in which one moment in our experience may lead us towards other moments which it will be worth while to have been led to. Primarily, and on the common-sense level, the truth of a state of mind means this function of A LEADING THAT IS WORTH WHILE. When a moment in our experience, of any kind whatever, inspires us with a thought that is true, that means that sooner or later we dip by that thought's guidance into the particulars of experience again and make advantageous connexion with them. This is a vague enough statement, but I beg you to retain it, for it is essential.

Our experience meanwhile is all shot through with regularities. One bit of it can warn us to get ready for another bit, can 'intend' or be 'significant of' that remoter object. The object's advent is the significance's verification. Truth, in these cases, meaning nothing but eventual verification, is manifestly incompatible with waywardness on our part. Woe to him whose beliefs play fast and loose with the order which realities follow in his experience: they will lead him nowhere or else make false connexions.

By 'realities' or 'objects' here, we mean either things of common sense, sensibly present, or else common-sense relations, such as dates, places, distances, kinds, activities. Following our mental image of a house along the cow-path, we actually come to see the house; we get the image's full verification. SUCH SIMPLY AND FULLY VERIFIED LEADINGS ARE CERTAINLY THE ORIGINALS AND PROTOTYPES OF THE TRUTH-PROCESS. Experience offers indeed other forms of truth-process, but they are all conceivable as being primary verifications arrested, multiplied or substituted one for another.

Take, for instance, yonder object on the wall. You and I consider it to be a 'clock,' altho no one of us has seen the hidden works that make it one. We let our notion pass for true without attempting to verify. If truths mean verification-process essentially, ought we then to call such unverified truths as this abortive? No, for they form the overwhelmingly large number of the truths we live by. Indirect as well as direct verifications pass muster. Where circumstantial evidence is sufficient, we can go without eye-witnessing. Just as we here assume Japan to exist without ever having been there, because it WORKS to do so, everything we know conspiring with the belief, and nothing interfering, so we assume that thing to be a clock. We USE it as a clock, regulating the length of our lecture by it. The verification of the assumption here means its leading to no frustration or contradiction. VerifiABIL-ITY of wheels and weights and pendulum is as good as verification. For one truth-process completed there are a million in our lives that function in this state of nascency. They turn us TOWARDS direct verification; lead us into the SURROUNDINGS of the objects they envisage; and then, if everything runs on harmoniously, we are so sure that verification is possible that we omit it, and are usually justified by all that happens.

Truth lives, in fact, for the most part on a credit system. Our thoughts and beliefs 'pass,' so long as nothing challenges them, just as bank-notes pass so long as nobody refuses them. But this all points to direct face-to-face verifications somewhere, without which the fabric of truth collapses like a financial system with no cash-basis whatever. You accept my verification of one thing, I yours of another. We trade on each other's truth. But beliefs verified concretely by SOMEBODY are the posts of the whole superstructure.

Another great reason—beside economy of time—for waiving complete verification in the usual business of life is that all things exist in kinds and not singly. Our world is found once for all to have that peculiarity. So that when we have once directly verified our ideas about one specimen of a kind, we consider ourselves free to apply them to other specimens without verification. A mind that habitually discerns the kind of thing before it, and acts by the law of the kind immediately, without pausing to verify, will be a 'true' mind in ninety-nine out of a hundred emergencies, proved so by its conduct fitting everything it meets, and getting no refutation.

INDIRECTLY OR ONLY POTENTIALLY VERIFYING PROCESSES MAY THUS BE TRUE AS WELL AS FULL VERIFICATION-PROCESSES. They work as true processes would work, give us the same advantages, and claim our recognition for the same reasons. All this on the common-sense level of, matters of fact, which we are alone considering.

But matters of fact are not our only stock in trade. RELATIONS AMONG PURELY MENTAL IDEAS form another sphere where true and false beliefs obtain, and here the beliefs are absolute, or unconditional. When they are true they bear the name either of definitions or of principles. It is either a principle or a definition that 1 and 1 make 2, that 2 and 1 make 3, and so on; that white differs less from gray than it does from black; that when the cause begins to act the effect also commences. Such propositions hold of all possible 'ones,' of all conceivable 'whites' and 'grays' and 'causes.' The objects here are mental objects. Their relations are perceptually obvious at a glance, and no sense-verification is necessary. Moreover, once true, always true, of those same mental objects. Truth here has an 'eternal' character. If you can find a concrete thing anywhere that is 'one' or 'white' or 'gray,' or an 'effect,' then your principles will everlastingly apply to it. It is but a case of ascertaining the kind, and then applying the law of its kind to the particular object. You are sure to get truth if you can but name the kind rightly, for your mental relations hold good of everything of that kind without exception. If you then, nevertheless, failed to get truth concretely, you would say that you had classed your real objects wrongly.

In this realm of mental relations, truth again is an affair of leading. We relate one abstract idea with another, framing in the end great systems of logical and mathematical truth, under the respective terms of which the sensible facts of experience eventually arrange themselves, so that our eternal truths hold good of realities also. This marriage of fact and theory is endlessly fertile. What we say is here already true in advance of special verification, IF WE HAVE SUBSUMED OUR OBJECTS RIGHTLY. Our ready-made ideal framework for all sorts of possible objects follows from the very structure of our thinking. We can no more play fast and loose with these abstract relations than we can do so with our sense-experiences. They coerce us; we must treat them consistently, whether or not we like the results. The rules of addition apply to our debts as rigorously as to our assets. The hundredth decimal of pi, the ratio of the circumference to its diameter, is predetermined ideally now, tho no one may have computed it. If we should ever need the figure in our dealings with an actual circle we should need to have it given rightly, calculated by the usual rules; for it is the same kind of truth that those rules elsewhere calculate.

Between the coercions of the sensible order and those of the ideal order, our mind is thus wedged tightly. Our ideas must agree with realities, be such realities concrete or abstract, be they facts or be they principles, under penalty of endless inconsistency and frustration. So far, intellectualists can raise no protest. They can only say that we have barely touched the skin of the matter.

Realities mean, then, either concrete facts, or abstract kinds of things and relations perceived intuitively between them. They, furthermore, and thirdly, mean as things that new ideas of ours must no less take account of the whole body of other truths already in our possession. But what now does 'agreement' with such three-fold realities mean? to use again the definition that is current.

Here it is that pragmatism and intellectualism begin to part company. Primarily, no doubt, to agree means to copy, but we saw that the mere word 'clock' would do instead of a mental picture of its works, and that of many realities our ideas can only be symbols and not copies. 'Past time,' 'power,' 'spontaneity'—how can our mind copy such realities?

To 'agree' in the widest sense with a reality, CAN ONLY MEAN TO BE GUIDED EITHER STRAIGHT UP TO IT OR INTO ITS SURROUNDINGS, OR TO BE PUT INTO SUCH WORK-ING TOUCH WITH IT AS TO HANDLE EITHER IT OR SOMETHING CONNECTED WITH IT BETTER THAN IF WE DISAGREED. Better either intellectually or practically! And often agreement will only mean the negative fact that nothing contradictory from the quarter of that reality comes to interfere with the way in which our ideas guide us elsewhere. To copy a reality is, indeed, one very important way of agreeing with it, but it is far from being essential. The essential thing is the process of being guided. Any idea that helps us to DEAL, whether practically or intellectually, with either the reality or its belongings, that doesn't entangle our progress in frustrations, that FITS, in fact, and adapts our life to the reality's whole setting, will agree sufficiently to meet the requirement. It will hold true of that reality.

Thus, NAMES are just as 'true' or 'false' as definite mental pictures are. They set up similar verification processes, and lead to fully equivalent practical results.

All human thinking gets discursified; we exchange ideas; we lend and borrow verifications, get them from one another by means of social intercourse. All truth thus gets verbally built out, stored up, and made available for everyone. Hence, we must TALK consistently just as we must THINK consistently: for both in talk and thought we deal with kinds. Names are arbitrary, but once understood they must be kept. We mustn't now call Abel 'Cain' or Cain 'Abel.' If we do, we ungear ourselves from the whole book of Genesis, and from all its connexions with the universe of speech and fact down to the present time. We throw ourselves out of whatever truth that entire system of speech and fact may embody.

The overwhelming majority of our true ideas admit of no direct or face-to-face verification-those of past history, for example, as of Cain and Abel. The stream of time can be remounted only verbally, or verified indirectly by the present prolongations or effects of what the past harbored. Yet if they agree with these verbalities and effects, we can know that our ideas of the past are true. AS TRUE AS PAST TIME ITSELF WAS, so true was Julius Caesar, so true were antediluvian monsters, all in their proper dates and settings. That past time itself is guaranteed by its coherence with everything that's present. True as the present is, the past was also.

Agreement thus turns out to be essentially an affair of leading—leading that is useful because it is into quarters that contain objects that are important. True ideas lead us into useful verbal and conceptual quarters as well as directly up to useful sensible termini. They lead to consistency, stability, and flowing human intercourse. They lead away from eccentricity and isolation, from foiled and barren thinking. The untrammeled flowing of the leading process, its general freedom from clash and contradiction, passes for its indirect verification; but all roads lead to Rome, and in the end and eventually, all true processes must lead to the face of directly verifying sensible experiences SOME-WHERE, which somebody's ideas have copied.

Such is the large loose way in which the pragmatist interprets the word agreement. He treats it altogether practically. He lets it cover any process of conduction from a present idea to a future terminus, provided it only runs prosperously. It is only thus that 'scientific' ideas, flying as they do beyond common sense, can be said to agree with their realities. It is, as I have already said, as if reality were made of ether, atoms, or electrons, but we mustn't think so literally. The term 'energy' doesn't even pretend to stand for anything 'objective.' It is only a way of measuring the surface of phenomena so as to string their changes on a simple formula.

Yet in the choice of these man-made formulas we cannot be capricious with impunity any more than we can be capricious at the practical common-sense level. We must find a theory that will WORK; and that means something extremely difficult; for our theory must mediate between all previous truths and certain new experiences. It must derange common sense and previous belief as little as possible, and it must lead to some sensible terminus or other that can be verified exactly. To 'work' means both these things; and the squeeze is so tight that there is little loose play for any hypothesis. Our theories are wedged and controlled as nothing else is. Yet sometimes alternative theoretic formulas are equally compatible with all the truths we know, and then we choose between them for subjective reasons. We choose the kind of theory to which we are already partial; we follow 'elegance' or 'economy.' Clerk Maxwell somewhere says it would be "poor scientific taste" to choose the more complicated of two equally well-evidenced conceptions; and you will all agree with him. Truth in science is what gives us the maximum possible sum of satisfactions, taste included, but consistency both with previous truth and with novel fact is always the most imperious claimant.

I have led you through a very sandy desert. But now, if I may be allowed so vulgar an expression, we begin to taste the milk in the coconut. Our rationalist critics here discharge their batteries upon us, and to reply to them will take us out from all this dryness into full sight of a momentous philosophical alternative.

Our account of truth is an account of truths in the plural, of processes of leading, realized in rebus, and having only this quality in common, that they PAY. They pay by guiding us into or toward some part of a system that dips at numerous points into sense-percepts, which we may copy mentally or not, but with which at any rate we are now in the kind of commerce vaguely designated as verification. Truth for us is simply a collective name for verification processes, just as health, wealth, strength, etc., are names for other processes connected with life, and also pursued because it pays to pursue them. Truth is MADE, just as health, wealth, and strength are made, in the course of experience.[4]

space

When does something become "satisfactorily related" to the other parts of our experience? Does a bell go off or something? Why is that the desired end? Why not discontinuity? Why is instrumentality or results-driven inquiries better than those that proceed from first principles? Are we simply to take it on faith that instrumentality is the way? I thought back to Ayer and his principle of verifiability. Is verifiability verifiable? If not, then the whole theory is based on something not proven.

I was confounded that I could arrive at a true conclusion supported by evidence outside of my knowledge of it. In the later work of the Austrian philosopher Ludwig Wiggtenstein, I found another answer I was not prepared for. I had been reading him about the time I was in theater production. I remember the director telling me "Depending on how you perform the line, it can mean a multitude of things." And it just dawned on me: that's basically Wittgenstein. It all depends upon the context. The word "help" can be a call for immediate assistance. Or it can put forth as a question like "Would you help me?" Or it can mean "Wow, that was great help." Or it can mean "Crap, I got no help." Or it can be an order. Or can be a prophecy as

---

[4] James, William. *Pragmatism: A New Way for Some Old Ways of Thinking*. Project Gutenberg. <https://www.gutenberg.org/ebooks/5116>.

in "help" will happen at some future date. It all depends on the language games we play. Those language games occur in specific contexts. More than that, there is no essence to anything. Meanings are determined by resemblance and not in any fixed way. Are jockeys athletes, for instance? That all depends upon where lines are drawn and what counts and doesn't count as a resemblance. If we say a jockey resembles a golfer and golfers are deemed athletes, then jockeys are athletes. But if we say jockeys don't resemble sprinters, football players, or swimmers, they are not athletes. It all depends upon the language game:

> But how many kinds of sentence are there? Say assertion, question, and command?—There are countless kinds: countless different kinds of use of what we call "symbols", "words", "sentences". And this multiplicity is not something fixed, given once for all; but new types of language, new language-games, as we may say, come into existence, and others become obsolete and get forgotten. . . .

Review the multiplicity of language-games in the following examples, and in others:

> Giving orders, and obeying them—
> Describing the appearance of an object, or giving its measurements.
> Constructing an object from a description (a drawing)—
> Reporting an event—
> Speculating about an event—
> Imagine a picture representing a boxer in a particular stance. Now, this picture can be used to tell someone how he should stand, should hold himself; or how he should not hold himself; or how a particular man did stand in such-and-such a place; and so on. . . .
> Forming and testing a hypothesis—
> Presenting the results of an experiment in tables and diagrams—
> Making up a story; and reading it—
> Play-acting—
> Singing catches—
> Guessing riddles—
> Making a joke; telling it—
> Solving a problem in practical arithmetic—
> Translating from one language to another—
> Asking, thanking, cursing, greeting, praying. —

It is interesting to compare the multiplicity of the tools in language and of the ways they are used, the multiplicity of kinds of words and sentences, with what logicians have said about the structure of language[5]

Yet the idea of language games cannot be verified. It becomes another one of those unproven assumptions—like the principle of verification, genuine testing, satisfactory relatability, and ideas and impressions. Not having money to buy *Parmenides* by Plato, I pulled up the text from Project Gutenberg. These lines leaped out at me. Understanding is not possible unless an idea can mean one thing:

> [I]f a man, fixing his attention on these and the like difficulties, does away with ideas of things and will not admit that every individual thing has its own determinate idea which is always one and the same, he will have nothing on which his mind can rest; and so he will utterly destroy the power of reasoning.[6]

---

[5] Wittgenstein, Ludwig. *Philosophical Investigations*. Trans. G. E. M. Anscombe. Oxford: Basil Blackwell, 1986.
[6] Plato. *Parmenides*. Project Gutenberg.

Maybe, just maybe, and I may be too young to go this far out on a limb, but "language-games" is the easy way out. Let us say that the meaning of words is dictated by their use in various contexts. There is no single meaning for any word. Apparently, that would apply to the word "language games" itself. But if it did, then it would render the term useless. If "language-games" had many meanings, then it could mean what we refer to as a dog, cat, chair, or anything else for that matter. If that were the case, then "language-games" can neither be understood nor implemented. The moment of understanding is one grasping a single meaning. If that holds, then whatever is not "language-games" is also understood. "Language games" is not "dog," "cat," or "chair" by virtue of understanding what these items as single meanings. Any kind of discrimination between things is between those held as single meanings. A word can have many meanings, but when grasped it is always its singular meaning. Even when facing as something notoriously ambiguous as a Rorschach test, we might say "I don't know what it is," but that statement is understandable as that conveying a single meaning. The toilet I regularly use has a different meaning from a similar toilet I find in an art gallery. These toilets have different meanings because of differing contexts: one is a device for the removal of waste and the other is a work of art. Yet the fact that the same "word" toilet has different meanings does not invalidate the idea that when the word "toilet" is grasped, it is grasped in its singular meaning.

MILLER
What you just took me through philosophically is more rigorous than the dancing we did.

MARGARET
It does take stamina.

MILLER
It's a different kind of stamina than say memorizing facts for a test.

MARGARET
You have to endure ambiguity. Many times, you're just pulled by the currents of your thinking and you never know where you'll end up.

MILLER
That's scary.

MARGARET
But rewarding. Exhilarating really.

MILLER
They're back to dancing.

MARGARET
You go. I got to get back to work.

MILLER
Big project, huh?

MARGARET
That I will never say.

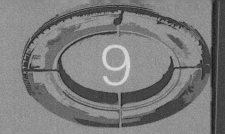

I met Evan at a Meet-Up event for people interested in "Philosophy in Real Time" near the River Walk in downtown Naperville, Illinois, USA. This was a not a planned interview, but once we started talking about the Cubs and agreed that they needed a leadoff hitter to go all the way, I felt comfortable to inquire whether he'd want to be part of my project. He wasn't one of those people who hemmed and hawed, and immediately agreed. I liked him from the start. He took long strides as we weaved in and out of crowds on the River Walk on a humid Saturday summer night. While sitting on a bench eating hot pretzels, he explained the importance of having a life's work instead of a vocation: that a job only got you from day to day, but a life's work extended through the whole of one's life. He owned his own small business, an animal shelter. He had very strong, callused hands, that's what I remember when we shook. He wore a nice green blazer and had a very determined look in his coal eyes and a sense of purpose in his movements and gestures, whether it was eating his pretzel or throwing away his trash.

MILLER
What got you into philosophy, Evan?

EVAN
I came from a family that didn't have a spiritual center and I felt I had no control in my life. I was way into drugs and alcohol and stuff like that but was searching.

MILLER
Searching for what?

EVAN
I didn't know what I was searching for and that was the problem. I dabbled in various religions and jobs and relationships, but came up empty. At the community college, I had my first exposure with philosophy and it clicked for me that this might be the right path.

MILLER
What made you think that?

EVAN
Philosophy was wide open and allowed me roam my own mind. In roaming my own mind, I started to see, slowly, that in order to have a purpose in life I had to find values that would not diminish me into a cowardly nay-sayer.

MILLER
Would you explain how this happened?

EVAN
It's not the most exciting story in the world. But okay. I start where all philosophers start: clarifying the issue. The main mistake in the meaning of life issue is that it is not about the meaning of life, but the value of the meaning:

> Man is encased, as though in a shell, in the particular ranking of the simplest values and value-qualities which represent the objective side of *ordo amoris*, values which have not yet been shaped into things and goods. He carries this shell wherever he goes and cannot escape from it no matter how quickly he runs. He perceives the world and himself through this shell, and perceives no more of the world, of himself, or anything else besides what these windows show him.[1]

People mistakenly say their lives have no meaning. More accurately, man is meaning and meaning is man. Meaning is a given for us. The worth of life has to do with its value. The statement "My life has no meaning" really means "I cannot find values in the meanings of my life." If I decide to tie my value to my fortune in life, disappointment and despair are likely, as Boethius says.

> What is it, then, poor mortal, that hath cast thee into lamentation and mourning? Some strange, unwonted sight, methinks, have thine eyes seen. Thou deemest Fortune to have changed towards thee; thou mistakest. Such ever were her ways, ever such her nature. Rather in her very mutability hath she preserved towards thee her true constancy. Such was she when she loaded thee with caresses, when she deluded thee with the allurements of a false happiness. Thou hast found out how changeful is the face of the blind goddess. She who still veils herself from others hath fully discovered to thee her whole character. If thou likest her, take her as she is, and do not complain. If thou abhorrest her perfidy, turn from her in disdain, renounce her, for baneful are her delusions. The very thing which is now the cause of thy great grief ought to have brought thee tranquillity. Thou hast been forsaken by one of whom no one can be sure that she will not forsake him. Or dost thou indeed set value on a happiness that is certain to depart? Again I ask, Is Fortune's presence dear to thee if she cannot be trusted to stay, and though she will bring sorrow when she is gone? Why, if she cannot be kept at pleasure, and if her flight overwhelms with calamity, what is this fleeting visitant but a token of coming trouble? Truly it is not enough to look only at what lies before the eyes; wisdom gauges the issues of things, and this same mutability, with its two aspects, makes the threats of Fortune void of terror, and her caresses little to be desired. Finally, thou oughtest to bear with whatever takes place within the boundaries of Fortune's demesne, when thou hast placed thy head beneath her yoke. But if thou wishes to impose a law of staying and departing on her whom thou hast of thine own accord chosen for thy mistress, art thou not acting wrongfully, art thou not embittering by impatience a lot which thou canst not alter? Didst thou commit thy sails to the winds, thou wouldst voyage not whither thy intention was to go, but whither the winds drave thee; didst thou entrust thy seed to the fields, thou wouldst set off the fruitful years against the barren. Thou hast resigned thyself to the sway

---

[1] Scheler, Max. *Selected Philosophical Essays*. Trans. David Lacterman. Evanston, IL: Northwestern University Press, 1973. 100.

of Fortune; thou must submit to thy mistress's caprices. What! art thou verily striving to stay the swing of the revolving wheel? Oh, stupidest of mortals, if it takes to standing still, it ceases to be the wheel of Fortune. [2]

Bad shit happens all the time. Such is life. But if we understand that the job of Fortune is to fuck us over, one day giving us everything and the next day taking it all away, we can develop an attitude that affirms everything in existence and become a yea-sayer:

For the New Year.—I still live, I still think; I must still live, for I must still think. *Sum, ergo cogito: cogito, ergo sum.* Today everyone takes the liberty of expressing his wish and his favourite thought: well, I also mean to tell what I have wished for myself to-day, and what thought first crossed my mind this year,—a thought which ought to be the basis, the pledge and the sweetening of all my future life! I want more and more to perceive the necessary characters in things as the beautiful:—I shall thus be one of those who beautify things. *Amor fati*: let that henceforth be my love! I do not want to wage war with the ugly. I do not want to accuse, I do not want even to accuse the accusers. Looking aside, let that be my sole negation! And all in all, to sum up: I wish to be at any time hereafter only a yea-sayer! [3]

Central to becoming a yea-sayer is to find the higher pleasures in life that both nourish our full humanity and form a basis for a spiritual perspective that shows us the greater good in everything. John Stuart Mill starts us off in that direction:

If I am asked, what I mean by difference of quality in pleasures, or what makes one pleasure more valuable than another, merely as a pleasure, except its being greater in amount, there is but one possible answer. Of two pleasures, if there be one to which all or almost all who have experience of both give a decided preference, irrespective of any feeling of moral obligation to prefer it, that is the more desirable pleasure. If one of the two is, by those who are competently acquainted with both, placed so far above the other that they prefer it, even though knowing it to be attended with a greater amount of discontent, and would not resign it for any quantity of the other pleasure which their nature is capable of, we are justified in ascribing to the preferred enjoyment a superiority in quality, so far outweighing quantity as to render it, in comparison, of small account.

Now it is an unquestionable fact that those who are equally acquainted with, and equally capable of appreciating and enjoying, both, do give a most marked preference to the manner of existence which employs their higher faculties. Few human creatures would consent to be changed into any of the lower animals, for a promise of the fullest allowance of a beast's pleasures; no intelligent human being would consent to be a fool, no instructed person would be an ignoramus, no person of feeling and conscience would be selfish and base, even though they should be persuaded that the fool, the dunce, or the rascal is better satisfied with his lot than they are with theirs. They would not resign what they possess more than he, for the most complete satisfaction of all the desires which they have in common with him. If they ever fancy they would, it is only in cases of unhappiness so extreme, that to escape from it they would exchange their lot for almost any other, however undesirable in their own eyes. A being of higher faculties requires more to make him happy, is capable probably of more acute suffering, and is certainly accessible to it at more points, than one of an inferior type;

[2] Boethius. *The Consolation of Philosophy*. Project Gutenberg. <https://www.gutenberg.org/ebooks/14328>.

[3] Nietzsche, Friedrich. *The Joyful Wisdom*. Project Gutenberg. <https://www.gutenberg.org/ebooks/52881>.

but in spite of these liabilities, he can never really wish to sink into what he feels to be a lower grade of existence. We may give what explanation we please of this unwillingness; we may attribute it to pride, a name which is given indiscriminately to some of the most and to some of the least estimable feelings of which mankind are capable; we may refer it to the love of liberty and personal independence, an appeal to which was with the Stoics one of the most effective means for the inculcation of it; to the love of power, or to the love of excitement, both of which do really enter into and contribute to it: but its most appropriate appellation is a sense of dignity, which all human beings possess in one form or other, and in some, though by no means in exact, proportion to their higher faculties, and which is so essential a part of the happiness of those in whom it is strong, that nothing which conflicts with it could be, otherwise than momentarily, an object of desire to them. Whoever supposes that this preference takes place at a sacrifice of happiness—that the superior being, in anything like equal circumstances, is not happier than the inferior—confounds the two very different ideas, of happiness, and content. It is indisputable that the being whose capacities of enjoyment are low, has the greatest chance of having them fully satisfied; and a highly-endowed being will always feel that any happiness which he can look for, as the world is constituted, is imperfect. But he can learn to bear its imperfections, if they are at all bearable; and they will not make him envy the being who is indeed unconscious of the imperfections, but only because he feels not at all the good which those imperfections qualify. It is better to be a human being dissatisfied than a pig satisfied; better to be Socrates dissatisfied than a fool satisfied. And if the fool, or the pig, is of a different opinion, it is because they only know their own side of the question. The other party to the comparison knows both sides.

It may be objected, that many who are capable of the higher pleasures, occasionally, under the influence of temptation, postpone them to the lower. But this is quite compatible with a full appreciation of the intrinsic superiority of the higher. Men often, from infirmity of character, make their election for the nearer good, though they know it to be the less valuable; and this no less when the choice is between two bodily pleasures, than when it is between bodily and mental. They pursue sensual indulgences to the injury of health, though perfectly aware that health is the greater good. It may be further objected, that many who begin with youthful enthusiasm for everything noble, as they advance in years sink into indolence and selfishness. But I do not believe that those who undergo this very common change, voluntarily choose the lower description of pleasures in preference to the higher. I believe that before they devote themselves exclusively to the one, they have already become incapable of the other. Capacity for the nobler feelings is in most natures a very tender plant, easily killed, not only by hostile influences, but by mere want of sustenance; and in the majority of young persons it speedily dies away if the occupations to which their position in life has devoted them, and the society into which it has thrown them, are not favourable to keeping that higher capacity in exercise. Men lose their high aspirations as they lose their intellectual tastes, because they have no time or opportunity for indulging them; and they addict themselves to inferior pleasures, not because they deliberately prefer them, but because they are either the only ones to which they have access, or the only ones which they are any longer capable of enjoying. It may be questioned whether any one who has remained equally susceptible to both classes of pleasures, ever knowingly and calmly preferred the lower; though many, in all ages, have broken down in an ineffectual attempt to combine both.

From this verdict of the only competent judges, I apprehend there can be no appeal. On a question which is the best worth having of two pleasures, or which of two modes of existence is the most grateful to the feelings, apart from its moral attributes and from its consequences, the judgment of those who are qualified by knowledge of both, or, if they differ, that of the majority among them, must be admitted as final. And there needs be the less hesitation to accept this judgment respecting the quality of pleasures, since there is no other tribunal to be referred to even on the question of quantity. What means are there of determining which is the acutest of two pains, or the intensest of two pleasurable sensations, except the general suffrage of those who are familiar with both? Neither pains nor pleasures are homogeneous, and pain is always heterogeneous with pleasure. What is there to decide whether a particular pleasure is worth purchasing at the cost of a particular pain, except the feelings and judgment of the experienced? When, therefore, those feelings and judgment declare the pleasures derived from the higher faculties to be preferable in kind, apart from the question of intensity, to those of which the animal nature, disjoined from the higher faculties, is susceptible, they are entitled on this subject to the same regard.[4]

But these higher pleasures have to be cultivated in a culture that does not constantly rob us of our spirituality. As Karl Marx points out, when people aren't fulfilled in their work , they become alienated and revert to their animal natures:

So far we have considered the alienation of the worker only from one aspect: namely, *his relationship with the products of his labour*. However, alienation appears not merely in the result but also in the *process of production*, within *productive activity* itself. How could the worker stand in an alien relationship to the product of its activity if he did not alienate himself in the production itself? The product is indeed a résumé of activity, of production. Consequently, if the product of labour is alienation, production itself must be active alienation—the alienation of activity and the activity of alienation. The alienation of the object of labour merely summarizes the alienation of the work activity itself.

What constitutes the alienation of labour? First, that the work is *external* to the worker, that it is not part of his nature; and that, consequently, he does not fulfill himself in his work but denies himself, has a feeling of misery rather than well-being, does not develop freely his mental and physical energies but is physically exhausted and mentally debased. The worker, therefore, feels himself at home only during his leisure time, whereas at work he feels homeless. . . .

We arrive at the result that man (the worker) finds himself to be freely active only in his animal functions—eating, drinking, and procreating, or at most also in his dwelling and in personal adornment—while in his human functions he is reduced to an animal.[5]

If we robotically go about our jobs instead of being fully invested in them, then a huge chunk of our lives is disvalued. We compensate for this lack of value in our work by overindulging in food, drugs, and sex and in the process reduce ourselves to animals. The overindulgence in the lower pleasures is less than fulfilling and contributes to the feeling our lives are valueless. We can be handsomely rewarded financially for our work, but if that work does not fulfill us, then alienation results.

Finding value in community is another way to invest our lives with value. But, as Paulo Freire points out, when people are forced into silence because of oppression, dialogue, the core of community, is excised:

Human existence cannot be silent, nor can it be nourished by false words, but only true words, with which men and women transform the world. To exist, humanly, is to *name* the world, to change it. Once named, the world in its turn reappears to the namers as a problem and requires them a new *naming*. Human beings are not built in silence, but in word, work, action, and reflection.

---

[4] Mill, John Stuart. *Utilitarianism*. Project Gutenberg. <http://www.gutenberg.org/cache/epub/11224/pg11224.txt>.
[5] Marx, Karl. "Economic and Philosophic Manuscripts (1844)." *Classics in Political Philosophy*. Ed. Jene M. Porter. Scarborough, Ontario: Prentice-Hall Canada Inc., 1989. 480, 481.

Dialogue is the encounter between men, mediated by the world, in order to name the world. Hence, dialogue cannot occur between those who want to name the world and those who do not wish this naming—between those who deny others the right to speak their word and those whose right to speak has been denied them.[6]

The more conscious we are of the universe, the more we feel overwhelmed by our lack of importance. However, if we value something more than our own individual mortality can make life completely worthwhile, as we see the case of Socrates, condemned to death but more interested in justice than his own skin. People get caught up with Socrates's advice not to fear what we don't know: death. But the bigger point is that he overcomes his own personal mortality by finding value in something bigger than it:

Not much time will be gained, O Athenians, in return for the evil name which you will get from the detractors of the city, who will say that you killed Socrates, a wise man; for they will call me wise, even although I am not wise, when they want to reproach you. If you had waited a little while, your desire would have been fulfilled in the course of nature. For I am far advanced in years, as you may perceive, and not far from death. I am speaking now not to all of you, but only to those who have condemned me to death. And I have another thing to say to them: you think that I was convicted because I had no words of the sort which would have procured my acquittal—I mean, if I had thought fit to leave nothing undone or unsaid. Not so; the deficiency which led to my conviction was not of words—certainly not. But I had not the boldness or impudence or inclination to address you as you would have liked me to do, weeping and wailing and lamenting, and saying and doing many things which you have been accustomed to hear from others, and which, as I maintain, are unworthy of me. I thought at the time that I ought not to do anything common or mean when in danger: nor do I now repent of the style of my defence; I would rather die having spoken after my manner, than speak in your manner and live. For neither in war nor yet at law ought I or any man to use every way of escaping death. Often in battle there can be no doubt that if a man will throw away his arms, and fall on his knees before his pursuers, he may escape death; and in other dangers there are other ways of escaping death, if a man is willing to say and do anything. The difficulty, my friends, is not to avoid death, but to avoid unrighteousness; for that runs faster than death. I am old and move slowly, and the slower runner has overtaken me, and my accusers are keen and quick, and the faster runner, who is unrighteousness, has overtaken them. And now I depart hence condemned by you to suffer the penalty of death,—they too go their ways condemned by the truth to suffer the penalty of villainy and wrong; and I must abide by my award—let them abide by theirs. I suppose that these things may be regarded as fated,—and I think that they are well.

And now, O men who have condemned me, I would fain prophesy to you; for I am about to die, and in the hour of death men are gifted with prophetic power. And I prophesy to you who are my murderers, that immediately after my departure punishment far heavier than you have inflicted on me will surely await you. Me you have killed because you wanted to escape the accuser, and not to give an account of your lives. But that will not be as you suppose: far otherwise. For I say that there will be more accusers of you than there are now; accusers whom hitherto I have restrained: and as they are younger they will be more inconsiderate with you, and you will be more offended at them. If you think that by killing men you can prevent someone from censuring your evil lives, you are mistaken;

---

[6] Freire, Paulo. *Pedagogy of the Oppressed*. Trans. Myra Bergman Ramos. New York: Continuum, 1993. 69.

that is not a way of escape which is either possible or honourable; the easiest and the noblest way is not to be disabling others, but to be improving yourselves. This is the prophecy which I utter before my departure to the judges who have condemned me.

Friends, who would have acquitted me, I would like also to talk with you about the thing which has come to pass, while the magistrates are busy, and before I go to the place at which I must die. Stay then a little, for we may as well talk with one another while there is time. You are my friends, and I should like to show you the meaning of this event which has happened to me. O my judges—for you I may truly call judges—I should like to tell you of a wonderful circumstance. Hitherto the divine faculty of which the internal oracle is the source has constantly been in the habit of opposing me even about trifles, if I was going to make a slip or error in any matter; and now as you see there has come upon me that which may be thought, and is generally believed to be, the last and worst evil. But the oracle made no sign of opposition, either when I was leaving my house in the morning, or when I was on my way to the court, or while I was speaking, at anything which I was going to say; and yet I have often been stopped in the middle of a speech, but now in nothing I either said or did touching the matter in hand has the oracle opposed me. What do I take to be the explanation of this silence? I will tell you. It is an intimation that what has happened to me is a good, and that those of us who think that death is an evil are in error. For the customary sign would surely have opposed me had I been going to evil and not to good.

Let us reflect in another way, and we shall see that there is great reason to hope that death is a good; for one of two things—either death is a state of nothingness and utter unconsciousness, or, as men say, there is a change and migration of the soul from this world to another. Now if you suppose that there is no consciousness, but a sleep like the sleep of him who is undisturbed even by dreams, death will be an unspeakable gain. For if a person were to select the night in which his sleep was undisturbed even by dreams, and were to compare with this the other days and nights of his life, and then were to tell us how many days and nights he had passed in the course of his life better and more pleasantly than this one, I think that any man, I will not say a private man, but even the great king will not find many such days or nights, when compared with the others. Now if death be of such a nature, I say that to die is gain; for eternity is then only a single night. But if death is the journey to another place, and there, as men say, all the dead abide, what good, O my friends and judges, can be greater than this? If indeed when the pilgrim arrives in the world below, he is delivered from the professors of justice in this world, and finds the true judges who are said to give judgment there, Minos and Rhadamanthus and Aeacus and Triptolemus, and other sons of God who were righteous in their own life, that pilgrimage will be worth making. What would not a man give if he might converse with Orpheus and Musaeus and Hesiod and Homer? Nay, if this be true, let me die again and again. I myself, too, shall have a wonderful interest in there meeting and conversing with Palamedes, and Ajax the son of Telamon, and any other ancient hero who has suffered death through an unjust judgment; and there will be no small pleasure, as I think, in comparing my own sufferings with theirs. Above all, I shall then be able to continue my search into true and false knowledge; as in this world, so also in the next; and I shall find out who is wise, and who pretends to be wise, and is not. What would not a man give, O judges, to be able to examine the leader of the great Trojan expedition; or Odysseus or Sisyphus, or numberless others, men and women too! What infinite delight would there be in conversing with them and asking them questions! In another world they do not put a man to death for asking questions: assuredly not. For besides being happier than we are, they will be immortal, if what is said is true.

Wherefore, O judges, be of good cheer about death, and know of a certainty, that no evil can happen to a good man, either in life or after death. He and his are not neglected by the gods; nor has my own approaching end happened by mere chance. But I see clearly that the time had arrived when it was better for me to die and be released from trouble; wherefore the oracle gave no sign. For which reason, also, I am not angry with my condemners, or with my accusers; they have done me no harm, although they did not mean to do me any good; and for this I may gently blame them.

Still I have a favour to ask of them. When my sons are grown up, I would ask you, O my friends, to punish them; and I would have you trouble them, as I have troubled you, if they seem to care about riches, or anything, more than about virtue; or if they pretend to be something when they are really nothing,—then reprove them, as I have reproved you, for not caring about that for which they ought to care, and thinking that they are something when they are really nothing. And if you do this, both I and my sons will have received justice at your hands.

The hour of departure has arrived, and we go our ways—I to die, and you to live. Which is better God only knows.[7]

Socrates values justice and virtue over his own immortality. This is evident when imagining his young sons to be grown up, he urges his friends to intervene should his offspring hold the wrong values.

Life is going to be filled with twists and turns, ups and downs, triumphs and disappointments. Such is Fortune. And death is always in the picture. In the final analysis, does anything we do matter? From the perspective of an outsider looking in on the universe (if that were possible), it would look like nothing matters. Life comes into and goes out of being. But this particular perspective of human beings on life makes us beings who can value things even higher than our own immortality, in the case of Socrates, for example, of doing the right thing. Even if doing the right thing only temporarily helps other people, we can create value. We can allow death to diminish our values or hold our values up in the face of death.

MILLER
It's great to see your breakthroughs.

EVAN
I've got to get back to my dogs and cats now.

MILLER
Thanks for sharing an evening with me.

---

[7] Plato. *Apology*. Project Gutenberg. <https://www.gutenberg.org/ebooks/1656>.

Nature or Nurture

A Slate Is Never Blank

I am a bit anxious maybe even a tad scared maybe even a lot terrified by my interview with Jin-Sun Park on a warm spring today the week before Easter. I hear gunshots as I enter the building and am frisked at least three times before I see Dr. Park. An up-and-coming counselor known to his friends and patients as the "Innatist," his ensemble is a sharp black sports jacket over yellow Lakers jersey and jeans. From a Lazy Boy recliner, he extends his long legs and they almost reach me as I kind of move on the couch so I can stretch my legs as well.

◇◇◇◇

JIN-SUN
I am surprised you decided to meet up.

MILLER
Why's that?

JIN-SUN
It's been a bloody two weeks.

MILLER
Humans are a violent lot.

JIN-SUN
Are you suggesting that people are born violent?

MILLER
Whether they learn it or are born that way, I really can't say.

JIN-SUN
I've been dealing with that question for most of my philosophical life.

MILLER
How long has your philosophical life been?

JIN-SUN
Not long in terms of years, but in intensity pretty long.

MILLER

What roped you into philosophy?

JIN-SUN

I became fascinated with the idea of *tabula rasa*, which I advocated early in my career.

MILLER

You mean two or three years ago,

JIN-SUN

Funny you are. ~~Yes.~~ The nature versus nurture issue was first introduced to me in Dr. Mark Bruner's philosophy of human nature class. For a whole semester, we studied two texts: the *Meno* by Plato and *An Essay Concerning Human Understanding* by John Locke. The subject resonated with me for a personal reason. I have like this sister who's a genius. She has a photographic memory and played Mozart on the piano before she was two after having only a few lessons. Everybody around us, my parents and friends, said she was like a sponge and could absorb things. One of my parents' bigmouth friends said each of us is a blank slate or a *tabula rasa* and that all we learn is from experience. That was problematic to me at the very least. How could my sister be such a music whiz at such an early age and have a photographic memory (I didn't have a photographic memory!), and learn all of this from experience. It didn't make sense. Her insane abilities were nurtured, but could only be nurtured if they were there in the first place in the same way a sun can nurture something like a seed and help it grow into a tree if that seed exists in the first place. I compared myself with my sister all the time and wondered how nurture by itself on a blank slate created this genius of a sister. Locke argues long and hard for *tabula rasa*, Plato for innatism. *Tabula rasa* seemed convincing at first, but even after years on the piano I couldn't come close to my sister and forget about memorizing things—she had me beat by a mile. But still Locke held sway in my mind for most of my teenage years.

1. The way shown how we come by any knowledge, sufficient to prove it not innate.

    It is an established opinion amongst some men, that there are in the understanding certain INNATE PRINCIPLES; some primary notions, KOIVAI EVVOIAI, characters, as it were stamped upon the mind of man; which the soul receives in its very first being, and brings into the world with it. It would be sufficient to convince unprejudiced readers of the falseness of this supposition, if I should only show (as I hope I shall in the following parts of this discourse) how men, barely by the use of their natural faculties may attain all the knowledge they have, without the help of any innate impressions; and may arrive at certainty, without any such original notions or principles. For I imagine any one will easily grant that it would be impertinent to suppose the ideas of colors innate in a creature to whom God hath given sight, and a power to receive them by the eyes from external objects: and no less unreasonable would it be to attribute several truths to the impressions of nature, and innate characters, when we may observe in ourselves faculties fit to attain as easy and certain knowledge of them as if they were originally imprinted on the mind.

    But because a man is not permitted without censure to follow his own thoughts in the search of truth, when they lead him ever so little out of the common road, I shall set down the reasons that made me doubt of the truth of that opinion, as an excuse for my mistake, if I be in one; which I leave to be considered by those who, with me, dispose themselves to embrace truth wherever they find it.

2. General assent, the great argument.

There is nothing more commonly taken for granted than that there are certain PRINCIPLES, both SPECULATIVE and PRACTICAL, (for they speak of both), universally agreed upon by all mankind: which therefore, they argue, must be the constant impressions which the souls of men receive in their first beings, and which they bring into the world with them, as necessarily and really as they do any of their inherent faculties.

3. Universal consent proves nothing innate.

This argument, drawn from universal consent, has this misfortune in it, that if it were true in matter of fact that there were certain truths wherein all mankind agreed, it would not prove them innate, if there can be any other way shown how men may come to that universal agreement, in the things they do consent in, which I presume may be done.

4. "What is is," and "it is possible for the same thing to be and not to be," not universally assented to.

But, which is worse, this argument of universal consent, which is made use of to prove innate principles, seems to me a demonstration that there are none such: because there are none to which all mankind give a universal assent. I shall begin with the speculative, and instance in those magnified principles of demonstration, "Whatsoever is, is," and "It is impossible for the same thing to be and not to be"; which, of all others, I think have the most allowed title to be innate. These have so settled a reputation of maxims universally received, and it will no doubt be thought strange if anyone should seem to question it. But yet I take the liberty to say that these propositions are so far from having a universal assent, that there are a great part of mankind to whom they are not so much as known.

5. Not on mind naturally imprinted, because not known to children, idiots, &c.

For, first, it is evident, that all children and idiots have not the least apprehension or thought of them. And the want of that is enough to destroy that universal assent which must needs be the necessary concomitant of all innate truths: it seeming to me near a contradiction to say, that there are truths imprinted on the soul, which it perceives or understands not: imprinting, if it signifies anything, being nothing else but the making certain truths to be perceived. For to imprint anything on the mind without the mind's perceiving it, seems to me hardly intelligible. If therefore children and idiots have souls, have minds, with those impressions upon them, THEY must unavoidably perceive them, and necessarily know and assent to these truths; which since they do not, it is evident that there are no such impressions. For if they are not notions naturally imprinted, how can they be innate? And if they are notions imprinted, how can they be unknown? To say a notion is imprinted on the mind, and yet at the same time to say, that the mind is ignorant of it, and never yet took notice of it, is to make this impression nothing. No proposition can be said to be in the mind which it never yet knew, which it was never yet conscious of. For if any one may, then, by the same reason, all propositions that are true, and the mind is capable ever of assenting to, may be said to be in the mind, and to be imprinted: since, if any one can be said to be in the mind, which it never yet knew, it must be only because it is capable of knowing it; and so the mind is of all truths it ever shall know. Nay, thus truths may be imprinted on the mind which it never did, nor ever shall know; for a man may live long, and die at last in ignorance of many truths which his mind was capable of knowing and that with certainty. So that if the capacity of knowing be the natural impression contended for, all the truths a man ever comes to know will, by this account, be every one of them innate; and this great point will amount to no more, but only to a very improper way of speaking; which, whilst it pretends to assert the contrary, says nothing different from those who deny innate principles. For nobody, I think, ever denied that the mind was capable of knowing several truths. The capacity, they say, is innate; the knowledge acquired. But then to what end such contest for certain innate maxims? If truths can be imprinted on the understanding without being perceived, I can see no difference there can be between any truths the mind is CAPABLE of knowing in respect of their original: they must all be innate or all adventitious: in vain shall a man go about to distinguish them. He therefore that talks of innate notions in the understanding, cannot (if he intend thereby any distinct sort of truths) mean such truths to be in the understanding as it never perceived, and is yet wholly ignorant of. For if these words "to be in the understanding" have any propriety, they signify to be understood. So that to be in the understanding, and not to be understood; to be in the mind and never to be perceived, is all one as to say anything is and is not in the mind or understanding. If therefore these two propositions, "Whatsoever is, is," and "It is impossible for the same thing to be and not to be," are by nature imprinted, children cannot be ignorant of them: infants, and all that have souls, must necessarily have them in their understanding, know the truth of them, and assent to it.

6. That men know them when they come to the use of reason answered.

   To avoid this, it is usually answered, that all men know and assent to them, WHEN THEY COME TO THE USE OF REASON; and this is enough to prove them innate. I answer:

7. Doubtful expressions, that have scarce signification, go for clear reasons to those who, being prepossessed, take not the pains to examine even what they themselves say. For, to apply this answer with any tolerable sense to our present purpose, it must signify one of these two things: either that as soon as men come to the use of reason these supposed native inscriptions come to be known and observed by them; or else, that the use and exercise of men's reason, assists them in the discovery of these principles, and certainly makes them known to them.

8. If reason discovered them, that would not prove them innate.

   If they mean, that by the use of reason men may discover these principles, and that this is sufficient to prove them innate; their way of arguing will stand thus, viz. that whatever truths reason can certainly discover to us, and make us firmly assent to, those are all naturally imprinted on the mind; since that universal assent, which is made a mark on them, amounts to no more but this—that by the use of reason we are capable of coming to a certain knowledge of and assent to them; and, by this means, there will be no difference between the maxims of the mathematicians and the theorems they deduce from them: all must be equally allowed innate; they being all discoveries made by the use of reason, and truths that a rational creature may certainly come to know, if he applies his thoughts rightly that way.

9. It is false that reason discovers them.

   But how can these men think the use of reason is necessary to discover principles that are supposed to be innate, when reason (if we may believe them) is nothing else but the faculty of deducing unknown truths from principles or propositions that are already known? That certainly can never be thought innate, which we have need of reason to discover; unless, as I have said, we will have all the certain truths that reason ever teaches us, to be innate. We may as well think the use of reason is necessary to make our eyes discover visible objects, as that there should be need for reason, or the exercise thereof, to make the understanding see what is originally engraven on it, and cannot be in the understanding before it be perceived by it. So that to make reason discover those truths thus imprinted, is to say, that the use of reason discovers to a man what he knew before: and if men have those innate impressed truths originally, and before the use of reason, and yet are always ignorant of them till they come to the use of reason, it is in effect to say, that men know and know them not at the same time.

10. No use made of reasoning in the discovery of these two maxims.

It will here perhaps be said that mathematical demonstrations, and other truths that are not innate, are not assented to as soon as proposed, wherein they are distinguished from these maxims and other innate truths. I shall have occasion to speak of assent upon the first proposing, more particularly by and by. I shall here only, and that very readily, allow, that these maxims and mathematical demonstrations are this different: that the one have need of reason, using proofs, to make them out and to gain our assent; but the other, as soon as understood, are, without the least reasoning, embraced and assented to. But I withal beg leave to observe, that it lays open the weakness of this subterfuge, which requires the use of reason for the discovery of these general truths: since it must be confessed that in their discovery there is no use made of reasoning at all. And I think those who give this answer will not be forward to affirm that the knowledge of this maxim, "That it is impossible for the same thing to be and not to be," is a deduction of our reason. For this would be to destroy that bounty of nature they seem so fond of, whilst they make the knowledge of those principles to depend on the labour of our thoughts. For all reasoning is search, and casting about, and requires pains and application. And how can it with any tolerable sense be supposed, that what was imprinted by nature, as the foundation and guide of our reason, should need the use of reason to discover it?

11. And if there were this would prove them not innate.

Those who will take the pains to reflect with a little attention on the operations of the understanding, will find that this ready assent of the mind to some truths, depends not, either on native inscription, or the use of reason, but on a faculty of the mind quite distinct from both of them, as we shall see hereafter. Reason, therefore, having nothing to do in procuring our assent to these maxims, if by saying, that "men know and assent to them, when they come to the use of reason," be meant, that the use of reason assists us in the knowledge of these maxims, it is utterly false; and were it true, would prove them not to be innate.

12. The coming of the use of reason not the time we come to know these maxims.

If by knowing and assenting to them "when we come to the use of reason," be meant, that this is the time when they come to be taken notice of by the mind; and that as soon as children come to the use of reason, they come also to know and assent to these maxims; this also is false and frivolous. First, it is false; because it is evident these maxims are not in the mind so early as the use of reason; and therefore the coming to the use of reason is falsely assigned as the time of their discovery. How many instances of the use of reason may we observe in children, a long time before they have any knowledge of this maxim, "That it is impossible for the same thing to be and not to be?" And a great part of illiterate people and savages pass many years, even of their rational age, without ever thinking on this and the like general propositions. I grant, men come not to the knowledge of these general and more abstract truths, which are thought innate, till they come to the use of reason; and I add, nor then neither. Which is so, because, till after they come to the use of reason, those general abstract ideas are not framed in the mind, about which those general maxims are, which are mistaken for innate principles, but are indeed discoveries made and verities introduced and brought into the mind by the same way, and discovered by the same steps, as several other propositions, which nobody was ever so extravagant as to suppose innate. This I hope to make plain in the sequel to this discourse. I allow therefore, a necessity that men should come to the use of reason before they get the knowledge of those general truths; but deny that men's coming to the use of reason is the time of their discovery.

13. By this they are not distinguished from other knowable truths.

In the meantime it is observable that this saying that men know and assent to these maxims "when they come to the use of reason," amounts in reality to no more but this,—that they are never known nor taken notice of before the use of reason, but may possibly be assented to some time after, during a man's life; but when is uncertain. And so may all other knowable truths, as well as these which therefore have no advantage nor distinction from other by this note of being known when we come to the use of reason; nor are thereby proved to be innate, but quite the contrary.

14. If coming to the use of reason were the time of their discovery, it would not prove them innate.

But, secondly, were it true that the precise time of their being known and assented to were, when men come to the use of reason; neither would that prove them innate. This way of arguing is as frivolous as the supposition itself is false. For, by what kind of logic will it appear that any notion is originally by nature imprinted in the mind in its first constitution, because it comes first to be observed and assented to when a faculty of the mind, which has quite a distinct province, begins to exert itself? And therefore the coming to the use of speech, if it were supposed the time that these maxims are first assented to, (which it may be with as much truth as the time when men come to the use of reason) would be as good a proof that they were innate, as to say they are innate because men assent to them when they come to the use of reason. I agree then with these men of innate principles, that there is no knowledge of these general and self-evident maxims in the mind, till it comes to the exercise of reason: but I deny that the coming to the use of reason is the precise time when they are first taken notice of; and if that were the precise time, I deny that it would prove them innate. All that can with any truth be meant by this proposition, that men 'assent to them when they come to the use of reason,' is no more but this,—that the making of general abstract ideas, and the understanding of general names, being a concomitant of the rational faculty, and growing up with it, children commonly get not those general ideas, nor learn the names that stand for them, till, having for a good while exercised their reason about familiar and more particular ideas, they are, by their ordinary discourse and actions with others, acknowledged to be capable of rational conversation. If assenting to these maxims, when men come to the use of reason, can be true in any other sense, I desire it may be shown; or at least, how in this, or any other sense, it proves them innate.

15. The steps by which the mind attains several truths.

The senses at first let in PARTICULAR ideas, and furnish the yet empty cabinet, and the mind by degrees growing familiar with some of them, they are lodged in the memory, and names got to them. Afterward, the mind proceeding further, abstracts them, and by degrees learns the use of general names. In this manner the mind comes to be furnished with ideas and language, the MATERIALS about which to exercise its discursive faculty. And the use of reason becomes daily more visible, as these materials that give it employment increase. But though the having of general ideas and the use of general words and reason usually grow together, yet I see not how this anyway proves them innate. The knowledge of some truths, I confess, is very early in the mind; but in a way that shows them not to be innate. For, if we will observe, we shall find it still to be about ideas, not innate, but acquired; it being about those first which are imprinted by external things, with which infants have the earliest to do, which make the most frequent impressions on their senses. In ideas thus got, the mind discovers that some agree and others differ, probably as soon as it has any use of memory; as soon as it is able to retain and perceive distinct ideas. But whether it be then or no, this is certain, it does so long before it has the use of words; or comes to that which we commonly call "the use of reason." For a child knows as certainly before it can speak the difference between the ideas of sweet and bitter (i.e. that sweet is not bitter), as it knows afterward (when it comes to speak) that wormwood and sugarplums are not the same thing.

16. Assent to supposed innate truths depends on having clear and distinct ideas of what their terms mean, and not on their innateness.

    A child knows not that three and four are equal to seven, till he comes to be able to count to seven, and has got the name and idea of equality; and then, upon explaining those words, he presently assents to, or rather perceives the truth of that proposition. But neither does he then readily assent because it is an innate truth, nor was his assent wanting till then because he wanted the use of reason; but the truth of it appears to him as soon as he has settled in his mind the clear and distinct ideas that these names stand for. And then he knows the truth of that proposition upon the same ground and by the same means, that he knew before that a rod and a cherry are not the same thing; and upon the same ground also that he may come to know afterwards "That it is impossible for the same thing to be and not to be," as shall be more fully shown hereafter. So that the later it is before anyone comes to have those general ideas about which those maxims are; or to know the signification of those generic terms that stand for them; or to put together in his mind the ideas they stand for; the later also will it be before he comes to assent to those maxims,—whose terms, with the ideas they stand for, being no more innate than those of a cat or a weasel he must stay till time and observation have acquainted him with them; and then he will be in a capacity to know the truth of these maxims, upon the first occasion that shall make him put together those ideas in his mind, and observe whether they agree or disagree, according as is expressed in those propositions. And therefore it is that a man knows that eighteen and nineteen are equal to thirty-seven, by the same self-evidence that he knows one and two to be equal to three: yet a child knows this not so soon as the other; not for want of the use of reason, but because the ideas the words eighteen, nineteen, and thirty-seven stand for, are not so soon got, as those which are signified by one, two, and three.

1. Idea is the object of thinking.

    Every man being conscious to himself that he thinks and that which his mind is applied about whilst thinking being the IDEAS that are there, it is past doubt that men have in their minds several ideas, such as are those expressed by the words whiteness, hardness, sweetness, thinking, motion, man, elephant, army, drunkenness, and others: it is in the first place then to be inquired, HOW HE COMES BY THEM?

    I know it is a received doctrine, that men have native ideas, and original characters, stamped upon their minds in their very first being. This opinion I have at large examined already; and, I suppose what I have said in the foregoing book will be much more easily admitted, when I have shown whence the understanding may get all the ideas it has; and by what ways and degrees they may come into the mind—for which I shall appeal to everyone's own observation and experience.

2. All ideas come from sensation or reflection.

Let us then suppose the mind to be, as we say, white paper, void of all characters, without any ideas—How comes it to be furnished? Whence comes it by that vast store which the busy and boundless fancy of man has painted on it with an almost endless variety? Whence has it all the MATERIALS of reason and knowledge? To this I answer, in one word, from EXPERIENCE. In that all our knowledge is founded, and from that it ultimately derives itself. Our observation employed either, about external sensible objects, or about the internal operations of our minds perceived and reflected on by ourselves, is that which supplies our understanding with all the MATERIALS of thinking. These two are the fountains of knowledge, from whence all the ideas we have, or can naturally have, do spring.

3. The objects of sensation one source of ideas

First, our senses, conversant about particular sensible objects, do convey into the mind several distinct perceptions of things, according to those various ways wherein those objects do affect them. And thus we come by those IDEAS we have of yellow, white, heat, cold, soft, hard, bitter, sweet, and all those which we call sensible qualities; which when I say the senses convey into the mind, I mean, they from external objects convey into the mind what produces those perceptions. This great source of most of the ideas we have, depending wholly upon our senses, and derived by them to the understanding, I call SENSATION.

4. The operations of our minds, the other sources of them.

Secondly, the other fountain from which experience furnisheth the understanding with ideas is the perception of the operations of our own mind within us, as it is employed about the ideas it has got, which operations, when the soul comes to reflect on and consider, do furnish the understanding with another set of ideas, which could not be had from things without. And such are perception, thinking, doubting, believing, reasoning, knowing, willing, and all the different actions stemming from our own minds, which we being conscious of, and observing in ourselves, do from these receive into our understanding as distinct ideas as we do from bodies affecting our senses. This source of ideas every man has wholly in himself; and though it be not sense, as having nothing to do with external objects, yet it is very like it, and might properly enough be called INTERNAL SENSE. But as I call the other sensation, so I call this REFLECTION, the ideas it affords being such only as the mind gets by reflecting on its own operations within itself. By reflection then, in the following part of this discourse, I would be understood to mean, that notice which the mind takes of its own operations, and the manner of them, by reason whereof there come to be ideas of these operations in the understanding. These two, I say, viz. external material things, as the objects of SENSATION, and the operations of our own minds within, as the objects of REFLECTION, are to me the only originals from whence all our ideas take their beginnings. The term OPERATIONS here I use in a large sense, as comprehending not barely the actions of the mind about its ideas, but some sort of passions arising sometimes from them, such as is the satisfaction or uneasiness arising from any thought.

5. All our ideas are of the one or of the other of these.

The understanding seems to me not to have the least glimmering of any ideas which it doth not receive from one of these two. EXTERNAL OBJECTS furnish the mind with the ideas of sensible qualities, which are all those different perceptions they produce in us; and THE MIND furnishes the understanding with ideas of its own operations.

These, when we have taken a full survey of them, and their several modes, and the compositions made out of them we shall find to contain all our whole stock of ideas; and that we have nothing in our minds which did not come in one of these two ways. Let any one examine his own thoughts, and thoroughly search into his understanding; and then let him tell me, whether all the original ideas he has there, are any other than of the objects of his senses, or of the operations of his mind, considered as objects of his reflection. And how great a mass of knowledge soever he imagines to be lodged there, he will, upon taking a strict view, see that he has not any idea in his mind but what one of these two have imprinted—though perhaps, with infinite variety compounded and enlarged by the understanding, as we shall see hereafter.

6. Observable in Children.

He that attentively considers the state of a child, at his first coming into the world, will have little reason to think him stored with plenty of ideas, that are to be the matter of his future knowledge. It is BY DEGREES he comes to be furnished with them. And though the ideas of obvious and familiar qualities imprint themselves before the memory begins to keep a register of time or order, yet it is often so late before some unusual qualities come in the way, that there are few men that cannot recollect the beginning of their acquaintance with them. And if it were worthwhile, no doubt a child might have but a very few, even of the ordinary ideas, when he grows up to a man. But all that are born into the world, being surrounded with bodies that perpetually and diversely affect them, variety of ideas, whether care be taken of it or not, are imprinted on the minds of children. Light and colors are everywhere, when the eye is but open; sounds and some tangible qualities fail not to solicit their proper senses, and force an entrance to the mind;—but yet, I think, it will be granted easily, that if a child were kept in a place where he never saw any other but black and white till he were a man, he would have no more ideas of scarlet or green, than he that from his childhood never tasted an oyster, or a pine-apple, has of those particular relishes.

7. Men are differently furnished with these, according to the different objects they converse with.

Men then come to be furnished with fewer or more simple ideas from without, accordingly as the objects they converse with afford greater or less variety; and from the operations of their minds within, accordingly as they more or less reflect on them. For, though he that contemplates the operations of his mind, cannot but have plain and clear ideas of them; yet, unless he turns his thoughts that way, and considers them attentively, he will no more have clear and distinct ideas of all the operations of his mind, and all that may be observed therein, than he will have all the particular ideas of any landscape, or of the parts and motions of a clock, who will not turn his eyes to it, and with attention heed all parts of it. The picture, or clock may be so placed, that they may come in his way every day; but yet he will have a confused idea of all the parts they are made up of, till he applies himself with attention, to consider them of each in particular.[1]

---

[1] Locke, John. *An Essay Concerning Human Understanding*. Project Gutenberg. <https://www.gutenberg.org/ebooks/10615>.

Locke is very thorough. I appreciate him for that. But there are some problems, as I see it:

1. Human creativity on a low and very high level depends upon comparing, contrasting, and synthesizing ideas. It is doubtful these abilities could be smuggled into the mind and must be originally there.
2. It makes little sense to say something comes from nothing. Nothing comes from nothing.
3. Other beings have innate gifts we do not have. A great shark can smell blood from as many as three miles away but cannot as far as we know write a poem. The marked difference is gifts point more to their innate than to their empirical origin.
4. Only the gifts of nature can be nurtured. No gifts, no nurturing.
5. Even if it is true that we can master any skill by devoting 10,000 hours to it, nonetheless the ability to do is innate.

When I read *Meno* by Plato I became convinced that all our ideas come from innate structures in our minds. In this dialogue, a slave boy unacquainted with geometry is able to understand the subject after only a few questions from Socrates. Critics might scoff and say that Socrates planted those ideas in the kid's head, but another scenario is that Socrates's questions help the kid give birth to those mathematical abilities, just as a midwife assists a woman in giving birth to a child.

SOCRATES: Some of them were priests and priestesses, who had studied how they might be able to give a reason for their profession: there have been poets also, who spoke of these things by inspiration, like Pindar, and many others who were inspired. And they say—mark, now, and see whether their words are true—they say that the soul of man is immortal, and at one time has an end, which is termed dying, and at another time is born again, but is never destroyed. And the moral is, that a man ought to live always in perfect holiness. 'For in the ninth year Persephone sends the souls of those from whom she has received the penalty of ancient crime back again from beneath into the light of the sun above, and these are they who become noble kings and mighty men and great in wisdom and are called saintly heroes in after ages.' The soul, then, as being immortal, and having been born again many times, and having seen all things that exist, whether in this world or in the world below, has knowledge of them all; and it is no wonder that she should be able to call to remembrance all that she ever knew about virtue, and about everything; for as all nature is akin, and the soul has learned all things; there is no difficulty in her eliciting or as men say learning, out of a single recollection all the rest, if a man is strenuous and does not faint; for all enquiry and all learning is but recollection. And therefore we ought not to listen to this sophistical argument about the impossibility of enquiry: for it will make us idle; and is sweet only to the sluggard; but the other saying will make us active and inquisitive. In that confiding, I will gladly enquire with you into the nature of virtue.

MENO: Yes, Socrates; but what do you mean by saying that we do not learn, and that what we call learning is only a process of recollection? Can you teach me how this is?

SOCRATES: I told you, Meno, just now that you were a rogue, and now you ask whether I can teach you, when I am saying that there is no teaching, but only recollection; and thus you imagine that you will involve me in a contradiction.

MENO: Indeed, Socrates, I protest that I had no such intention. I only asked the question from habit; but if you can prove to me that what you say is true, I wish that you would.

SOCRATES: It will be no easy matter, but I will try to please you to the utmost of my power. Suppose that you call one of your numerous attendants, that I may demonstrate on him.

MENO: Certainly. Come hither, boy.

SOCRATES: He is Greek, and speaks Greek, does he not?

MENO: Yes, indeed; he was born in the house.

SOCRATES: Attend now to the questions which I ask him, and observe whether he learns of me or only remembers.

MENO: I will.

SOCRATES: Tell me, boy, do you know that a figure like this is a square?

BOY: I do.

SOCRATES: And you know that a square figure has these four lines equal?

BOY: Certainly.

SOCRATES: And these lines which I have drawn through the middle of the square are also equal?

BOY: Yes.

SOCRATES: A square may be of any size?

BOY: Certainly.

SOCRATES: And if one side of the figure be of two feet, and the other side be of two feet, how much will the whole be? Let me explain: if in one direction the space was of two feet, and in the other direction of one foot, the whole would be of two feet taken once?

BOY: Yes.

SOCRATES: But since this side is also of two feet, there are twice two feet?

BOY: There are.

SOCRATES: Then the square is of twice two feet?

BOY: Yes.

SOCRATES: And how many are twice two feet? Count and tell me.

BOY: Four, Socrates.

SOCRATES: And might there not be another square twice as large as this, and having like this the lines equal?

BOY: Yes.

SOCRATES: And of how many feet will that be?

BOY: Of eight feet.

SOCRATES: And now try and tell me the length of the line which forms the side of that double square: this is two feet—what will that be?

BOY: Clearly, Socrates, it will be double.

SOCRATES: Do you observe, Meno, that I am not teaching the boy anything, but only asking him questions; and now he fancies that he knows how long a line is necessary in order to produce a figure of eight square feet; does he not?

MENO: Yes.

SOCRATES: And does he really know?

MENO: Certainly not.

SOCRATES: He only guesses that because the square is double, the line is double.

MENO: True.

SOCRATES: Observe him while he recalls the steps in regular order. (To the boy:) Tell me, boy, do you assert that a double space comes from a double line? Remember that I am not speaking of an oblong, but of a figure equal every way, and twice the size of this—that is to say of eight feet; and I want to know whether you still say that a double square comes from a double line?

BOY: Yes.

SOCRATES: But does not this line become doubled if we add another such line here?

BOY: Certainly.

SOCRATES: And four such lines will make a space containing eight feet?

BOY: Yes.

SOCRATES: Let us describe such a figure: Would you not say that this is the figure of eight feet?

BOY: Yes.

SOCRATES: And are there not these four divisions in the figure, each of which is equal to the figure of four feet?

BOY: True.

SOCRATES: And is not that four times four?

BOY: Certainly.

SOCRATES: And four times is not double?

BOY: No, indeed.

SOCRATES: But how much?

BOY: Four times as much.

SOCRATES: Therefore the double line, boy, has given a space, not twice, but four times as much.

BOY: True.

SOCRATES: Four times four are sixteen—are they not?

BOY: Yes.

SOCRATES: What line would give you a space of eight feet, as this gives one of sixteen feet—do you see?

BOY: Yes.

SOCRATES: And the space of four feet is made from this half line?

BOY: Yes.

SOCRATES: Good; and is not a space of eight feet twice the size of this, and half the size of the other?

BOY: Certainly.

SOCRATES: Such a space, then, will be made out of a line greater than this one, and less than that one?

BOY: Yes; I think so.

SOCRATES: Very good; I like to hear you say what you think. And now tell me, is not this a line of two feet and that of four?

BOY: Yes.

SOCRATES: Then the line that forms the side of eight feet ought to be more than this line of two feet, and less than the other of four feet?

BOY: It ought.

SOCRATES: Try and see if you can tell me how much it will be.

BOY: Three feet.

SOCRATES: Then if we add a half to this line of two, that will be the line of three. Here are two and there is one; and on the other side, here are two also and there is one: and that makes the figure of which you speak?

BOY: Yes.

SOCRATES: But if there are three feet this way and three feet that way, the whole space will be three times three feet?

BOY: That is evident.

SOCRATES: And how much are three times three feet?

BOY: Nine.

SOCRATES: And how much is the double of four?

BOY: Eight.

SOCRATES: Then the figure of eight is not made out of a line of three?

BOY: No.

SOCRATES: But from what line? Tell me exactly, and if you would rather not reckon, try and show me the line.

BOY: Indeed, Socrates, I do not know.

SOCRATES: Do you see, Meno, what advances he has made in his power of recollection? He did not know at first, and he does not know now, what is the side of a figure of eight feet: but then he thought that he knew, and answered confidently as if he knew, and had no difficulty; now he has a difficulty, and neither knows nor fancies that he knows.

MENO: True.

SOCRATES: Is he not better off in knowing his ignorance?

MENO: I think that he is.

SOCRATES: If we have made him doubt, and given him the 'torpedo's shock,' have we done him any harm?

MENO: I think not.

SOCRATES: We have certainly, as would seem, assisted him in some degree to the discovery of the truth; and now he will wish to remedy his ignorance, but then he would have been ready to tell all the world again and again that the double space should have a double side.

MENO: True.

SOCRATES: But do you suppose that he would ever have enquired into or learned what he fancied that he knew, though he was really ignorant of it, until he had fallen into perplexity under the idea that he did not know, and had desired to know?

MENO: I think not, Socrates.

SOCRATES: Then he was the better for the torpedo's touch?

MENO: I think so.

SOCRATES: Mark now the farther development. I shall only ask him, and not teach him, and he shall share the enquiry with me: and do you watch and see if you find me telling or explaining anything to him, instead of eliciting his opinion. Tell me, boy, is not this a square of four feet which I have drawn?

BOY: Yes.

SOCRATES: And now I add another square equal to the former one?

BOY: Yes.

SOCRATES: And a third, which is equal to either of them?

BOY: Yes.

SOCRATES: Suppose that we fill up the vacant corner?

BOY: Very good.

SOCRATES: Here, then, there are four equal spaces?

BOY: Yes.

SOCRATES: And how many times larger is this space than this other?

BOY: Four times.

SOCRATES: But it ought to have been twice only, as you will remember.

BOY: True.

SOCRATES: And does not this line, reaching from corner to corner, bisect each of these spaces?

BOY: Yes.

SOCRATES: And are there not here four equal lines which contain this space?

BOY: There are.

SOCRATES: Look and see how much this space is.

BOY: I do not understand.

SOCRATES: Has not each interior line cut off half of the four spaces?

BOY: Yes.

SOCRATES: And how many spaces are there in this section?

BOY: Four.

SOCRATES: And how many in this?

BOY: Two.

SOCRATES: And four is how many times two?

BOY: Twice.

SOCRATES: And this space is of how many feet?

BOY: Of eight feet.

SOCRATES: And from what line do you get this figure?

BOY: From this.

SOCRATES: That is, from the line which extends from corner to corner of the figure of four feet?

BOY: Yes.

SOCRATES: And that is the line which the learned call the diagonal. And if this is the proper name, then you, Meno's slave, are prepared to affirm that the double space is the square of the diagonal?

BOY: Certainly, Socrates.

SOCRATES: What do you say of him, Meno? Were not all these answers given out of his own head?

MENO: Yes, they were all his own.

SOCRATES: And yet, as we were just now saying, he did not know?

MENO: True.

SOCRATES: But still he had in him those notions of his—had he not?

MENO: Yes.

SOCRATES: Then he who does not know may still have true notions of that which he does not know?

MENO: He has.

SOCRATES: And at present these notions have just been stirred up in him, as in a dream; but if he were frequently asked the same questions, in different forms, he would know as well as any one at last?

MENO: I dare say.

SOCRATES: Without any one teaching him he will recover his knowledge for himself, if he is only asked questions?

MENO: Yes.

SOCRATES: And this spontaneous recovery of knowledge in him is recollection?

MENO: True.

SOCRATES: And this knowledge which he now has must he not either have acquired or always possessed?

MENO: Yes.

SOCRATES: But if he always possessed this knowledge he would always have known; or if he has acquired the knowledge he could not have acquired it in this life, unless he has been taught geometry; for he may be made to do the same with all geometry and every other branch of knowledge. Now, has anyone ever taught him all this? You must know about him, if, as you say, he was born and bred in your house.[2]

---

[2] Plato. *Meno*. Project Gutenberg. <https://www.gutenberg.org/ebooks/1643>.

MILLER
This issue has consumed you.

JIN-SUN
It has. And it has changed my viewpoint on a number of issues.

MILLER
Like what?

JIN-SUN
Like people don't learn to be gay, but are born that way as a popular singer says.

MILLER
And what else?

JIN-SUN
That people are unequally gifted and in teaching them we have to recognize the variety of distinct gifts people have as well as the degree to which people possess them. We must teach unequally or differently to each person according to their degree of giftedness.

MILLER
Your sister may be a gift of music, but you certainly have the gift of philosophy.

JIN-SUN
You think so.

MILLER
I do. Now tell me: are people born violent or do they learn it.

JIN-SUN
That may be more a complicated issue for another day.

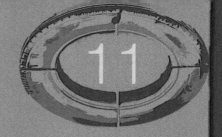

11

Physicalism

Is Consciousness More Than Matter?

In Reykjavik, Iceland, I am lucky enough to meet one of architects of the equal pay legislation, a young **1** member of Iceland's parliament. It was one of those times when "you know somebody who knows somebody who knows somebody." Dark-haired with serious brown eyes, we meet on a bike path on the north side of the city with the beautiful North Atlantic Ocean as a backdrop. The air is fresh and Katrin still wears hear helmet and black one-piece biking gear.

◇◇◇◇

MILLER
You are nice to carve some time for me from your schedule. What got you into philosophy?

KATRIN
I have always been what is called a "political animal." I was class president every year in school except once. I have always noted how other people use arguments.

MILLER
So the political philosophy intrigued you? Aristotle, Machiavelli, Rawls. **3**

KATRIN
Political philosophy was my path into philosophy. As a politician, I am used to everyone having an agenda. It goes with the territory. It came as a terrible shock to me to discover philosophers pushed their own agendas as well. But at least some of us know we're pushing for things. When people say in the free market system that winners and losers are not picked ahead of time, I have to restrain myself from laughing so hard that my belt will burst. You mean the billions of dollars to oil companies, pharmaceuticals, and defense contractors rather than infrastructure, environment, and the arts is somehow not picking winners and losers?

MILLER
And you found this to be the case among philosophers?

KATRIN
In all areas. I became interested in consciousness and immediately saw that there was an agenda in reducing consciousness to matter. Most philosophers were picking a winner, physicalism. They were shaping the economy of their philosophical thinking to make it a winner.

121

MILLER

They weren't open-minded?

KATRIN

Who is really totally open-minded, honestly? We all take sides, politically, philosophically, morally, spiritually. It's important as a philosopher to realize everyone has a favorite theory and idea, including yourself.

MILLER

And what is your favorite idea regarding consciousness?

KATRIN

That consciousness cannot be reduced to materialism.

MILLER

Can you prove that philosophically?

KATRIN

If you have time, I can elaborate.

MILLER

Sure.

KATRIN

I love to go head-to-head with the most powerful concepts. Gives me a rush. In this era, probably the most powerful concept is physicalism. But not quite. Yet consciousness cannot be so easily reduced to the physical, although physicalists like J.J.C. Smart think there's a way around this problem. Smart assumes the predominant scientific worldview that everything in the universe is material, including consciousness. The material world and consciousness are strictly identical, in the same way that the person who is now president and the person who was a gameshow host are strictly identical. Furthermore, just because the logic of statements about consciousness are different from statements about the physical universe does not necessarily mean that consciousness is above "over and above" the physical world.

> Suppose that I report that I have at this moment a roundish, blurry-edged after-image which is yellowish toward its edge and is orange toward its center. What is it that I am reporting?' One answer to this question might be that I am not reporting anything, that when I say that it looks to me as though there is a roundish yellowy orange patch of light on the wall I am expressing some sort of temptation, the temptation to say that there is a roundish yellowy orange patch on the wall (though I may know that there is not such a patch on the wall). This is perhaps Wittgenstein's view in *Philosophical Investigations* (see paragraphs 367, 370). Similarly, when I "report" a pain, I am not really reporting anything (or, if you like, I am reporting in a queer sense of "reporting"), but am doing a sophisticated sort of wince. (See paragraph 244: "The verbal expression of pain replaces crying and does not describe it." Nor does it describe anything else?) I prefer most of the time to discuss an afterimage rather than a pain, because the word "pain" brings in something which is irrelevant to my purpose: the notion of "distress." I think that "he is in pain" entails "he is in distress," that is, that he is in a

certain agitation-condition. Similarly, to say "I am in pain" may be to do more than "replace pain behavior": it may be partly to report something, though this something is quite nonmysterious, being an agitation-condition, and so susceptible of behavioristic analysis. The suggestion I wish if possible to avoid is a different one, namely that "I am in pain" is a genuine report, and that what it reports is an irreducibly psychical something. And similarly the suggestion I wish to resist is also that to say "I have a yellowish orange after-image" is to report something irreducibly psychical.

Why do I wish to resist this suggestion? Mainly because of Occam's razor. It seems to me that science is increasingly giving us a viewpoint whereby organisms are able to be seen as physico-chemical mechanisms: it seems that even the behavior of man himself will one day be explicable in mechanistic terms. There does seem to be, so far as science is concerned, nothing in the world but increasingly complex arrangements of physical constituents. All except for one place: in consciousness. That is, for a full description of what is going on in a man you would have to mention not only the physical processes in his tissue, glands, nervous system, and so forth, but also his states of consciousness: his visual, auditory, and tactual sensations, his aches and pains. That these should be correlated with brain processes does not help, for to say that they are correlated is to say that they are something "over and above." You cannot correlate something with itself. You correlate footprints with burglars, but not Bill Sikes the burglar with Bill Sikes the burglar. So sensations, states of consciousness, do seem to be the one sort of thing left outside the physicalist picture, and for various reasons I just cannot believe that this can be so. That everything should be explicable in terms of physics (together of course with descriptions of the ways in which the parts are put together-roughly, biology is to physics as radio-engineering is to electromagnetism) except the occurrence of sensations seems to me to be frankly unbelievable. Such sensations would be "nomological danglers," to use Feigl's expression. It is not often realized how odd would be the laws whereby these nomological danglers would dangle. It is sometimes asked, "Why can't there be psycho-physical laws which are of a novel sort, just as the laws of electricity and magnetism were novelties from the standpoint of Newtonian mechanics?" Certainly we are pretty sure in the future to come across new ultimate laws of a novel type, but I expect them to relate simple constituents: for example, whatever ultimate particles are then in vogue. I cannot believe that ultimate laws of nature could relate simple constituents to configurations consisting of perhaps billions of neurons (and goodness knows how many billions of ultimate particles) all put together for all the world as though their main purpose in life was to be a negative feedback mechanism of a complicated sort. Such ultimate laws would be like nothing so far known in science. They have a queer "smell" to them. I am just unable to believe in the nomological danglers themselves, or in the laws whereby they would dangle. If any philosophical arguments seemed to compel us to believe in such things, I would suspect a catch in the argument. In any case it is the object of this paper to show that there are no philosophical arguments which compel us to be dualists.

The above is largely a confession of faith, but it explains why I find Wittgenstein's position (as I construe it) so congenial. For on this view there are, in a sense, no sensations. A man is a vast arrangement of physical particles, but there are not, over and above this, sensations or states of consciousness. There are just behavioral facts about this vast mechanism, such as that it expresses a temptation (behavior disposition)—to say "there is a yellowish-red patch on the wall" or that it goes through a sophisticated sort of wince, that is, says "I am in pain." Admittedly Wittgenstein says that though the sensation "is not a something," it is nevertheless "not a nothing either" (paragraph 304), but this need only mean that the word "ache" has a use. An ache is a thing, but only in the innocuous sense in which the plain man, in the first paragraph of Frege's *Foundations of Arithmetic*, answers the question "what is the number one?" by "a thing." It should be noted that when I assert that to say "I have a yellowish-orange after-image" is to express a temptation to assert the physical-object statement "there is a yellowish-orange patch on the wall," I mean that saying "I have a yellowish-orange after-image" is (partly) the exercise of the disposition which is the temptation. It is not to report that I have the temptation, any more than is "I love you" normally a report that I love someone. Saying "I love you" is just part of the behavior that is the exercise of the disposition of loving someone.

Though, for the reasons given above, I am very receptive to the above "expressive" account of sensation statements, I do not feel that it will quite do the trick. Maybe this is because I have not thought it out sufficiently, but it does seem to me as though, when a person says "I have an after-image," he is making a genuine report, and that when he says "I have a pain," he is doing more than "replace pain-behavior," and that "this more" is not just to say that he is in distress. I am not so sure, however, that to admit this is to admit that there are nonphysical correlates of brain processes. Why should not sensations just be brain processes of a certain sort? There are, of course, well-known (as well as lesser-known) philosophical objections to the view that reports of sensations are reports of brain-processes, but I shall try to argue that these arguments are by no means as cogent as is commonly thought to be the case.

Let me first try to state more-accurately the thesis that sensations are brain processes. It is not the thesis that, for example, "after-image" or "ache" means the same as "brain process of sort X" (where "X" is replaced by a description of a certain sort of brain process). It is that, in so far as "after-image" or "ache" is a report of a process, it is a report of a process that happens to be a brain process. It follows that the thesis does not claim that sensation statements can be translated into statements about brain processes. Nor does it claim that the logic of a sensation statement is the same as that of a brain-process state; Wittgenstein did not like the word "disposition." I am using it to put in a nutshell (and perhaps inaccurately) the view which I am attributing to Wittgenstein. I should like to repeat that I do not wish to claim that my interpretation of Wittgenstein is correct. Some of those who knew him do not interpret him in this way. It is merely a view which I find myself extracting from his printed words and which I think is important and worth discussing for its own sake. All it claims is that in so far as a sensation statement is a report of something, that something is in fact a brain process. Sensations are nothing over and above brain processes. Nations are nothing "over and above" citizens, but this does not prevent the logic of nation statements being very different from the logic of citizen statements, nor does it insure the translatability of nation statements into citizen statements. (I do not, however, wish to assert that the relation of sensation statements to brain-process statements is very similar to that of nation statements to citizen statements. Nations do not just happen to be nothing over and above citizens, for example. I bring in the "nations" example merely to make a negative point: that the fact that the logic of A-statements is different from that of B-statements does not insure that A's are anything over and above B's.)

Remarks on identity. When I say that a sensation is a brain process or that lightning is an electric discharge, I am using "is" in the sense of strict identity. (Just as in this case, the necessary-proposition "is identical with the smallest prime number greater than 5.") When I say that a sensation is a brain process or that lightning is an electric discharge I do not mean just that the sensation is somehow spatially or temporally continuous with the brain process or that the lightning is just spatially or temporally continuous with the discharge. When on the other hand I say that the successful general is the same person as the small boy who stole the apples I mean only that the successful general I see before me is a time slice of the same four-dimensional object of which the small boy stealing apples is an earlier time slice. However, the four-dimensional object which has the general-I-see-before-me for its late time slice is identical in the strict sense with the four-dimensional object which has the small-boy-stealing-apples for an early time slice. I distinguish these two senses of "is identical with" because I wish to make it clear that the brain-process doctrine asserts identity in the strict sense.[1]

From The Philosophical Review, Vol. 68, No. 2, April 1959 by J.J.C. Smart. Copyright © 1959 by Duke University Press. Reprinted by permission.

Smart wants to use the idea of language-games borrowed from Wittgenstein to prove that consciousness is materialistic. Just because the logic of statements about consciousness ~~are~~ different from statements about the physical universe, he claims, does not necessarily mean that consciousness is ~~above~~ "over and above" the physical world. Yet by playing a different language-game, it can be argued that consciousness is above and beyond the physical world. By another language-game, it can be argued that consciousness is different from the material world. According to Thomas Nagel, looking at the world from a ~~single~~ point-of-view is different in kind from material things. Nagel emphasizes this point by imagining what it is like to be a bat. Since humans don't have sonar as bats do, we can never understand the perspective of a bat. We can talk about sonar until we lose our voices, but never understand the experience of sonar from the bat's perspective. The bat's perspective is irreducible to physicalist descriptions in the same way all consciousness is irreducible to physicalist descriptions:

> Any reductionist program has to be based on an analysis of what is to be reduced. If the analysis leaves something out, the problem will be falsely posed. It is useless to base the defense of materialism on any analysis of mental phenomena that fails to deal explicitly with their subjective character. For there is no reason to suppose that a reduction that seems plausible when no attempt is made to account for consciousness can be extended to include consciousness. Without some idea, therefore, of what the subjective character of experience is, we cannot know what is required of a physicalist theory. . . .
>
> But when we examine their subjective character it seems that such a result is impossible. The reason is that every subjective phenomenon is essentially connected with a single point of view, and it seems inevitable that an objective, physical theory will abandon that point of view. . . .
>
> Now we know that most bats (the microchiroptera, to be precise) perceive the external world primarily by sonar, or echolocation, detecting the reflections, from objects within the range, of their own rapid, subtly modulated, high-frequency shrieks. Their brains are designed to correlate the outgoing impulses with the subsequent echoes, and the information thus acquired enables bats to make precise discriminations of distance, size, shape, motion, and texture comparable to those we make by vision. But bat sonar, though clearly a form of perception, is not similar in its operation to any sense that we possess.[2]

Point-of-view cannot be reduced material objectivity—this is another way to look at consciousness. Or what does this point-of-view consist? Would a point-of-view consist of the manipulation of symbols or would it include cognition, perception, understanding, and thinking? For John Searle, manipulation of symbols refers to the syntax and actually understanding them refers to semantics. There is a world of

---

[1] Smart, J. J. C. "Sensations and Brain Processes." *The Philosophical Review* 68.2 (April, 1959): 141-5.
[2] Nagel, Thomas. "What Is It Like to Be a Bat?" *The Philosophical Review* 83.4 (October, 1974): 436-9, 441-3.

difference between manipulating symbols and knowing the meaning of them. If someone hands me sym-bols from a language I do not know asking what my favorite color is, I can go to a rule-book to another set of symbols I do not know and point to another symbol I don't understand that means "blue." I follow the rules such that when X occurs, I must respond with a Y, without knowing what either X or Y mean:

Imagine that people outside the room who understand Chinese hand in small bunches of symbols and that in response I manipulate the symbols according to the rule book and hand back more small bunches of symbols. Now, the rule book is the "computer program." The people who wrote it are "programmers," and I am the "computer." The baskets full of symbols are the "data base," the small bunches that are handed in to me are "questions" and the bunches I then hand out are "answers."

Now suppose that the rule book is written in such a way that my "answers" to the "questions" are indistinguishable from those of a native Chinese speaker. For example, the people outside might hand me some symbols that unknown to me mean, "What's your favorite color?" and I might after going through the rules give back symbols that, also unknown to me, mean, "My favorite is blue, but I also like green a lot." I satisfy the Turing test for understanding Chinese. All the same, I am totally ignorant of Chinese. And there is no way I could come to understand Chinese in the system as de-scribed, since there is no way that I can learn the meanings of any of the symbols. Like a computer, I manipulate symbols, but I attach no meaning to the symbols.

The point of the thought experiment is this: if I do not understand Chinese solely on the basis of running a computer program for understanding Chinese, then neither does any other digital com-puter solely on that basis. Digital computers merely manipulate formal symbols according to the rules of a program.

What goes for Chinese goes for other forms of cognition as well. Just manipulating the symbols is not by itself enough to guarantee cognition, perception, understanding, thinking, and so forth. And since computers, qua computers, are symbol-manipulating devices, merely running the computer program is not enough to guarantee cognition.

This simple argument is decisive against the claims of strong AI. The first premise of the argu-ment simply states the formal character of a computer program. Programs are defined in terms of symbol manipulations, and the symbols are purely formal, or "syntactic." The formal character of the program, by the way, is what makes computers so powerful. The same program can be run on an indefinite variety of hardware, and one hardware system can run an indefinite range of computer programs. Let me abbreviate this "axiom" as

Axiom 1. *Computer programs are formal (syntactic).*

This point is so crucial that it is worth explaining in more detail. A digital computer pro-cesses information by first encoding it in the symbolism that the computer uses and then manip-ulating the symbols through a set of precisely stated rules. These rules constitute the program. For example, in Turing's early theory of computers, the symbols were simply O's and 1's, and the rules of the program said such things as, "Print a 0 on the tape, move one square to the left and erase a 1." The astonishing thing about computers is that any information that can be stated in a language can be encoded in such a system, and any information processing task that can be solved by explicit rules can be programmed.

Two further points are important. First, symbols and programs are purely abstract notions: they have no essential physical properties to define them and can be implemented in any physical medium whatsoever. The O's and 1's, qua symbols, have no essential physical properties and a fortiori have no physical, causal properties. I emphasize this point because it is tempting to identify computers with some specific technology, say, silicon chips and to think that the issues are about the physics of silicon chips or to think that syntax identifies some physical phenomenon that might have as yet unknown causal powers, in the way that actual physical phenomena such as electromagnetic radiation or hydrogen atoms have physical, causal properties. The second point is that symbols are manipulated without reference to any meanings. The symbols of the program can stand for anything the programmer or user wants. In this sense the program has syntax but no semantics.

The next axiom is just a reminder of the obvious fact that thoughts, perceptions, understandings, and so forth have a mental content. By virtue of their content they can be about objects and states of affairs in the world. If the content involves language, there will be syntax in addition to semantics, but linguistic understanding requires at least a semantic framework. If, for example, I am thinking about the last presidential election, certain words will go through my mind, but the words are about the election only because I attach specific meanings to these words, in accordance with my knowledge of English. In this respect they are unlike Chinese symbols for me. Let me abbreviate this axiom as

Axiom 2. *Human minds have mental contents (semantics).*

Now let me add the point that the Chinese room demonstrated. Having the symbols by themselves-just having the syntax is not sufficient for having the semantics. Merely manipulating symbols is not enough to guarantee knowledge of what they mean. I shall abbreviate this as

Axiom 3. *Syntax by itself is neither constitutive of nor sufficient for semantics.*

At one level this principle is true by definition. One might, of course, define the terms syntax and semantics differently. The point is that there is a distinction between formal elements, which have no intrinsic meaning or content, and those phenomena that have intrinsic content. From these premises it follows that

Conclusion 1. *Programs are neither constitutive of nor sufficient for minds. And that is just another way of saying that strong AI is false....*

All of these arguments share a common feature: they are all inadequate because they fail to come to grips with the actual Chinese room argument. That argument rests on the distinction between the formal symbol manipulation that is done by the computer and the mental contents biologically produced by the brain, a distinction I have abbreviated-I hope not misleadingly as the distinction between syntax and semantics.[3]

If we don't know sign language and someone signs "How are you?" and we are told by someone else to sign "I'm fine" without knowing what either of those and gestures mean, we do not know sign language any more than we know how to dance if we are told to move our feet here and then there. In each perspective meaning is marshalled. Meaning cannot be reduced to the material. Meaning eschews the material.

---

[3] Searle, John R. "Is the Brain's Mind a Computer Program?" *Scientific American* 262.1 (January, 1990): 26-7, 30.

The manifestation of meaning marginalizes the material. Meaning is the "more than" that often occurs to people when they think about existence. This "more than" constitutes a point-of-view over and beyond the material, allowing us the vantage point of even saying there is a material.

MILLER
That is quite a radical viewpoint.

KATRIN
Yes, it is. Is meaning identical with matter? I have problems of equating the two. I don't think matter has what it takes to produce meaning. It's inadequate to the task.

MILLER
Inadequate to the task. Nice phrase.

KATRIN
Such a good phrase that I'll use it again. Matter is also inadequate to the task of producing perspective, subjectivity.

MILLER
May I take this where I think you're going? It's exciting.

KATRIN
Yes, please.

MILLER
Matter is also inadequate to the task of producing changing perspectives.

KATRIN
Do you know why I think matter's inadequate in all these cases?

MILLER
I am not sure about that one. I can help you finish your thoughts, but not much more.

KATRIN
In each case, there is transcendence. Meaning transcends matter; perspective transcends matter; shifting perspectives transcends matter. Transcendence doesn't go away. You can't wish it away or philosophize it away. It is like a big blot in the middle of philosophy. Everybody wants to wipe it up, but the more we try to wipe it up the more it's spread to other areas of philosophy, just like the Dr. Seuss story. As much as the physicalists try, there is no solution to transcendence. This is where I have my fun as a philosopher. They can't touch transcendence as much might as they put into destroying it.

MILLER
By transcendent you mean?

KATRIN
Follow me more closely, Miller. Follow me more closely. Transcendence means irreducible.

MILLER
Your philosophical problem is transcendence or what you call the irreducible. You can't seem to shake the problem.

KATRIN
Yes. Whenever people have problems, they create agendas to solve those problems. When philosophers have problems, they develop philosophical agendas to solve those problems. And like everyone else, they'll stick to the script until they think enough evidence exists to undermine their agendas and then they'll quit.

MILLER
How much evidence does it take for a philosopher to change a view? For people, there never seems to be enough evidence. You can hit them of the head with a stick over and over again and they'll still stay faithful.

KATRIN
That is a question for another one of your interviewees. By the way: how is this interviewing going?

MILLER
Wonderful, I'm learning a lot about myself and the process of interviewing.

KATRIN
I wish you well—and how did you get my name?

MILLER
Your friend Henry once had a relationship with one of the cousins of one of my colleagues I didn't know so well and didn't like and he mentioned it to my mother during a chance meeting at Target.

KATRIN
That's interesting.

MILLER
Be careful riding back. It's dark now.

KATRIN
No problem for me. I see like a hawk. It was fun.

The Cat in Hat Comes Back

see things in different
ways, from different
perspective Mobility
~~~~~ and shift perspective

Shift perspective by willing it demonstrat
another persona not according to
Job description

1) receive symbols one cannot decypher
2) use a rulebook that ~~tells you~~
3) ~~informing you~~ respond A
    tells you ~~how~~ to ~~answer~~

~~On~~ indecipherable symbol 1
~~~~~~~~~~~~ with indecipherable
                symbol ?

3) Never understand the mean
of either of those symbols,
even though symbol 1
asks "what is the color?" and
symbol 2 is the response. The
will never be accused of
~~understanding~~ ~~simply~~ that only manipulat
symbols

Diversity and Free Speech
Who's Woke and What's Broke

While in Wales, I visit the birth home of the great poet, Dylan Thomas. During the tour of the birth home, I strike up a conversation with one of the guides. "Woke" (that's what it says on his nametag) and I broach a number of topics, but return to the notion of freedom of speech, diversity, and political correctness. Woke is an immigrant from Ireland finishing his doctorate in philosophy (defense shortly). He's a tall lad with an engaging lilt who strides around the premises like a person with a mission. Wild brown hair crops up an old-timey cap and faintest green studs recede into his earlobes. He has worked on newspapers, in public relations, and lately in cyber security.

⟡⟡⟡

MILLER
Your name really is "Woke"?

WOKE
That's the name mom and dad gave me.

MILLER
What is your main philosophical concern?

WOKE
Each age thinks it's the shit and the previous generation a bunch of idiots. In truth, human beings of all ages and times act foolishly because they fail to recognize they fall into the same patterns of errors as their parents did. My age thinks it's so woke because people are beginning to realize that zoos and circuses are institutionalized violence and cruelty against animals, a topic they discuss incidentally while consuming meat that was once an animal confined in the vilest conditions for all of its life and terrorized on the way to a brutal death.

MILLER
It takes a while for people to get woke.

WOKE
Yes, and I am learning that, but it angers me when philosophy becomes religious faith. Philosophy is not about ending dialogue, but beginning it, always going back to the beginning, reexamining one's premises. Without that reexamination, you can't begin to be woke. Philosophical reexamination is the manner in which the blinds are drawn and the eyes opened. *the mind is opened.*

131

MILLER

And as you and I were talking about during the tour, political correctness is destroying the freedom of speech that is at the core of reexamination.

WOKE

It's gotten to be ridiculous. I saw a student expelled for clapping in a class.

MILLER

What? Why?

WOKE

Because his clapping triggered one of the students and *retraumatized* her. He wasn't applauding for the rape culture, but only because one of other students had said something funny about the soup tasting horribly. It's beyond words that can get you in trouble. Even if sarcasm slips into your voice, you better watch out.

MILLER

Why do you think we've reached this point?

WOKE

Because diversity has become corrupted. I agree, by the way, in the basic premises of diversity: to includes ideas and literature from peoples who had not had their voices heard. That to me is what a university is all about: to hear as many perspectives as possible. Also, it's vital for people who have marginalized and oppressed to see themselves portrayed in a positive way and encounter ideas that resonate for them. Charles Taylor explains this wonderfully:

> Precognition of others, and so a person or group of people can suffer real damage, real distortion, if the people or society around them mirror back to them a confining or demeaning or contemptible picture of themselves. Nonrecognition or misrecognition can inflict harm, can be a form of oppression, imprisoning someone in a false, distorted, and reduced mode of being. Thus some feminists have argued that women in patriarchal societies have been induced to adopt a depreciatory image of themselves. They have internalized a picture of their own inferiority, so that even when some of the objective obstacles to their advancement fall away, they may be incapable of taking advantage of the new opportunities. And beyond this, they are condemned to suffer the pain of low self-esteem. An analogous point has been made in relation to Blacks: that White society has for generations projected a demeaning image of them, which some of them have been unable to resist adopting. Their own self-depreciation, on this view, becomes one of the most potent instruments of their own oppression. Their first task ought to be to purge themselves of this imposed and destructive identity. Recently, a similar point has been made in relation to indigenous and colonized people in general. It is held that since 1492 Europeans have projected an image of such people as somehow inferior, "uncivilized," and through the force of conquest have often been able to impose.[1]

---

[1] Taylor, Charles. "The Politics of Recognition." *Multiculturalism*. Ed. Amy Gutmann. Princeton, NJ: Princeton University Press, 1994.

Inclusivity makes sense to people like myself who want a richer curriculum as well as a society that speaks to a wide range of people. But diversity devolved from a philosophy into an article of faith. Any hint of disagreement with the screed and off with your head. You are presumed guilty and convicted—no trial. Feeling replaces reason. If something makes you feel horrible, it must be that that person is purposely making you feel that way and is an oppressor. Philosophy dies when there is no critical distance and hysteria becomes the norm. At least at the Salem Witch Trials, there was an "objective" test for whether a woman was a witch or not. In the PC world, it's just what you feel. And if someone makes you feel uncomfortable or offends you, then that person is deliberately doing it to destroy you.

> Worse, I tend to be ironic—I like irony; it helps you think because it gives you critical distance on a thing. Irony doesn't sit very well in the current climate, especially when it comes to irony about the current climate. Critical distance itself is out of fashion—not exactly a plus when it comes to intellectual life (or education itself). Feelings are what's in fashion. I'm all for feelings; I'm a standard-issue female, after all. But this cult of feeling has an authoritarian underbelly: feelings can't be questioned or probed, even while furnishing the rationale for sweeping new policies, which can't be questioned or probed either. (I speak from experience here.) The result is that higher education has been so radically transformed that the place is almost unrecognizable. There are plenty of transformations I'd applaud: more diversity in enrollments and hiring; need-blind admissions; progress toward gender equity. But personally, I dislike being told what I can and can't say. Beyond that, there are pretty important freedoms at stake that are worth fighting to preserve.[2]

This feel-first philosophy (if you can call it that) of political correctness is anti-philosophical, shutting down instead of opening up thinking. It makes people scared to death to even clap in class for fear of offending other people:

> It is vital to understand that political correctness is immune to evidence—and I do not mean resistant to evidence, nor do I mean blindly dogmatic such that PC requires an overwhelming weight of evidence to be convinced; but I mean utterly and completely immune to evidence such that unanimity of incontrovertible evidence against PC is still insufficient to induce significant re-evaluation. This is important to realize; since it makes clear that time, energy, and personal resources expended on trying to convince PC advocates with evidence is just so much time and energy down-the-drain and lost-precious resources that could potentially have been expended constructively elsewhere. The reason that PC is absolutely evidence-proof is that it operates at a wholly abstract level. But the reason that it superficially appears that PC might potentially be open to evidential refutation is that, although abstract, PC is concerned exclusively with material proxy-measures of its abstractions. That is the distinctive move which sets PC apart from any preceding ideology. Political correctness operates on the assumption that an abstract system of allocation is intrinsically superior to the lack of such a system; and the details can be worked-out in the fullness of time. The reason why politically correct people believe in objective moral progress is that moral progress is equated with systematic altruism. . . . This is why effectiveness is of no interest, outcomes are of no concern and evidence has no relevance.[3]

---

[2] Kipnis, Laura. *Unwanted Advances*. New York: HarperCollins, 2017.

[3] Charlton, Bruce G.. *Thought Prison*. Buckingham: University of Buckingham Press, 2015.

Can't talk about hell

Maybe the end-game of PC is not systemic altruism, but something else: to create a world where nobody is offended and all feelings are spared. PC is a theology of over-sensitization consisting of hair-triggered hysteria that it is right and the rest of the world is wrong. That overall philosophy immediately leads, for the betterment of all it believes, to censorship. I once studied the censorship standards in the American film industry. Woke people now probably think how could these unwoke people think this way? But they had the same reasons for censorship as the PC people do: we censor to make society a better place for all. In the same way, clapping is not PC, neither was a sarcastic cheer, what is called a "Bronx Cheer," for the motion picture moralists, among many, many other things.

Pointed profanity and every other profane or vulgar expression, however used, is forbidden.

(1) No approval by the Production Code Administration shall be given to the use of words and phrases in motion pictures including, but not limited to, the following:

Alley cat (applied to a woman); bat (applied to a woman); broad (applied to a woman); Bronx cheer (the sound); chippie; cocotte; God, Lord, Jesus, Christ (unless used reverently); cripes; fanny; fairy (in a vulgar sense); finger (the); fire, cries of; Gawd; goose (in a vulgar sense); "hold your hat" or "hats"; hot (applied to a woman); "in your hat"; louse; lousy; Madam (relating to prostitution); nance, nerts; nuts (except when meaning crazy); pansy; razzberry (the sound); slut (applied to a woman); SOB.; son-of-a; tart; toilet gags; tom cat (applied to a man); traveling salesman and farmer's daughter jokes; whore; damn; hell (excepting when the use of said last two words shall be essential and required for portrayal, in proper historical context, of any scene or dialogue based upon historical fact or folklore, or for the presentation in proper literary context of a Biblical, or other religious quotation, or a quotation from a literary work provided that no such use shall he permitted which is intrinsically objectionable or offends good taste).[4]

The paradox of PC-driven diversity is that its mission is to eliminate fundamental diversity in human expression and establish a single pure language free of negativity, which now seems to mean what would "upset" another person. Yet human expression is multi-layered and extremely diverse. A single word can have multiple meanings according to its *specific* context. If that context is not established, then we don't have a clue what the speaker means. And contexts are further muddled by how other people interpret those contexts according to their belief systems. (Even PC people argue rather inconsistently that a word with a historically negative connotation is okay if used by members of that historically oppressed class.) A single word might have several meanings according to context: an order, report, hypothesis, play-acting, guessing riddles, translating one language into another, thanking, cursing, and greeting, as Wittgenstein suggests.

For PC, diversity in human expression is scrapped and their idea of a "perfect" society is where anything that is considered a negative connotation is removed, much the way Plato sees his ideal society. This should send shudders down the spines of any of us who want to continue with PC. This is our future should PC strangle free speech:

Then the first thing will be to establish a censorship of the writers of fiction, and let the censors receive any tale of fiction which is good, and reject the bad; and we will desire mothers and nurses to tell their children the authorised ones only. Let them fashion the mind with such tales, even more

---

[4] The Motion Picture Production Code. *The Production Code of the Motion Picture Industry (1930-1967)*. <https://productioncode.dhwritings.com/multipleframes_productioncode.php>.

fondly than they mould the body with their hands; but most of those which are now in use must be discarded. Of what tales are you speaking? he said.

You may find a model of the lesser in the greater, I said; for they are necessarily of the same type, and there is the same spirit in both of them.

Very likely, he replied; but I do not as yet know what you would term the greater.

Those, I said, which are narrated by Homer and Hesiod, and the rest of the poets, who have ever been the great story-tellers of mankind. But which stories do you mean, he said; and what fault do you find with them?

A fault which is most serious, I said; the fault of telling a lie, and, what is more, a bad lie.

But when is this fault committed?

Whenever an erroneous representation is made of the nature of gods and heroes,—as when a painter paints a portrait not having the shadow of a likeness to the original.

Yes, he said, that sort of thing is certainly very blamable; but what are the stories which you mean?

First of all, I said, there was that greatest of all lies, in high places, which the poet told about Uranus, and which was a bad lie too,—I mean what Hesiod says that Uranus did, and how Cronus retaliated on him. The doings of Cronus, and the sufferings which in turn his son inflicted upon him, even if they were true, ought certainly not to be lightly told to young and thoughtless persons; if possible, they had better be buried in silence. But if there is an absolute necessity for their mention, a chosen few might hear them in a mystery, and they should sacrifice not a common [Eleusinian] pig, but some huge and unprocurable victim; and then the number of the hearers will be very few indeed.

Why, yes, said he, those stories are extremely objectionable.

Yes, Adeimantus, they are stories not to be repeated in our State; the young man should not be told that in committing the worst of crimes he is far from doing anything outrageous; and that even if he chastises his father when does wrong, in whatever manner, he will only be following the example of the first and greatest among the gods. I entirely agree with you, he said; in my opinion those stories are quite unfit to be repeated.

Neither, if we mean our future guardians to regard the habit of quarrelling among themselves as of all things the basest, should any word be said to them of the wars in heaven, and of the plots and fightings of the gods against one another, for they are not true. No, we shall never mention the battles of the giants, or let them be embroidered on garments; and we shall be silent about the innumerable other quarrels of gods and heroes with their friends and relatives. If they would only believe us we would tell them that quarrelling is unholy, and that never up to this time has there been any, quarrel between citizens; this is what old men and old women should begin by telling children; and when they grow up, the poets also should be told to compose for them in a similar spirit. But the narrative of Hephaestus binding Hera his mother, or how on another occasion Zeus sent him flying for taking her part when she was being beaten, and all the battles of the gods in Homer—these tales must not be admitted into our State, whether they are supposed to have an allegorical meaning or not. For a young person cannot judge what is allegorical and what is literal; anything that he receives into his mind at that age is likely to become indelible and unalterable; and therefore it is most important that the tales which the young first hear should be models of virtuous thoughts.

There you are right, he replied; but if anyone asks where are such models to be found and of what tales are you speaking—how shall we answer him?

I said to him, You and I, Adeimantus, at this moment are not poets, but founders of a State: now the founders of a State ought to know the general forms in which poets should cast their tales, and the limits which must be observed by them, but to make the tales is not their business.

Very true, he said; but what are these forms of theology which you mean? Something of this kind, I replied: God is always to be represented as he truly is, whatever be the sort of poetry, epic, lyric, or tragic, in which the representation is given.

Right.

And is he not truly good? And must he not be represented as such?

Certainly.

And no good thing is hurtful?

No, indeed.

And that which is not hurtful hurts not?

Certainly not.

And that which hurts not does no evil?

No.

And can that which does no evil be a cause of evil?

Impossible.

And the good is advantageous?

Yes.

And therefore the cause of well-being?

Yes.

It follows therefore that the good is not the cause of all things, but of the good only?

Assuredly.

Then God, if he be good, is not the author of all things, as the many assert, but he is the cause of a few things only, and not of most things that occur to men. For few are the goods of human life, and many are the evils, and the good is to be attributed to God alone; of the evils the causes are to be sought elsewhere, and not in him.

That appears to me to be most true, he said.

Then we must not listen to Homer or to any other poet who is guilty of the folly of saying that two casks

Lie at the threshold of Zeus, full of lots, one of good, the other of evil lots,

and that he to whom Zeus gives a mixture of the two

Sometimes meets with evil fortune, at other times with good;

but that he to whom is given the cup of unmingled ill,

Him wild hunger drives o'er the beauteous earth.

And again

Zeus, who is the dispenser of good and evil to us.

And if anyone asserts that the violation of oaths and treaties, which was really the work of Pandarus, was brought about by Athene and Zeus, or that the strife and contention of the gods was instigated by Themis and Zeus, he shall not have our approval; neither will we allow our young men to hear the words of Aeschylus, that

God plants guilt among men when he desires utterly to destroy a house.

And if a poet writes of the sufferings of Niobe—the subject of the tragedy in which these iambic verses occur—or of the house of Pelops, or of the Trojan war or on any similar theme, either we must not permit him to say that these are the works of God, or if they are of God, he must devise some explanation of them such as we are seeking; he must say that God did what was just and right, and they were the better for being punished; but that those who are punished are miserable, and that God is the author of their misery—the poet is not to be permitted to say; though he may say that the wicked are miserable because they require to be punished, and are benefited by receiving punishment from God; but that God being good is the author of evil to anyone is to be strenuously denied, and not to be said or sung or heard in verse or prose by anyone whether old or young in any well-ordered commonwealth. Such a fiction is suicidal, ruinous, impious.

I agree with you, he replied, and am ready to give my assent to the law.

Let this then be one of our rules and principles concerning the gods, to which our poets and reciters will be expected to conform—that God is not the author of all things, but of good only.

That will do, he said.

And what do you think of a second principle? Shall I ask you whether God is a magician, and of a nature to appear insidiously now in one shape, and now in another—sometimes himself changing and passing into many forms, sometimes deceiving us with the semblance of such transformations; or is he one and the same immutably fixed in his own proper image?

I cannot answer you, he said, without more thought.

Well, I said; but if we suppose a change in anything, that change must be effected either by the thing itself, or by some other thing?

Most certainly.

And things which are at their best are also least liable to be altered or discomposed; for example, when healthiest and strongest, the human frame is least liable to be affected by meats and drinks, and the plant which is in the fullest vigour also suffers least from winds or the heat of the sun or any similar causes.

Of course.

And will not the bravest and wisest soul be least confused or deranged by any external influence?

True.

And the same principle, as I should suppose, applies to all composite things—furniture, houses, garments; when good and well made, they are least altered by time and circumstances.

Very true.

Then everything which is good, whether made by art or nature, or both, is least liable to suffer change from without?

True.

But surely God and the things of God are in every way perfect?

Of course they are.

Then can he be compelled by an external influence to take many shapes?

He cannot.

But may he not change and transform himself?

Clearly, he said, that must be the case if he is changed at all.

And will he then change himself for the better and fairer, or for the worse and more unsightly?

If he change at all he can only change for the worse, for we cannot suppose him to be deficient either in virtue or beauty.

Very true, Adeimantus; but then, would anyone, whether God or man, desire to make himself worse?

Impossible.

Then it is impossible that God should ever be willing to change; being, as is supposed, the fairest and best that is conceivable, every god remains absolutely and forever in his own form.

That necessarily follows, he said, in my judgment.

Then, I said, my dear friend, let none of the poets tell us that

The gods, taking the disguise of strangers from other lands,

walk up and down cities in all sorts of forms;

and let no one slander Proteus and Thetis, neither let anyone, either in tragedy or in any other kind of poetry, introduce Hera disguised in the likeness of a priestess asking for alms

For the life-giving daughters of Inachus the river of Argos;

—let us have no more lies of that sort. Neither must we have mothers under the influence of the poets scaring their children with a bad version of these myths—telling how certain gods, as they say, 'Go about by night in the likeness of so many strangers and in diverse forms'; but let them take heed lest they make cowards of their children, and at the same time speak blasphemy against the gods.

Heaven forbid, he said.

But although the gods are themselves unchangeable, still by witchcraft and deception they may make us think that they appear in various forms?

Perhaps, he replied.

Well, but can you imagine that God will be willing to lie, whether in word or deed, or to put forth a phantom of himself?

I cannot say, he replied.

Do you not know, I said, that the true lie, if such an expression may be allowed, is hated of gods and men?

What do you mean? he said.

I mean that no one is willingly deceived in that which is the truest and highest part of himself, or about the truest and highest matters; there, above all, he is most afraid of a lie having possession of him.

Still, he said, I do not comprehend you.

The reason is, I replied, that you attribute some profound meaning to my words; but I am only saying that deception, or being deceived or uninformed about the highest realities in the highest part of themselves, which is the soul, and in that part of them to have and to hold the lie, is what mankind least like;—that, I say, is what they utterly detest.

There is nothing more hateful to them.

And, as I was just now remarking, this ignorance in the soul of him who is deceived may be called the true lie; for the lie in words is only a kind of imitation and shadowy image of a previous affection of the soul, not pure unadulterated falsehood. Am I not right?

Perfectly right.

The true lie is hated not only by the gods, but also by men?

Yes.

Whereas the lie in words is in certain cases useful and not hateful; in dealing with enemies—that would be an instance; or again, when those whom we call our friends in a fit of madness or illusion are going to do some harm, then it is useful and is a sort of medicine or preventive; also in the tales of mythology, of which we were just now speaking—because we do not know the truth about ancient times, we make falsehood as much like truth as we can, and so turn it to account.

Very true, he said.

But can any of these reasons apply to God? Can we suppose that he is ignorant of antiquity, and therefore has recourse to invention?

That would be ridiculous, he said.

Then the lying poet has no place in our idea of God?

I should say not.

Or perhaps he may tell a lie because he is afraid of enemies?

That is inconceivable.

But he may have friends who are senseless or mad?

But no mad or senseless person can be a friend of God.

Then no motive can be imagined why God should lie?

None whatever.

Then the superhuman and divine is absolutely incapable of falsehood?

Yes.

Then is God perfectly simple and true both in word and deed; he changes not; he deceives not, either by sign or word, by dream or waking vision.

Your thoughts, he said, are the reflection of my own.

You agree with me then, I said, that this is the second type or form in which we should write and speak about divine things. The gods are not magicians who transform themselves, neither do they deceive mankind in any way.

I grant that.

Then, although we are admirers of Homer, we do not admire the lying dream which Zeus sends to Agamemnon; neither will we praise the verses of Aeschylus in which Thetis says that Apollo at her nuptials

Was celebrating in song her fair progeny whose days were to be long, and to know no sickness. And when he had spoken of my lot as in all things blessed of heaven he raised a note of triumph and cheered my soul. And I thought that the word of Phoebus being divine and full of prophecy, would not fail. And now he himself who uttered the strain, he who was present at the banquet, and who said this—he it is who has slain my son.

These are the kind of sentiments about the gods which will arouse our anger; and he who utters them shall be refused a chorus; neither shall we allow teachers to make use of them in the instruction of the young, meaning, as we do, that our guardians, as far as men can be, should be true worshippers of the gods and like them.

I entirely agree, he said, in these principles, and promise to make them my laws.

Book III

Socrates—Adeimantus

SUCH then, I said, are our principles of theology—some tales are to be told, and others are not to be told to our disciples from their youth upwards, if we mean them to honour the gods and their parents, and to value friendship with one another.

Yes; and I think that our principles are right, he said.

But if they are to be courageous, must they not learn other lessons besides these, and lessons of such a kind as will take away the fear of death? Can any man be courageous who has the fear of death in him?

Certainly not, he said.

And can he be fearless of death, or will he choose death in battle rather than defeat and slavery, who believes the world below to be real and terrible?

Impossible.

Then we must assume a control over the narrators of this class of tales as well as over the others, and beg them not simply to but rather to commend the world below, intimating to them that their descriptions are untrue, and will do harm to our future warriors.

That will be our duty, he said.

Then, I said, we shall have to obliterate many obnoxious passages, beginning with the verses,

I would rather he a serf on the land of a poor and portionless man than rule over all the dead who have come to nought.

We must also expunge the verse, which tells us how Pluto feared,

Lest the mansions grim and squalid which the gods abhor should be seen both of mortals and immortals.

And again:

O heavens! verily in the house of Hades there is soul and ghostly form but no mind at all!

Again of Tiresias:

To him even after death did Persephone grant mind, that he alone should be wise; but the other souls are flitting shades.

Again:

The soul flying from the limbs had gone to Hades, lamenting her fate, leaving manhood and youth.

Again:

And the soul, with shrilling cry, passed like smoke beneath the earth.

And,

As bats in hollow of mystic cavern, whenever any of the has dropped out of the string and falls from the rock, fly shrilling and cling to one another, so did they with shrilling cry hold together as they moved.

And we must beg Homer and the other poets not to be angry if we strike out these and similar passages, not because they are unpoetical, or unattractive to the popular ear, but because the greater the poetical charm of them, the less they meet for the ears of boys and men who are meant to be free, and who should fear slavery more than death.

Undoubtedly.

Also we shall have to reject all the terrible and appalling names that describe the world below—Cocytus and Styx, ghosts under the earth, and sapless shades, and any similar words of which the very mention causes a shudder to pass through the inmost soul of him who hears them. I do not say that these horrible stories may not have a use of some kind; but there is a danger that the nerves of our guardians may be rendered too excitable and effeminate by them.

There is a real danger, he said.

Then we must have no more of them.

True.

Another and a nobler strain must be composed and sung by us.

Clearly.

And shall we proceed to get rid of the weepings and wailings of famous men?

They will go with the rest.

But shall we be right in getting rid of them? Reflect: our principle is that the good man will not consider death terrible to any other good man who is his comrade.

Yes; that is our principle.[5]

---

[5] Plato. *Republic*. Project Gutenberg. <https://www.gutenberg.org/ebooks/150>.

"Woke" people don't endorse censorship. They can be wrong and for that reason want to hear other perspectives. Diversity depends upon diverse ideas, even if those ideas are unpopular and "negative." Diversity cannot be maintained without a diversity of ideas. That kind of diversity is hollow and superficial. Not surprisingly, the essay that speaks to me most is *On Liberty* by John Stuart Mill, who recognizes how society benefits by being challenged by unpopular views.

If all mankind minus one, were of one opinion, and only one person were of the contrary opinion, mankind would be no more justified in silencing that one person, than he, if he had the power, would be justified in silencing mankind. Were an opinion a personal possession of no value except to the owner; if to be obstructed in the enjoyment of it were simply a private injury, it would make some difference whether the injury was inflicted only on a few persons or on many. But the peculiar evil of silencing the expression of an opinion is that it is robbing the human race; posterity as well as the existing generation; those who dissent from the opinion, still more than those who hold it. If the opinion is right, they are deprived of the opportunity of exchanging error for truth: if wrong, they lose, what is almost as great a benefit, the clearer perception and livelier impression of truth, produced by its collision with error.

It is necessary to consider separately these two hypotheses, each of which has a distinct branch of the argument corresponding to it. We can never be sure that the opinion we are endeavouring to stifle is a false opinion; and if we were sure, stifling it would be an evil still.

First: the opinion which it is attempted to suppress by authority may possibly be true. Those who desire to suppress it, of course deny its truth; but they are not infallible. They have no authority to decide the question for all mankind, and exclude every other person from the means of judging. To refuse a hearing to an opinion, because they are sure that it is false, is to assume that their certainty is the same thing as absolute certainty. All silencing of discussion is an assumption of infallibility. Its condemnation may be allowed to rest on this common argument, not the worse for being common.

Unfortunately for the good sense of mankind, the fact of their fallibility is far from carrying the weight in their practical judgment, which is always allowed to it in theory; for while everyone well knows himself to be fallible, few think it necessary to take any precautions against their own fallibility, or admit the supposition that any opinion, of which they feel very certain, may be one of the examples of the error to which they acknowledge themselves to be liable. Absolute princes, or others who are accustomed to unlimited deference, usually feel this complete confidence in their own opinions on nearly all subjects. People more happily situated, who sometimes hear their opinions disputed, and are not wholly unused to be set right when they are wrong, place the same unbounded reliance only on such of their opinions as are shared by all who surround them, or to whom they habitually defer: for in proportion to a man's want of confidence in his own solitary judgment, does he usually repose, with implicit trust, on the infallibility of "the world" in general. And the world, to each individual, means the part of it with which he comes in contact; his party, his sect, his church, his class of society: the man may be called, by comparison, almost liberal and large-minded to whom it means anything so comprehensive as his own country or his own age. Nor is his faith in this collective authority at all shaken by his being aware that other ages, countries, sects, churches, classes, and parties have thought, and even now think, the exact reverse. He devolves upon his own world the responsibility of being in the right against the dissentient worlds of other people; and it never troubles him that mere accident has decided which of these numerous worlds is the object of his reliance, and that the same causes which make him a Churchman in London, would have made him a Buddhist or a Confucian in Pekin. Yet it is as evident in itself as any amount of argument can make it, that ages are no more infallible than individuals; every age having held many opinions which subsequent ages

— happily situated
people privileged

have deemed not only false but absurd; and it is as certain that many opinions, now general, will be rejected by future ages, as it is that many, once general, are rejected by the present.

The objection likely to be made to this argument, would probably take some such form as the following. There is no greater assumption of infallibility in forbidding the propagation of error, than in any other thing which is done by public authority on its own judgment and responsibility. Judgment is given to men that they may use it. Because it may be used erroneously, are men to be told that they ought not to use it at all? To prohibit what they think pernicious, is not claiming exemption from error, but fulfilling the duty incumbent on them, although fallible, of acting on their conscientious conviction. If we were never to act on our opinions, because those opinions may be wrong, we should leave all our interests uncared for, and all our duties unperformed. An objection which applies to all conduct, can be no valid objection to any conduct in particular. It is the duty of governments, and of individuals, to form the truest opinions they can; to form them carefully, and never impose them upon others unless they are quite sure of being right. But when they are sure (such reasoners may say), it is not conscientiousness but cowardice to shrink from acting on their opinions, and allow doctrines which they honestly think dangerous to the welfare of mankind, either in this life or in another, to be scattered abroad without restraint, because other people, in less enlightened times, have persecuted opinions now believed to be true. Let us take care, it may be said, not to make the same mistake: but governments and nations have made mistakes in other things, which are not denied to be fit subjects for the exercise of authority: they have laid on bad taxes, made unjust wars. Ought we therefore to lay on no taxes, and, under whatever provocation, make no wars? Men, and governments, must act to the best of their ability. There is no such thing as absolute certainty, but there is assurance sufficient for the purposes of human life. We may, and must, assume our opinion to be true for the guidance of our own conduct: and it is assuming no more when we forbid bad men to pervert society by the propagation of opinions that we regard as false and pernicious.

I answer that it is assuming very much more. There is the greatest difference between presuming an opinion to be true, because, with every opportunity for contesting it, it has not been refuted, and assuming its truth for the purpose of not permitting its refutation. Complete liberty of contradicting and disproving our opinion is the very condition which justifies us in assuming its truth for purposes of action; and on no other terms can a being with human faculties have any rational assurance of being right.

When we consider either the history of opinion, or the ordinary conduct of human life, to what is it to be ascribed that the one and the other are no worse than they are? Not certainly to the inherent force of the human understanding; for, on any matter not self-evident, there are ninety-nine persons totally incapable of judging of it, for one who is capable; and the capacity of the hundredth person is only comparative; for the majority of the eminent men of every past generation held many opinions now known to be erroneous, and did or approved numerous things which no one will now justify. Why is it, then, that there is on the whole a preponderance among mankind of rational opinions and rational conduct? If there really is this preponderance—which there must be, unless human affairs are, and have always been, in an almost desperate state—it is owing to a quality of the human mind, the source of everything respectable in man either as an intellectual or as a moral being, namely, that his errors are corrigible. He is capable of rectifying his mistakes, by discussion and experience. Not by experience alone. There must be discussion, to show how experience is to be interpreted. Wrong opinions and practices gradually yield to fact and argument: but facts and arguments, to produce any effect on the mind, must be brought before it. Very few facts are able to tell their own story, without comments to bring out their meaning. The whole strength and value, then, of human judgment, depending on the one property, that it can be set right when it is wrong, reliance can be placed on it only when the means of setting it right are kept constantly at hand. In the case of any person whose judgment is really deserving of confidence, how has it become so? Because he has kept his mind open to criticism of his opinions and conduct. Because it has been his practice to listen to all that could be said against him; to profit by as much of it as was just, and expound to himself, and upon occasion to others, the fallacy of what was fallacious. Because he has felt, that the only way in which a human being can make some approach to knowing the whole of a subject, is by hearing what can be said about it by persons of every variety of opinion, and studying all modes in which it can be looked at by every character of mind. No wise man ever acquired his wisdom in any mode but this; nor is it in the nature of human intellect to become wise in any other manner. The steady habit of correcting and completing his own opinion by collating it with those of others, so far from causing doubt and hesitation in carrying it into practice, is the only stable foundation for a just reliance on it: for, being cognisant of all that can, at least obviously, be said against him, and having taken up his position against all gainsayers—knowing that he has sought for objections and difficulties, instead of avoiding them, and has shut out no light which can be thrown upon the subject from any quarter—he has a right to think his judgment better than that of any person, or any multitude, who have not gone through a similar process.

It is not too much to require that what the wisest of mankind, those who are best entitled to trust their own judgment, find necessary to warrant their relying on it, should be submitted to by that miscellaneous collection of a few wise and many foolish individuals, called the public. The most intolerant of churches, the Roman Catholic Church, even at the canonisation of a saint, admits, and listens patiently to, a "devil's advocate." The holiest of men, it appears, cannot be admitted to posthumous honours, until all that the devil could say against him is known and weighed. If even the Newtonian philosophy were not permitted to be questioned, mankind could not feel as complete assurance of its truth as they now do. The beliefs which we have most warrant for, have no safeguard to rest on, but a standing invitation to the whole world to prove them unfounded. If the challenge is not accepted, or is accepted and the attempt fails, we are far enough from certainty still; but we have done the best that the existing state of human reason admits of; we have neglected nothing that could give the truth a chance of reaching us: if the lists are kept open, we may hope that if there be a better truth, it will be found when the human mind is capable of receiving it; and in the meantime we may rely on having attained such approach to truth, as is possible in our own day. This is the amount of certainty attainable by a fallible being, and this the sole way of attaining it.

Strange it is, that men should admit the validity of the arguments for free discussion, but object to their being "pushed to an extreme;" not seeing that unless the reasons are good for an extreme case, they are not good for any case. Strange that they should imagine that they are not assuming infallibility, when they acknowledge that there should be free discussion on all subjects which can possibly be doubtful, but think that some particular principle or doctrine should be forbidden to be questioned because it is so certain, that is, because they are certain that it is certain. To call any proposition certain, while there is anyone who would deny its certainty if permitted, but who is not permitted, is to assume that we ourselves, and those who agree with us, are the judges of certainty, and judges without hearing the other side.

In the present age—which has been described as "destitute of faith, but terrified at scepticism"—in which people feel sure, not so much that their opinions are true, as that they should not know what to do without them—the claims of an opinion to be protected from public attack are rested not so much on its truth, as on its importance to society. There are, it is alleged, certain beliefs, so useful, not to say indispensable to well-being, that it is as much the duty of governments to uphold those beliefs, as to protect any other of the interests of society. In a case of such necessity, and so directly in the line of their duty, something less than infallibility may, it is maintained, warrant, and even bind, governments, to act on their own opinion, confirmed by the general opinion of mankind. It is also often argued, and still oftener thought, that none but bad men would desire to weaken these salutary beliefs; and there can be nothing wrong, it is thought, in restraining bad men, and prohibiting what only such men would wish to practise. This mode of thinking makes the justification of restraints on discussion not a question of the truth of doctrines, but of their usefulness; and flatters itself by that means to escape the responsibility of claiming to be an infallible judge of opinions. But those who thus satisfy themselves do not perceive that the assumption of infallibility is merely shifted from one point to another. The usefulness of an opinion is itself a matter of opinion: as disputable, as open to discussion, and requiring discussion as much, as the opinion itself. There is the same need of an infallible judge of opinions to decide an opinion to be noxious, as to decide it to be false, unless the opinion condemned has full opportunity of defending itself. And it will not do to say that the heretic may be allowed to maintain the utility or harmlessness of his opinion, though forbidden to maintain its truth. The truth of an opinion is part of its utility. If we would know whether or not it is desirable that a proposition should be believed, is it possible to exclude the consideration of whether or not it is true? In the opinion, not of bad men, but of the best men, no belief which is contrary to truth can be really useful: and can you prevent such men from urging that plea, when they are charged with culpability for denying some doctrine which they are told is useful, but which they believe to be false? Those who are on the side of received opinions, never fail to take all possible advantage of this plea; you do not find them handling the question of utility as if it could be completely abstracted from that of truth: on the contrary, it is, above all, because their doctrine is "the truth," that the knowledge or the belief of it is held to be so indispensable. There can be no fair discussion of the question of usefulness, when an argument so vital may be employed on one side, but not on the other. And in point of fact, when law or public feeling do not permit the truth of an opinion to be disputed, they are just as little tolerant of a denial of its usefulness. The utmost they allow is an extenuation of its absolute necessity, or of the positive guilt of rejecting it.

In order more fully to illustrate the mischief of denying a hearing to opinions because we, in our own judgment, have condemned them, it will be desirable to fix down the discussion to a concrete case; and I choose, by preference, the cases which are least favourable to me—in which the argument against freedom of opinion, both on the score of truth and on that of utility, is considered the strongest. Let the opinions impugned be the belief in a God and in a future state, or any of the commonly received doctrines of morality. To fight the battle on such ground, gives a great advantage to an unfair antagonist; since he will be sure to say (and many who have no desire to be unfair will say it internally). Are these the doctrines that you do not deem sufficiently certain to be taken under the protection of law? Is the belief in a God one of the opinions, to feel sure of which, you hold to be assuming infallibility? But I must be permitted to observe, that it is not the feeling sure of a doctrine (be it what it may) which I call an assumption of infallibility. It is the undertaking to decide that question for others, without allowing them to hear what can be said on the contrary side. And I denounce and reprobate this pretension not the less, if put forth on the side of my most solemn convictions. However positive anyone's persuasion may be, not only of the falsity, but of the pernicious consequences—not only of the pernicious consequences, but (to adopt expressions which I altogether condemn) the immorality and impiety of an opinion; yet if, in pursuance of that private judgment, though backed by the public judgment of his country or his contemporaries, he prevents the opinion from being heard in its defence, he assumes infallibility. And so far from the assumption being less objectionable or less dangerous because the opinion is called immoral or impious, this is the case of all others in which it is most fatal. These are exactly the occasions on which the men of one generation commit those dreadful mistakes, which excite the astonishment and horror of posterity. It is among such that we find the instances memorable in history, when the arm of the law has been employed to root out the best men and the noblest doctrines; with deplorable success as to the men, though some of the doctrines have survived to be (as if in mockery) invoked, in defence of similar conduct towards those who dissent from them, or from their received interpretation.

Mankind does not need to be too often reminded that there was once a man named Socrates, between whom and the legal authorities and public opinion of his time, there took place a memorable collision. Born in an age and country abounding in individual greatness, this man has been handed down to us by those who best knew both him and the age, as the most virtuous man in it; while we know him as the head and prototype of all subsequent teachers of virtue, the source equally of the lofty inspiration of Plato and the judicious utilitarianism of Aristotle, *"i maëstri di color che sanno,"* the two headsprings of ethical as of all other philosophy. This acknowledged master of all the eminent thinkers who have since lived—whose fame, still growing after more than two thousand years, all but outweighs the whole remainder of the names which make his native city illustrious—was put to death by his countrymen, after a judicial conviction, for impiety and immorality. Impiety, in denying the gods recognised by the State; indeed his accuser asserted (see the "Apologia") that he believed in no gods at all. Immorality, in being, by his doctrines and instructions, a "corruptor of youth." Of these charges filed by the tribunal, there is every ground for believing, honestly found him guilty, and condemned the man who probably of all then born had deserved best of mankind, to be put to death as a criminal.

To pass from this to the only other instance of judicial iniquity, the mention of which, after the condemnation of Socrates, would not be an anticlimax: the event which took place on Calvary rather more than eighteen hundred years ago. The man who left on the memory of those who witnessed his life and conversation, such an impression of his moral grandeur, that eighteen subsequent centuries have done homage to him as the Almighty in person, was ignominiously put to death, as what? As a blasphemer. Men did not merely mistake their benefactor; they mistook him for the exact contrary of what he was, and treated him as that prodigy of impiety, which they themselves are now held to be, for their treatment of him. The feelings with which mankind now regard these lamentable transactions, especially the later of the two, render them extremely unjust in their judgment of the unhappy actors. These were, to all appearance, not bad men—not worse than men commonly are, but rather the contrary; men who possessed in a full, or somewhat more than a full measure, the religious, moral, and patriotic feelings of their time and people: the very kind of men who, in all times, our own included, have every chance of passing through life blameless and respected. The high-priest who rented his garments when the words were pronounced, which, according to all the ideas of his country, constituted the blackest guilt, was in all probability quite as sincere in his horror and indignation, as the generality of respectable and pious men now are in the religious and moral sentiments they profess; and most of those who now shudder at his conduct, if they had lived in his time, and been born Jews, would have acted precisely as he did. Orthodox Christians who are tempted to think that those who stoned to death the first martyrs must have been worse men than they themselves are, ought to remember that one of those persecutors was Saint Paul.[6]

If you're woke you're philosophizing. If you're philosophizing, you're always going back to the beginning to retrace your steps and wondering whether the path you took is the right one. This involves the positive as well as the negative, the whole range of human thoughts and emotions, which PC severely limits. Then you're woke.

MILLER
Thanks, Woke.

---

[6] Mill, John Stuart. *On Liberty*. Project Guttenberg. <https://www.gutenberg.org/ebooks/34901>.

I like to use these six philosophical approaches together rather than using one. For example not I might start with a few insights or a line of poetry and from that constructy an insight argument apology and subsequently be moderately and then radically skeptical of it

cut around the edge of the argument
    then
        with moderate and then radical
skepticism. But That order can
    be different. Maybe I start out with
radical skepticism, realize The argument
approach is a perfect place to free-form
loosely associated insight. The poetic
approach allows you to express yourself
in ways that dry prose cannot. These base
insights can be expanded with argument and go
approach that take on depth and
allows it to grow in new direction.
From that an apology
can be fashioned and tunneled with
radical and moderate skepticism.

"Left is short" →

wisdom
statements
truth concerning human nature and the universe
study a short header
suggestively

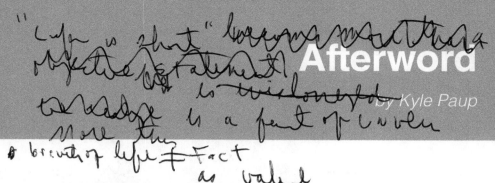

Afterword

by Kyle Paup

As a philosophy student of Dr. George Miller for the past four years, I knew that I could comfortably expect two things to come from this book. First and foremost, I knew that I could expect a radical, almost wild text that would be blatantly unlimited by any preconceived social constraints. Second, and more importantly, I knew that it would be revolutionary.

This text is nothing less than an essential guideline for any introductory level philosophy student. It cleverly introduces a number of indispensable philosophical texts, simplifying them before their appearance through the retellings of twelve powerful, new voices of young philosophers. The variety of voices encourages each student reading it to, in turn, find their own voice as a young philosopher as well.

Presenting the philosophical works in this manner allows students to understand the countless different ways of approaching philosophy, preparing them to see and hear philosophy in the way that works best for them as individuals. As they read through the text, they will undoubtedly find works of the old and voices of the new that resonate with them personally, enlightening them with newfound wisdom and permitting them to shape strong philosophical positions. Students will gravitate toward certain issues in a way that will plant the seeds for a deep passion for philosophy.

Not only will the text spark interest in beginning philosophers, but they will be constantly reminded of the greater significance of studying and practicing the subject as well. Personally, as all twelve voices ahead will affirm, philosophy is a life-changing experience. It allows us to reflect on ourselves as much as it allows us to reflect on the world. The person I am as a result of philosophical learning, a person who questions the nature of the world, questions the ethics behind our every action, questions what we can do to make the world a better place, and questions the limits of my own mind, is not the same person I was before being subject to it. Dr. Miller's text highlights the importance of this learning, is an ode to the philosophical experience itself, and is a call to action for revolutionaries to be.

Contributed by Kyle Paup. © Kendall Hunt Publishing Company.

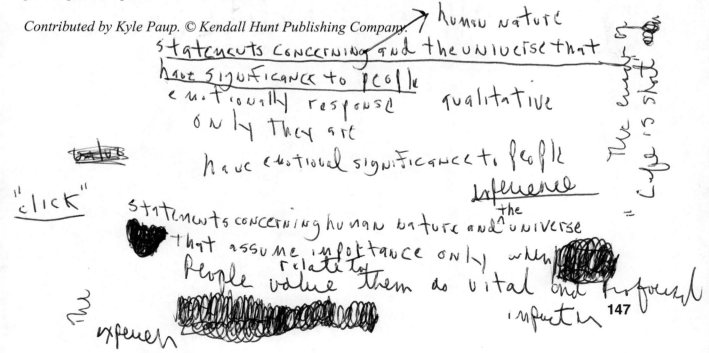

unexamined life ≠ living
understood

is made into wisdom only
when we realize this
vital, impactful, and
profound to ___ ___

It's not a remote possibility that a
statement like "The unexamined life is not worth living"
May ~~be wisdom for one person but not for another~~.
One person may consider it wisdom and another
may not. It depends on ~~whether the person~~ whether the person
relates and values it as profoundly vital,
impactful, and profound. It is quite possible
that for one person a Taylor Swift lyric
is wisdom, while "Socrates's" "an examined
constitul   life is not worth living" is
not.

Here is your Job description:

(1) Receive symbols that you cannot decyph

(2) Go to a rulebook

(3)

(4)

20 20 | 2

20
—————
240

chapter 1 - 11 - 20

chapter 2 - 30

* 20 annotations per chapter

* 1 chapter with 30

150 Total = Commesh

annotation Interptation

(1) Comment critique, response

(2)

Information

Basics - words you don't know a

research words, persons, places, events, then you don't know

CPSIA information can be obtained
at www.ICGtesting.com
Printed in the USA
JSHW022302210120
3728JS00003B/64